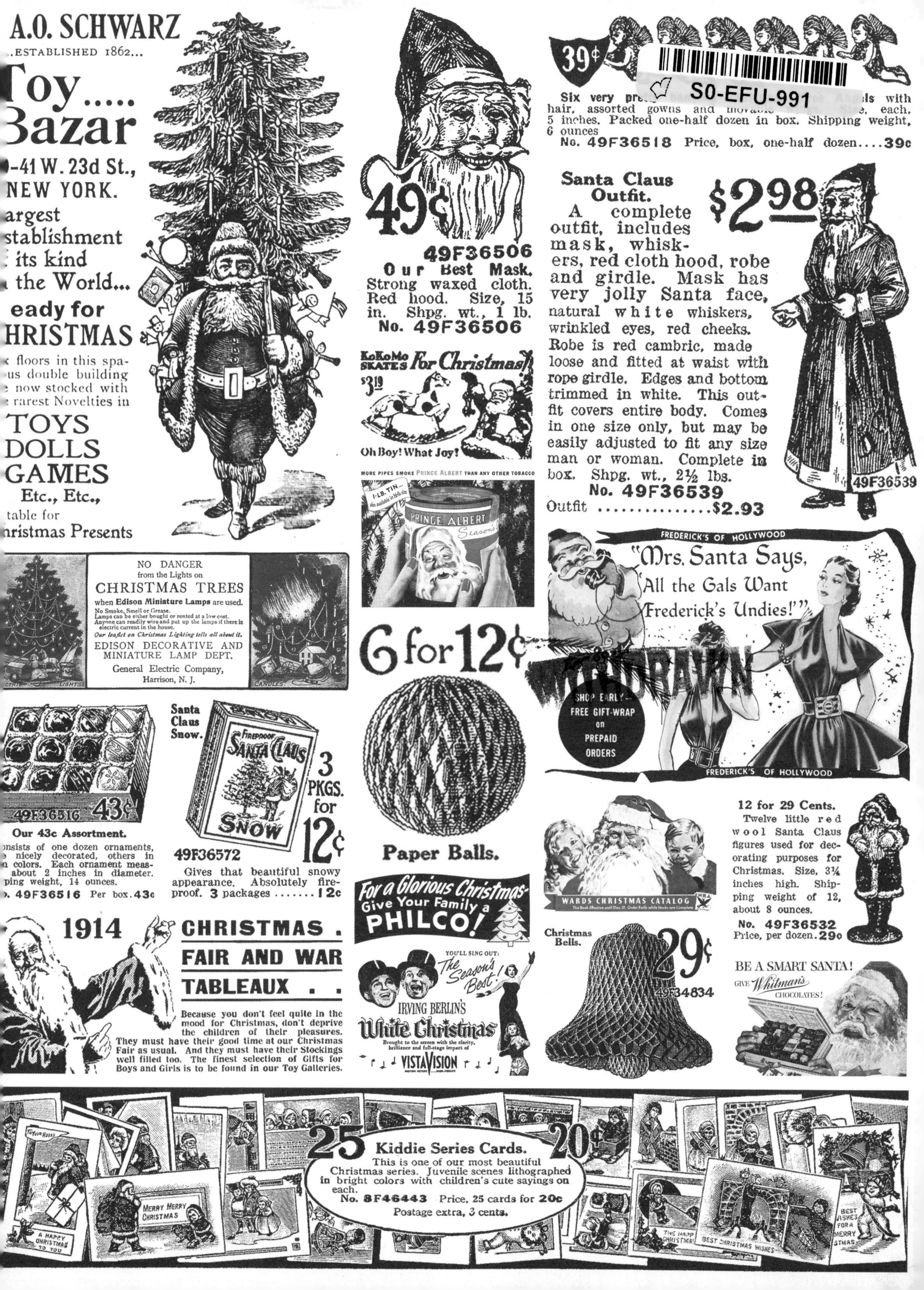

A.O. SCHWARZ
..ESTABLISHED 1862...
Toy.....
Bazar
-41 W. 23d St.,
NEW YORK.
argest
stablishment
its kind
the World...
eady for
HRISTMAS
floors in this spa-
us double building
now stocked with
rarest Novelties in
TOYS
DOLLS
GAMES
Etc., Etc.,
table for
hristmas Presents
49¢
49F36506
Our Best Mask.
Strong waxed cloth. Red hood. Size, 15 in. Shpg. wt., 1 lb.
No. 49F36506
39¢
Six very pre... hair, assorted gowns and movable ... each, 5 inches. Packed one-half dozen in box. Shipping weight, 6 ounces
No. 49F36518 Price, box, one-half dozen....39c
Santa Claus Outfit.
$2.98
A complete outfit, includes mask, whiskers, red cloth hood, robe and girdle. Mask has very jolly Santa face, natural white whiskers, wrinkled eyes, red cheeks. Robe is red cambric, made loose and fitted at waist with rope girdle. Edges and bottom trimmed in white. This outfit covers entire body. Comes in one size only, but may be easily adjusted to fit any size man or woman. Complete in box. Shpg. wt., 2½ lbs.
No. 49F36539
Outfit $2.93
49F36539
KoKoMo SKATES For Christmas
$3.19
Oh Boy! What Joy!
MORE PIPES SMOKE PRINCE ALBERT THAN ANY OTHER TOBACCO
1-LB. TIN
PRINCE ALBERT
NO DANGER
from the Lights on
CHRISTMAS TREES
when Edison Miniature Lamps are used.
No Smoke, Smell or Grease.
Lamps can be either bought or rented at a low cost.
Anyone can readily wire and put up the lamps if there is electric current in the house.
Our leaflet on Christmas Lighting tells all about it.
EDISON DECORATIVE AND MINIATURE LAMP DEPT.
General Electric Company,
Harrison, N. J.
6 for 12¢
Paper Balls.
FREDERICK'S OF HOLLYWOOD
"Mrs. Santa Says,
All the Gals Want
Frederick's Undies!"
WITHDRAWN
SHOP EARLY
FREE GIFT-WRAP
on
PREPAID
ORDERS
FREDERICK'S OF HOLLYWOOD
49F36516 43¢
Our 43c Assortment.
onsists of one dozen ornaments, nicely decorated, others in colors. Each ornament measures about 2 inches in diameter. ping weight, 14 ounces.
49F36516 Per box.43c
Santa Claus Snow.
FIREPROOF SANTA CLAUS SNOW
3 PKGS. for 12¢
49F36572
Gives that beautiful snowy appearance. Absolutely fireproof. 3 packages 12c
WARDS CHRISTMAS CATALOG
12 for 29 Cents.
Twelve little red wool Santa Claus figures used for decorating purposes for Christmas. Size, 3¼ inches high. Shipping weight of 12, about 8 ounces.
No. 49F36532
Price, per dozen. 29c
1914
CHRISTMAS .
FAIR AND WAR
TABLEAUX . .
Because you don't feel quite in the mood for Christmas, don't deprive the children of their pleasures. They must have their good time at our Christmas Fair as usual. And they must have their Stockings well filled too. The finest selection of Gifts for Boys and Girls is to be found in our Toy Galleries.
For a Glorious Christmas-
Give Your Family a
PHILCO!
YOU'LL SING OUT:
The Season's Best!
IRVING BERLIN'S
White Christmas
VISTAVISION
Christmas Bells.
29¢
49F34834
BE A SMART SANTA!
GIVE Whitman's CHOCOLATES!
25
20¢
Kiddie Series Cards.
This is one of our most beautiful Christmas series. Juvenile scenes lithographed in bright colors with children's cute sayings on each.
No. 8F46443 Price, 25 cards for 20c
Postage extra, 3 cents.
MERRY MERRY CHRISTMAS
A HAPPY CHRISTMAS TO YOU
BEST CHRISTMAS WISHES
BEST WISHES FOR A MERRY XMAS

"Christmas Day will always be, just as long as we have we."
— Theodor Geisel

Holly Jolly

Celebrating Christmas Past in Pop Culture

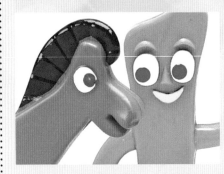

Holly Jolly
Celebrating Christmas Past in Pop Culture
by Mark Voger

Written and designed by: Mark Voger
Publisher: John Morrow
Proofreader: Scott Peters

Front cover: Santa Claus Funnies, a.k.a. Four Color #958 (1958) cover illustration by uncredited artist © Dell Publishing; elf decoration, spinning light for aluminum Christmas tree, and Humpty Dumpty decoration, manufacturers unknown © current copyright holders; "Rudolph the Red-Nosed Reindeer" book © Little Golden Books/ Western Publishing Company, Inc.; "leg lamp" novelty item based on "A Christmas Story" sequence © Metro-Goldwyn-Mayer; Frosty Sno-Man Sno-Cone Machine © Hasbro

Back cover: Santa doll © Bijou Toys; Tri-Ang Gyro Cycle © Tri-Ang; Classics Illustrated © Gilberton Co. Inc.; "Santa Claus" (1959) © Azteca Films; "The Spirit of Christmas" © Bell Telephone Co.; "Dominick the Donkey" © Roulette Records

Every effort has been made to verify the ownership or source of all illustrated material. We regret any errors of attribution, and will make the appropriate corrections in future editions.

For Kim

"Holly Jolly: Celebrating Christmas Past in Pop Culture" © 2020 Mark Voger

ISBN-13: 978-1-60549-097-7
First printing, November 2020
Printed in China

Published by:
TwoMorrows Publishing
10407 Bedfordtown Drive
Raleigh, North Carolina 27614
www.twomorrows.com

Introduction

In a way, your first memory of life is when your life begins.

Think about it. Before that, you're an amoeba, a mere speck. You don't know nuthin' about nuthin' except eating, crying and eliminating. Then one day, something crazy happens that imprints itself on your brain for the rest of your life ... and your life begins.

My earliest memory — my *very first memory of life* — came a few days before Christmas in, I'm guessing, 1960. I would have been going on 3 (it's a very foggy memory), putting my sister Bobbi at 3 months and my brother Brian at yet-to-come.

My parents had stashed all of our Christmas toys into the downstairs powder room, where they'd be handy to put under the tree on Christmas Eve. One afternoon that week, I was wandering around the house, when I stumbled into this room full of toys.

Whoa! My young eyes had never seen anything like this. Toys everywhere! It was a fantasy-land.

One of the toys was a Popeye Punch-Me — a cheap, inflated, plastic punching bag for kids. It was a lot taller than me. I bumped into it, causing it to teeter back and forth. I was transfixed by Popeye's scowling mug as he teetered backward and forward, backward and forward. My eyes were wide and my jaw was dropped. I was in an altered state. I made some sort of exclamations. I don't know if they were in English.

My mom rushed in, calmly ushered me out of the room, and without a word, closed the powder-room door behind her.

It all happened so quickly that I couldn't swear that it happened at all.

Well, I didn't possess much logic yet. I didn't know, honestly, anything about Christmas. Adults in my presence were probably saying, "Christmas is coming," and there were pretty lights and decorations around the neighborhood, and I was maybe seeing the scary (to a toddler) bearded face of Santa Claus at the supermarket or on our snowy, black-and-white TV. But I hadn't yet grasped the concept of Dec. 25th.

When the Big Day finally came, my parents woke us, gathered us at the top of the rec-room stairs and said, "It's Christmas morning! Go down and see what Santa left you!" We were half asleep, and I had no idea what they were talking about. I walked warily down the steps (my dad carried my sister) and into the rec room.

Suddenly, I spotted it: the Popeye Punch-Me.

It was surrounded by all the other toys, and behind them was a sparkling tree that wasn't there before. Instantly, that weird euphoria came back. Only *this* time, Popeye and his fellow toys didn't go away. They stuck around all morning — Christmas morning. My dad demonstrated how to punch Popeye, and then *I* did it, and the teetering thing happened again. My subconscious thought was: I must have made a wish, and it came true.

THE FOLLOWING YEAR IS WHEN I BEGAN putting it together — that once it got colder outside and I started seeing pretty lights and decorations and Santa's scary bearded face, it meant that this thing the adults called "Christmas" was coming. Christmas, the Day of Many Toys.

And I started noticing that, besides seeing Santa Claus everywhere, there was a glowing baby in a hay crib with a golden circle around his tiny head and a winged lady floating above him and a bunch of animals and people from the olden days standing around, staring at him. I thought: Is that some kind of magic Christmas baby?

THE WONDROUS AND MYSTERIOUS thing about Christmas is that for one day a year, we live in the past as well as the present. (Is this phenomenon attributable to Charles Dickens' "A Christmas Carol," with its Ghosts of Christmas Past and Present? I've always wondered.) We break out the same decorations, many that go back decades. We observe the same traditions. We're always saying things like, "Remember that Christmas back in '78?" or whenever. But each year, we add a few new decorations, traditions and memories — which, of course, are revisited in ensuing Christmases.

It's like one day that we live again and again. Following are some of the memories that, for me, keep coming back ...

Why, you! Popeye Punch-Me. © King Features Syndicate

From left: Cousin Alfie, my sister Bobbi, Santa, my brother Brian (in vest) and myself in 1963. Family photo

ONE YEAR WHEN I WAS LITTLE, I GOT A WOOD-burning kit for Christmas. My advice to parents: Never give your child a device that plugs in and gets hot enough to sear human flesh unless you determine, with a high degree of certainty, that your child fully comprehends the device's purpose and safe usage.

I looked at the box blankly. My dad said, "It's a wood-burning kit." I didn't know what he was talking about. (My parents probably bought it for me because I could cartoon a little as a kid, and wood-burning was an "artistic" activity.) My dad told me that you plug it in and the tip gets hot, and it comes with these little squares of balsa wood with designs on them that you press the hot tip against, and it burns the designs into the wood, and that's about it. That's what it does. So my dad plugged it in.

"It's very, very important that you never touch this part of the wood-burner," he said, pointing to the tip. "Don't ever touch that."

But I wasn't catching his drift, exactly. I thought what my dad meant was: "Don't touch it, or you will get in a whole lot of trouble." I didn't know that what he *really* meant was: "Don't touch it, or it will sear your flesh."

My dad watched as I burned some designs into a balsa-wood square. It wasn't much fun, or particularly creative, but it smelled nice. Satisfied for the moment, my dad then went upstairs.

The minute he was gone, I called out to my little brother, *"Here! Grab this!"* and held out the wood-burner. Oh, boy, I thought, is *he* going to get into trouble when Dad finds out he touched the tip of the wood-burner! Brian trustingly wrapped his tiny hand around the tip, and it seared his flesh. He screamed, as anyone would whose flesh has been seared.

My dad was back in a flash, and saw my screaming brother's red, blistered hand, and looked at me like I was the anti-Christ. He got ice on my brother's hand, swatted me, grabbed the wood-burning kit, and threw it out the front door. There was snow outside, and steam rose up from the spot where the wood-burner landed.

WE WERE AN IRISH-CATHOLIC FAMILY WITH OUR own live-in Irish-Catholic immigrant, my maternal grandfather, Henry Patrick Kelly, who hailed from the tight-knit farming village of Gort in County Galway. It was Henry who once tearfully insisted to my mother that we little ones attend Catholic school.

Soon after I was enrolled at Holy Rosary School in the Diocese of Camden in New Jersey, I found out who that magic Christmas baby was. The fact that there were "two" kinds of Christmases — the Santa Claus kind and the Baby Jesus kind — was a bit confusing. But when toys and cookies are at stake, you don't ask questions.

MR. BOTENSTEN, WHO MY DAD
called "Billy Bubblegum," helped us trim our
tree every year. He'd wipe dust from the colored glass Christmas balls and, to the tune of
"Silent Night," he'd sing: *"Jingle-a-fotz, polish
the balls ..."* Billy Bubblegum was not tall, not
slim, and without question, he was the funniest
man I've ever known. Every sentence he uttered
had one purpose: to make you laugh. He *looked*
like a comedian. This guy could've been on TV.
My dad was a pretty serious fella. He'd laugh
when the situation warranted it, but never to
excess. But when Uncle Bubblegum was around,
my dad would be in stitches.

Every year between Christmas and New Year's
Day, all my Irish-side cousins, uncles and aunts
would stay over. They'd travel to South Jersey
from Long Island, Pennsylvania, Detroit and
sometimes Phoenix. We'd all go out to dinner at a
big place called Dunbarton Oaks Restaurant &
Cocktail Lounge on the White Horse Pike ("somewhere in the swamps of Jersey," as Bruce
Springsteen put it). We would commandeer a din-
ing room with a long table. The proprietor was a
short, stout, bespectacled woman named
Christine with an impenetrable German accent. She
served us a turkey dinner with German potato salad
(sour), German cole slaw (*more* sour) and pitchers of
cola (which turned us kids into caffeinated maniacs).
Christine was a little like S.Z. "Cuddles" Sakall — the fat little
Hungarian guy who abetted Humphrey Bogart in "Casablanca"
and Barbara Stanwyck in "Christmas in Connecticut."

One year, we all came back from Dunbarton Oaks to find an
unexpected guest. While we were gone, Uncle Bubblegum snuck
into our house. He was downstairs, pretending to sleep in a lounge
chair, dressed as Santa Claus and cradling a Santa doll. Some of
the cousins were so little, they believed he really *was* Santa.

OUR FAMILY TRADITIONS WERE SIMPLE AND
kinda sweet. As one sibling activity, we made cookies in the
shape of Christmas trees, candy canes and Santa, but without
using cookie cutters. We shaped (*mis*-shaped?) them by hand and
painted them with this awful-tasting icing my mom made in red,
yellow, white and green. (The icing was concocted from powdered
sugar and water, and the food coloring imbued it with an icky
aftertaste.) Adults pretended to like the cookies, but you could
detect a shadow falling across their faces as they tasted that icing.

We'd make Christmas-y things during school and scouting
activities. With the Cub Scouts, I made a soup-can candle for my
mom, which was solid red with a schmear of white wax "snow"
around the top and a stab of plastic holly on the side. Problem
was, there was no getting around the fact that this candle was
formed from a soup can. The size, shape and ridges just *screamed*
Campbell's Chicken Noodle. Still, my mom put that soup-can
candle out every year like it was a Fabergé heirloom.

My brother made a Christmas angel out of the cardboard tube
from a toilet-paper roll. The "Toilet-Paper Angel," as we came to
call it, topped our Christmas tree every year, which was fine, as
long as you didn't think *too* hard about what that angel was made
out of. The Toilet-Paper Angel held its place of honor atop the
tree long after we were jaded teenagers immune to its "cuteness."

**"Billy Bubblegum" as Santa with my Irish-side cousins (1967).
At center rear is our grandfather from the old country.** Family photo

FROM A YOUNG AGE, WE CHILDREN WERE
encouraged to save our pennies, nickels and dimes all year to buy
Christmas presents for one other. The first Christmas presents I
ever gave were two of those small, tin, kiddie watercolor paint
sets — one each for my little sister and brother. So I got off for a
mere 19 cents apiece. They were also the first presents I ever
wrapped, and I did a lousy job; I only taped Christmas wrap
across the lids of the paint sets, so what lay beneath wasn't exactly a mystery. My sister informed me, in a voice devoid of diplo-
macy, "We know what you got us."

As we got older, we did our gift shopping, not at the *chi-chi*
Cherry Hill Mall, but where our precious coins went the farthest:
a dingy, scrappy, wonderful bargain center known as the Berlin
Farmers Market and Auction. You wouldn't find Jacqueline
Kennedy or Margaret Drysdale there, but to us, it was Disneyland.

The Berlin Mart had a slogan that could be taken several ways:
"Where shopping is an adventure." When Rod Stewart sings
*"Take me back / carry me back / down the Gasoline Alley / where
I started from,"* I think of the Berlin Mart.

There was no place on Earth like the Mart at Christmastime.
Small gestures like strings of colored lights and old Christmas
songs playing through tinny speakers transformed the drab milieu
into something magical. The Mart's sometimes forlorn denizens
moved with a bit more purpose, and even some joviality. At the
lamp shop, the animated "bleeding Jesus" framed art (remember
those?) took on extra significance.

One store at the Mart, which we called "the Dece Store" (for
"decent"), had its many tight aisles crammed to the ceiling with
remainder, expired, off-brand, no-brand, unclaimed, unwanted and

Seasons Greetings FROM THE BERLIN FARMERS MARKET

Your Christmas-shopping dollar could go the farthest at the good old Berlin Farmers Market and Auction in Berlin, N.J.

unloved products. This is where we always bought gifts for Bud and Pat — our big brother, 19 years older than me (we had different moms), and his wife. Bud would get cologne, Pat would get perfume. God knows what Dece Store cologne and perfume smelled like, how old it was, what country it was manufactured in, what safety standards it failed to meet, what punishment it inflicted on one's skin. But it cost just north of a buck, and it looked classy and expensive when you unwrapped it, and after all, cologne and perfume are classy things, and Bud and Pat always acted like it was the Best Christmas Present Ever, and Pat would say, "I'm going to get some use out of *this*," and who knows? Maybe it came in handy killing bugs in the spring.

ONE REASON SO MANY PEOPLE RELATE TO THE 1983 movie "A Christmas Story" is its central theme of the little boy's obsessive desire for a Christmas gift in the form of a Daisy Air Rifle. Nerdy Ralphie (Peter Billingsley) has fantasies in which, clad in a spangly cowboy getup, he protects his family from ornery outlaws using Daisy's popular BB gun. In Ralphie's mind, the air rifle becomes something more than a mere toy. It represents his very sense of self. At that tender age, we all yearn to *be* something, but we don't yet know what.

The toy I wanted more than any other — my version of "A Christmas Story's" Daisy Air Rifle — was Captain Action. He was like G.I. Joe, but with superhero costumes and accessories instead of military uniforms and accessories. Cap could become Batman, Superman, Aquaman, Captain America, Buck Rogers, the Phantom. (An interesting aside for fellow comic-book geeks: Captain Action was the first-ever DC/Marvel crossover, an important distinction usually bestowed upon the 1976 comic book *Superman vs. the Amazing Spider-Man*. But I digress.) During the week before Christmas 1966, when I was 8, I thought about Captain Action at every waking moment. If I hadn't gotten Captain Action for Christmas, I would still wear the psychic scars.

But there he was on Christmas morning, with his confident expression and spiffy cowlick, sitting in a chair at his Batcave-like console, ready for, well, *action*. (The Captain Action console was a Sears-exclusive accoutrement, I'll have you know.) My no-nonsense, World War II-veteran dad, who I doubt had many toys growing up, set up this little tableau for his undeserving son.

SO HERE COMES A CONFESSION.

For me, the big day wasn't Christmas, really. It was Christmas *Eve*. That was the day of anticipation. Studies show that delayed gratification is a character-building exercise for children. And isn't Christmas Eve the ultimate in delayed gratification?

Our house would be a whirlwind of activity, since my parents always threw a big open-house party on Dec. 24th. (More about that later.) There was the high-pitched *whrrrrr* of clam dip being blended, the low-tide odor of oyster stew bubbling on the stove. We'd put those awful cookies on a big plate, adorned with candy canes and Hershey's Kisses, to foist upon unsuspecting company.

Every Christmas Eve, Philadelphia TV celebrity "Wee Willie" Webber hosted an annual special on Channel 17 titled something like "The World's Most Expensive Christmas Toys." Mind you, these weren't fun toys that you played with. They were gigantic animated figures — like a great big bear, for instance — that you could only look at. "Glad *we're* not rich kids," we used to say.

Our mom allowed us to open one present on Christmas Eve: the one mailed to us by our Aunt Peggy from Long Island. It was usually, like, pajamas, robes or slippers, not some cool, battery-operated toy. But anyway, it qualified as a Christmas present.

So pardon the blasphemy, but Christmas Eve was more fun than Christmas Day. Because at a certain point on Dec. 25th, usually around mid-afternoon, it would dawn on you that no further surprises awaited, and you couldn't possibly eat another morsel, and you were already beginning to experience that weird malaise which hadn't yet been named called "post-holiday depression."

EVERYTHING WE'VE DISCUSSED THUS FAR HAS more to do with the Scary Bearded Guy than the Magic Christmas Baby. This work called "Holly Jolly" leans overwhelmingly toward the former, without question. But once in a while, so as not to incur the wrath of the nuns at Holy Rosary School (regardless of the fact that they are all likely deceased), I'll acknowledge the — quote, unquote — "true meaning of Christmas" in a way that's (hopefully) respectful and (just as hopefully) inclusive of people of all faiths, or *no* faith. After all — to borrow from the slogan for Levi's Real Jewish Rye — you don't have to be Christian to love Christmas. Hark!

Mark

READ ALOUD AND BEGINNING READER STORIES

HUMPTY DUMPTY'S

MAGAZINE FOR LITTLE CHILDREN

DECEMBER 1963 · 50¢

COMMENDED by PARENTS MAGAZINE

THE BAD LUCK CAT
and other stories

THINGS TO DO
GAMES · CUTOUTS
PICTURES TO COLOR

A long white beard is no disguise,
For an egg of Humpty's size.
Dressed like Santa he tries his tricks,
But in the chimney top he sticks!

"Who, and what are you?" "I am the Ghost of Christmas Past."

Few topics have inspired as much art and culture as Christmas. Think about it. Paintings, etchings, stained-glass windows, sculpture, hymns, poems, songs, books, plays, decorations, movies, greeting cards, TV, food, drink, cartoons, cookies, candy, toys ...

Did I mention cartoons, cookies, candy and toys?

All of this has been inspired by a holiday that began as a religious observance, and grew exponentially over the course of millennia to touch anyone with — at the risk of sounding like a Care Bear — an open heart. *Or* a sweet tooth.

It's hardly a revelation to say that Christmas is for everybody, regardless of your religion (or lack thereof). Atheists, agnostics, Satanists, snake worshippers, Kennedy Republicans, Reagan Democrats — anybody can love Christmas if they wanna.

And everybody, it seems, has a favorite Christmas *something*. A favorite Christmas special ... Christmas song ... Christmas movie ... Christmas TV episode ... Christmas toy ...

Finish this sentence: It wouldn't be Christmas without (blank).

Your answer could be a delicacy: stroopwafels, chrusciki, pizzelles, even Little Debbie's Christmas Tree Cakes, which are made with love ... and mononitrate, sodium aluminum phosphate, carnauba wax, mono- and diglycerides, titanium dioxide, sorbitan monostearate, and polysorbate 80.

These shared experiences — having eaten the same delicacies, listened to the same music, watched the same movies and TV shows, played with the same toys — can unite us, if we let them. See if you remember the following Christmas somethings.

In music: Bing Crosby's whistling solo on Irving Berlin's "White Christmas" ... Nat King Cole's silky voice and the plinky piano on "The Christmas Song" ... Hank Garland's rockin' guitar on Bobby Helms' "Jingle Bell Rock" ... Boots Randolph's swingin' sax on Brenda Lee's "Rockin' Around the Christmas Tree" ... the "hee-haw!" refrain on "Dominick the Christmas Donkey" ... John and Yoko joined by a Harlem choir on "Happy Christmas (War is Over)" ... Bruce asking Clarence if he's been practicing his saxophone on "Santa Claus is Comin' to Town" ... and strange bedfellows Crosby and David Bowie harmonizing (and bridging a generational gap) on "Little Drummer Boy/Peace on Earth."

In movies: Stannie Dum and Ollie Dee playing with peewees and fighting bogeymen ... Barbara Stanwyck's complicated Connecticut charade ... Kris Kringle's New York City "trial" to determine if he's the "one and only Santa Claus" ... Jimmy Stewart and Donna Reed dancing the Charleston ... Zuzu's petals ... Michael Horden bellowing, *"Mankind* was my bus-i-ness!"* ... Bing Crosby and Danny Kaye rescuing the Old Man's resort ... Santa Claus fighting the devil ... Santa Claus fighting the Martians ... "You'll shoot your eye out!" ... and, of course, Cousin Eddie's heartwarming greeting, "Merry Christmas! S***er was full!"

In television: Ralph's excitement when Alice opens her gift (what could it be?) ... Lucy, Ricky, Fred and Ethel in Santa suits ... Gomez, Morticia, Fester, Grandmama, Lurch and Cousin Itt in Santa suits ... Art Carney's drunken, down-and-out Santa ... Aunt Bee serving Christmas dinner to crotchety old Ben Weaver in the Mayberry jailhouse ... the Monkees singing "Ríu Chíu" a capella ... Cindy Brady asking Santa to heal her mother's voice in time for the Christmas morning church service ... and Santa saying yes.

In animation: Gerald McBoing-Boing "as" Tiny Tim singing the refrain "with razzle-berry dressing" ... Clarice telling Rudolph he's cute ... Linus reciting from Luke in answer to the question

Superman gets the spirit in the store giveaway Superman's Christmas Adventure (1940). Opposite: Dan Lawler's cover for Humpty Dumpty's Magazine for Little Children (1963).

"What is the true meaning of Christmas?" ... the Charlie Brown Christmas tree ... the Grinch's heart growing three sizes ... and those battling Miser brothers. (Will they *never* get along?)

In print: "Babar and Father Christmas" by Jean de Brunhoff ... "Madeline's Christmas" by Ludwig Bemelmans ... "How the Grinch Stole Christmas!" by Dr. Seuss ... holiday puzzles and fiction in *Jack and Jill, Highlights for Children* and *Humpty Dumpty's Magazine for Little Children* ... DC Comics' giveaway *Superman's Christmas Adventure* ... Dell's *Santa Claus Funnies* ... *Archie's Christmas Stocking* ... *Betty and Veronica's Christmas Spectacular* ... and comic books featuring Disney and Warner Bros. characters.

Ah, shared memories.

SPEAKING OF DICKENS — *WERE* WE SPEAKING OF Dickens? — there's the question of how one defines "Christmas Past." To cut it fine, a given Christmas transitions into "Christmas Past" the split-second it ends, when the clock strikes midnight on Christmas night, yielding to the wee moments of Dec. 26.

So remember *that* each Christmas Yet to Come. It's only 24 out of the 8,760 hours in a year. Considering average life expectancies, one can't hope for many more than 75 Christmases over a lifetime. But — here comes that Care Bear threat again — we can carry all of our Christmas Pasts with us each remaining day.

Was that depressing? Have a stroopwafel.

Timeline

What? We'd already had Christmas trees, Christmas cards, Christmas carols and the prototype for Santa Claus — all by as early as the 1600s? It's amazing, looking back over millennia, how far into the past our holiday traditions go.

4 B.C.: Go tell it on the mountain: Jesus Christ is born. Dec. 25, however, is an arbitrarily selected date.

50 A.D.: The first documents that will coalesce into the New Testament begin to appear.

270: St. Nicholas is born. His penchant for giving gifts to the poor makes him the inspiration for Santa Claus.

11th century: The term "Christmas" (for "Christ's Mass") is coined.

16th century: The first Christmas trees originate in Germany.

1824: "O Tannenbaum" (in English, "O Christmas Tree") debuts.

1823: "The First Noël" debuts.

1822: The poem "A Visit From St. Nicholas" debuts.

1821: The poem "Old Santeclaus with Much Delight" debuts, with the first known published illustrations of "Santeclaus."

12/24/1818: "Silent Night" debuts.

18th century: "God Rest Ye Merry Gentlemen," "O Come, All Ye Faithful" and "Joy to the World" debut.

1670: Candy canes are introduced by the choirmaster of Cologne Cathedral as a way to keep young singers behaved.

1650s: "Hark! The Herald Angels Sing" debuts.

1611: The first known Christmas card is sent to King James I of England (and his son) by German physician Michael Maier.

1843: The first commercially printed Christmas card is introduced with art by John Callcott Horsley.

12/19/1843: The novella "A Christmas Carol" by Charles Dickens is published.

1847: "O Holy Night" debuts.

1847: The British novelty "Christmas crackers" is introduced by confectioner Tom Smith.

1849: "It Came Upon the Midnight Clear" debuts.

1853: "Good King Wenceslas" debuts.

1857: "Jingle Bells" debuts.

1861: "O Come, O Come, Emmanuel" debuts.

1862: "Angels We Have Heard on High" and "Deck the Halls" debut.

1880: Thomas Edison invents the first strand of electric lights, which will eventually become known and used as Christmas lights.

6/1870: President Ulysses S. Grant makes Christmas a federal holiday.

12/12/1868: "O Little Town of Bethlehem" debuts.

1865: "Go Tell It on the Mountain" and "What Child is This" debut.

12/25/1863: The poem "Christmas Bells" is written by Henry Wadsworth Longfellow, inspiring the carol "I Heard the Bells on Christmas Day."

1/3/1863: Harper's Weekly magazine publishes political cartoonist Thomas Nast's influential illustrations of Santa Claus.

1863: "We Three Kings of Orient Are" debuts.

1881: "Jolly Old Saint Nicholas" is published.

12/22/1882: Edward Hibberd Johnson displays the first electric lights on a Christmas tree.

1882: "Away in a Manger" debuts.

1889: President Benjamin Harrison hosts the first Christmas tree at the White House.

1890: James Edgar of Brockton, Massachusetts, becomes the first store Santa.

1892: Tchaikovsky's "The Nutcracker" debuts.

9/21/1897: When young reader Virginia O'Hanlon questions the existence of Santa Claus, The New York Sun publishes an unsigned editorial (by Francis P. Church) replying, "Yes, Virginia, there is a Santa Claus."

1897: "The Parade of Tin Soldiers" debuts.

1933: Sears, Roebuck and Co. issues the Sears Christmas Book, its first Christmas catalog. (It is renamed The Wish Book in 1968.)

1932: The first Coca-Cola ad featuring Santa Claus painted by artist Haddon Sundblom appears.

10/24/1929: The stock market crash signals the start of the Great Depression in America.

12/25/1924: The first Macy's Day Parade is held in New York City.

1903: General Electric begins manufacturing electric Christmas lights.

1901: The silent film "Scrooge; or Marley's Ghost," the earliest surviving film adaptation of Charles Dickens' tale, is released.

11/1898: The silent movie "Santa Claus" presents the first known filmic depiction of Santa.

11/1934: The song "Santa Claus is Comin' to Town" is introduced by Eddie Cantor on his radio show.

12/14/1934: The movie "March of the Wooden Soldiers" starring Stan Laurel and Oliver Hardy is released.

11/30/1935: The movie "Scrooge" starring Seymour Hicks is released.

12/16/1938: The movie "A Christmas Carol" starring Reginald Owen is released.

1939: "Rudolph the Red-Nosed Reindeer" debuts as a store mascot.

1939: President Franklin Delano Roosevelt moves Thanksgiving to the fourth Thursday of the month, giving Depression-era retailers more shopping time.

1940: DC Comics publishes the giveway Superman's Christmas Adventure.

7/30/1942: Irving Berlin's "White Christmas" recorded by Bing Crosby is released by Decca. For many decades to follow, Crosby's version remains the biggest-selling single.

1942: The comic book Santa Claus Funnies is introduced by Dell, which publishes it annually for the next 20 years.

12/25/1941: Bing Crosby gives the first public performance of Irving Berlin's song "White Christmas" over the radio.

12/7/1941: Japan bombs Pearl Harbor, bringing the United States into World War II (a conflict begun in 1939). The war has many reverberations in Christmas Culture.

1940: The children's book "Babar and Father Christmas" by Jean de Brunhoff is published.

9/4/1942: "Holiday Inn" starring Bing Crosby, the first movie in which the song "White Christmas" is heard, is released.

1943: Blumstein's department store in Harlem introduces its first black Santa Claus.

11/22/1944: The movie "Meet Me in St. Louis," in which Judy Garland introduces the song "Have Yourself a Merry Little Christmas," is released.

8/11/1945: The movie "Christmas in Connecticut" starring Barbara Stanwyck is released.

11/1946: "The Christmas Song" recorded by radio's King Cole Trio (with lead vocals by Nat King Cole) is released.

12/20/1946: Frank Capra's movie "It's a Wonderful Life" starring James Stewart is released.

6/4/1947: The movie "Miracle on 34th Street," starring Edmund Gwenn as a man who believes he is the "one and only Santa Claus," is released.

1949: The instrumental "Sleigh Ride" (the one with the "horse-y" sounds) is recorded by the Boston Pops Orchestra debuts.

9/1/1949: The song "Rudolph the Red-Nosed Reindeer" recorded by Gene Autry debuts. It becomes a #1 hit, however briefly .

1947: The song "Here Comes Santa Claus," recorded and co-written by movie cowboy Gene Autry, debuts.

12/6/1947: "All I Want For Christmas (Is My Two Front Teeth)," recorded by Spike Jones and His City Slickers, debuts.

12/1947: The Disney character Scrooge McDuck debuts in writer-artist Carl Barks' story "Christmas on Bear Mountain," in Dell's Four Color Comics #178. (Twenty years later, the character will cross over into animated film.)

FROSTY the SNOW MAN
GENE AUTRY
WHEN SANTA CLAUS GETS YOUR LETTER
COLUMBIA RECORD

1950: The song "Frosty the Snowman" recorded by Gene Autry debuts.

10/1950: The song "Silver Bells" recorded by Bing Crosby debuts.

1951: The song "The Little Drummer Boy" recorded by the Trapp Family Singers debuts.

9/18/1951: The song "It's Beginning to Look a Lot Like Christmas" recorded by Perry Como debuts.

12/2/1951: The movie "Scrooge" starring Alastair Sim is released.

Mid 1950s: Silver-colored aluminum trees are marketed. Christmas will never be the same!

1954: Archie's Christmas Stocking debuts from Archie Comics.

12/24/1956: The "I Love Lucy" Christmas episode, in which the Ricardos and the Mertzes suit up as Santa, airs.

MADELINE'S CHRISTMAS
LUDWIG BEMELMANS

1956: "Madeline's Christmas" by Ludwig Bemelmans debuts as a magazine insert (published as a stand-alone book in 1985.)

12/24/1955: "The Honeymooners" Christmas episode about Ralph's gift goof-up airs.

11/15/1954: The movie "White Christmas" starring Bing Crosby and Rosemary Clooney is released.

1954: The song "Home for the Holidays" is published. (It is first recorded by Perry Como.)

1957: The songs "Santa, Bring My Baby Back to Me" and "Blue Christmas" recorded by Elvis Presley debut.

HOW THE GRINCH STOLE CHRISTMAS!
By Dr. Seuss

1957: The children's book "How the Grinch Stole Christmas!" by Dr. Seuss is published.

1957: The song "Mistletoe and Holly" co-written and recorded by Frank Sinatra debuts.

10/1957: The song "Jingle Bell Rock" recorded by Bobby Helms debuts.

1958: The song "Run Rudolph Run" recorded by Chuck Berry debuts.

10/19/1958: The song "Rockin' Around the Christmas Tree" recorded by Brenda Lee debuts.

12/19/1958: Walt Disney's "From All of Us to All of You," a harbinger of Christmas television specials, airs.

12/18/1962: "Mr. Magoo's Christmas Carol," the first animated Christmas special made specifically for television, premieres.

1962: The song "Do You Hear What I Hear?" recorded by the Harry Simeone Chorale is released.

1962: The first of seven Christmas song compilation albums from the Firestone Tire and Rubber Company debuts.

1961: The first of 17 Christmas song compilation albums from the Goodyear Tire and Rubber Company debuts.

LOU MONTE

12/1960: The song "Dominick the Donkey" recorded by Lou Monte debuts. Hee-haw!

12/19/1960: "The Andy Griffith Show" Christmas episode about Mayberry's own Scrooge airs.

1959: The charming (albeit, bizarre) Mexican kiddie film "Santa Claus" is released.

12/20/1962: The first Christmas episode of "The Andy Williams Show" airs and becomes an annual tradition.

10/14/1963: The song "The Most Wonderful Time of the Year" recorded by Andy Williams debuts.

11/22/63: The song "Christmas (Baby Please Come Home)," co-written by Phil Spector and recorded by Darlene Love, debuts.

The Official Beatles FAN CLUB
45
Another Beatles Christmas Record

12/6/1963: The Beatles release a recorded Christmas greeting for fan club members. The band continues this tradition until its final Christmas as a group in 1969.

12/9/63: The song "Little Saint Nick" recorded by the Beach Boys is released.

11/14/1964: The kiddie sci-fi movie "Santa Claus Conquers the Martians" is released.

12/25/1967: The Christmas episode of "The Monkees" airs, with the group's a capella rendition of the hymn "Ríu Chíu."

1967: The song "Snoopy's Christmas" recorded by the Royal Guardsmen debuts.

12/18/1966: The animated TV special "How the Grinch Stole Christmas!" premieres.

12/9/1965: The animated TV special "A Charlie Brown Christmas" premieres.

10/1965: Burl Ives releases the album "Have a Holly Jolly Christmas," with a redo of the title track (which Ives sang for the special "Rudolph the Red-Nosed Reindeer").

12/6/1964: The animated TV special "Rudolph the Red-Nosed Reindeer" premieres.

1968: "Santa Claus Go Straight to the Ghetto" recorded by James Brown debuts.

12/19/1968: The animated TV special "The Little Drummer Boy" premieres.

12/7/1969: The animated TV special "Frosty the Snowman" premieres.

12/19/1969: "The Brady Bunch" Christmas episode in which Cindy asks Santa to grant a special wish airs.

12/1/1970: The movie "Scrooge" starring Albert Finney is released.

12/14/1970: The animated TV special "Santa Claus is Comin' to Town," "starring" Fred Astaire in puppet form, premieres.

11/30/1977: The Bing Crosby-David Bowie duet "Little Drummer Boy/Peace on Earth" airs.

12/12/75: Bruce Springsteen records his live version of "Santa Claus is Comin' to Town," which becomes a radio perennial.

12/10/1974: The animated TV special "The Year Without a Santa Claus" premieres.

1974: KFC Japan rolls out its "Kentucky for Christmas" promotion, making buckets of KFC fried chicken a Christmas tradition in Japan.

12/1/1971: The song "Happy Christmas (War is Over)" recorded by John Lennon and Yoko Ono debuts.

11/17/1978: TV's "Star Wars Holiday Special" premieres. An infamous bomb, the show does not air again for decades.

11/16/1979: The song "Simply Having a Wonderful Christmastime" recorded by Paul McCartney debuts.

1981: The song "Christmas Wrapping" recorded by the Waitresses is released.

11/18/1983: The movie "A Christmas Story" starring Peter Billingsley is released.

12/3/1984: The song (and video) "Do They Know It's Christmas," recorded by the musical collective Band Aid to benefit Ethiopian famine victims, debuts.

Thereafter: Many more Christmas milestones are established, with many more to come. Ho, ho, ho!

12/11/1992: "The Muppets Christmas Carol" proves yet again that Dickens' Scrooge is enduring — and adaptable.

12/17/1989: TV's "The Simpsons" debuts with a Christmas episode.

12/1/1989: The movie "National Lampoon's Christmas Vacation" starring Chevy Chase is released.

11/25/1987: The song "Christmas in Hollis" recorded by Run-DMC debuts.

The firstest Noël

The very first instance of Christmas media — millennia before "A Very Brady Christmas" and "Grandma Got Run Over by a Reindeer" — was found in the New Testament.

That's a pretty big meatball. Not being anything approaching a Bible scholar, I'm going to tread lightly. I only have two thin possible credentials in this regard: having attended approximately 1,000 Catholic Masses, and the fact that my old college roommate wrote "Ken's Guide to the Bible" (1995, Blast Books).

The New Testament was written, the scholars reckon, between 50 and 62 A.D., and first published in, oh, 1611. Of course, it has been handed down, translated and re-translated many times over many centuries. I'm using a venerable volume, practically an heirloom, borrowed from a real-deal observant family (they're Southerners): The Thompson Chain-Reference Bible, published by the B.B. Kirkbride Bible Company of Indianapolis in 1964, King James version, 63rd printing, first edition published in 1908.

I'm leaving nothing to chance.

To my thinking, Luke gave us the sweet, "Silent Night"-ish vision of the First Noël, leaving out the mass infanticide (a fancy term for baby-killing), while Matthew squarely took on that grim reality.

Following are the events of the first Christmas as reported in Luke 2. (For fellow non-scholars, I've joined paragraphs, removed the little numbers, added ellipses when skipping ahead, updated the archaic punctuation, and capitalized Wise Men for clarity.)

"And it came to pass in those days, that there went out a decree from Caesar Augustus, that all the world should be taxed. ... And Joseph also went up from Galilee, out of the city of Nazareth, into Judaea, unto the city of David, which is called Bethlehem (because he was of the house and lineage of David); To be taxed with Mary his espoused wife, being great with child."

Hmmm, "great with child." I remember how, in Catholic school, the word "virgin" was always stressed — the "virgin mother," the "virgin birth." Of course, we were children, and had no idea what the nuns were talking about. We just obediently accepted what we were told, which is what Catholic schoolchildren did in those days.

We were also told that Jesus was born of the "immaculate conception" without "original sin," but that all of us were born *with* "original sin." And there was nothing we could do about it. This sounded unfair, but again, we didn't know exactly what the nuns were getting at. Back to Luke:

"And she brought forth her firstborn son, and wrapped him in swaddling clothes, and laid him in a manger; because there was no room for them in the inn. And there were in the same country shepherds abiding in the field, keeping watch over their flock by night. And, lo, the angel of the Lord came upon them ... And the angel said unto them, Fear not: for, behold, I bring you good tidings of great joy, which shall be to all people. For unto you is born this day in the city of David a Saviour, which is Christ the Lord."

Can't you just hear Linus speaking those words on the stage during the pageant rehearsal? Eight years of Catholic school, and I got most of my Bible-learnin' from "A Charlie Brown Christmas" and "Jesus Christ Superstar." Back to Luke 2:

"And this shall be a sign unto you; Ye shall find the babe wrapped in swaddling clothes, lying in a manger. And suddenly there was with the angel a multitude of the heavenly host praising God, and saying, Glory to God in the highest, and on earth peace, good will toward men. ... the shepherds said one to another, Let us now go even unto Bethlehem, and see this thing which is come to pass, which the Lord hath made known unto us. And they came with haste, and found Mary, and Joseph, and the babe lying in a manger. ... And the shepherds returned, glorifying and praising God for all the things that they had heard and seen, as it was told unto them. And when eight days were accomplished for the circumcising of the child, his name was called JESUS, which was so named of the angel before he was conceived in the womb."

(Forgive me, but the word "circumcising" always gives me pause, especially when set centuries before laser surgery.)

LET'S NOW SWITCH OVER TO MATTHEW, CHAPTER

2 as well, in which King Herod dispatches the Wise Men to find Baby Jesus. (A foreboding musical theme is heard here.)

"When (Herod) had gathered all the chief priests and scribes of the people together, he demanded of them where Christ should be born. And they said unto him, in Bethlehem of Judaea: for thus it is written by the prophet, And thou Bethlehem, in the land of Juda ... for out of thee shall come a Governor, that shall rule my people Israel."

Herod gives every impression that he welcomes this news. And that *he* wants to get in on the worshipping, too.

"Then Herod, when he had privily called the Wise Men, enquired of them diligently what time the star appeared. And he sent them to Bethlehem and said, Go and search diligently for the young child; and when ye have found him, bring me word again, that I may come and worship him also."

Sounds like a nice fella, eh? The Wise Men make the trek, and present Baby Jesus with history's first-ever Christmas gifts.

"When they (the Wise Men) had heard the king, they departed; and, lo, the star, which they saw in the east, went before them, till it came and stood over where the young child was. When they saw the star, they rejoiced with exceeding great joy ... they saw the young child with Mary his mother, and fell down, and worshipped him: and when they had opened their treasures, they presented unto him gifts; gold, and frankincense, and myrrh."

WE LITTLE KIDS KNEW WHAT GOLD WAS, BUT

what were frankincense and myrrh? One of us asked Sister, who told us they were fragrances. (I later learned that myrrh was used for burials — a foreshadowing?)

Of course, in catechism class, my first-grade ears heard "Frankenstein" instead of "frankincense," and I got excited for a moment. Was one of the Wise Men giving Baby Jesus a Frankenstein toy for Christmas?

Persnickety ex-Catholic-school boy that I am, I still say "gold, Frankenstein and myrrh" on those improbable occasions when the Gifts of the Magi come up in conversation. Because that's what persnickety ex-Catholic-school boys do.

Back to Matthew. It'd been nice if the story of the first Noël wrapped here, but things take a dark turn. Herod is a liar. He sent the Wise Men to Bethlehem for a nefarious purpose. Thank God, literally, for dreams and angelic visions:

"And being warned of God in a dream that they should not return to Herod, they (the Wise Men) departed into their own country in another way. And when they were departed, behold, the angel of the Lord appeareth to Joseph in a dream, saying, Arise, and take the young child and his mother, and flee into Egypt, and be thou there until I bring thee word: for Herod will seek the young child to destroy him."

Now comes the really bad part.

"Then Herod, when he saw that he was mocked by the Wise Men, was exceedingly wroth, and sent forth, and slew all the children that were in Bethlehem, and in all the coasts thereof, from two years old and under, according to the time which he had diligently enquired of the Wise Men. ... In Rama there was a voice heard, lamentation, and weeping, and great mourning, Rachel weeping for her children, and would not be comforted, because they are not."

So there was a bloodbath. Herod committed mass infanticide, which Baby Jesus survived with inside information from an angel.

Still, in miniature Nativity sets, lawn Nativity sets, dramatic

A holy card from Italy depicts the Madonna and Baby Jesus.

recreations of the first Christmas and especially the beloved hymns we hear every year at Christmastime, we are not usually reminded of Herod's murderous campaign and Jesus' flight.

This is not to sound righteous. Considering Christ's torturous death 33 years later, it's a good thing to memorialize that earliest time when, for one silent night, all was calm and all was bright.

I'll lay out some lyrics. You'll know the melodies.

"With angelic host proclaim / Christ is born in Bethlehem ..."

"'Round young virgin mother and child ..."

"Remember Christ thy savior was born on Christmas day ..."

"O holy night, the stars are brightly shining / It is the night of our dear Savior's birth ..."

Whether one believes Christ is the son of God, or a historical figure, or a just a character in a sweet story about no room at the inn, we can cling to that all-is-calm moment in Bethlehem, with Baby Jesus laying on the straw, while Mary, Joseph, the Wise Men, the shepherds, the animals, an angel of the Lord — and possibly a little drummer boy — were frozen in rapt adoration.

The 'two' Christmases

One takes place at a manger in Bethlehem. The other, at a toy factory at the North Pole.

BEING A CATHOLIC SCHOOL BOY, I WAS BUT A squirt when it dawned on me that there were "two" Christmases — the sacred one with Baby Jesus, and the *commercial* one with Santa Claus, Rudolph and the caroling residents of Who-ville.

This was decades before the slogan "Keep Christ in Christmas" would appear on lawn signs and bumper stickers every December.

But in the still surprisingly repressed middle 1960s, the intrepid nuns at Holy Rosary School in the Diocese of Camden darned near coined that phrase themselves. For starters, they informed us that "Christmas" was a shortening of "Christ's Mass."

Even the word "holiday" was a subject of scrutiny.

Christmas, the nuns stressed at every opportunity, was a *"holy day,"* not a "holiday." They spoke of another semantic sin — one I feared my own family was guilty of.

In advertising and on occasional correspondence, you would notice the use of the spelling "Xmas" instead of "Christmas." To we tadpoles, it was a mere abbreviation — one we'd gotten used to — and we didn't give it much thought. But one day, the nuns warned us *never* to use the word Xmas, because it's a tool of godless heathens to "X" out, or cross out, Christ.

Could this be? I'd noticed that at home, the boxes of Christmas decorations we unearthed from the crawlspace every year were marked "Xmas" in my father's crude hand. I asked him if he meant to cross out Christ. He said no, the word Xmas was used to save time when marking boxes to pack up the decorations.

I didn't think of my father as a godless heathen, so I accepted his word over the nuns'. It was an early instance of applying shades-of-gray in my little black-and-white world.

Another area in which you noticed the divide was in Christmas songs. Compare "O Come All Ye Faithful" to "Jingle Bells." Or

"Hark! The Herald Angels Sing" to "Rudolph the Red-Nosed Reindeer." Or "The First Noël" to "Santa Claus is Comin' to Town." During Sunday Mass, of course, we didn't sing any of the "fun" Christmas songs — just the "holy" ones.

At Holy Rosary School, they would put up decorations which fostered Christmas-is-coming excitement. But again, these were more "holy day"-ish than "holiday"-ish.

Around the school, you would see something called Advent wreaths, Advent being a four-week observance in advance of Christmas. The wreath had four candles, three pink (for the 21 days prior to Christmas week) and one purple (for the Big Week).

But there were *some* concessions to the commercial Christmas.

WHEN I WAS IN THE SECOND GRADE, WE HAD A Christmas pageant at which I finally learned a fundamental skill that had eluded me all my young life: how to tell my left from my right. Try as I might, I couldn't grasp the concept. Grownups would say, "This is your left and this is your right," and I wouldn't know what in the world they were talking about.

For the pageant, I was one of three boys chosen to play toy soldiers under the tree on Christmas morning. A fifth-grade girl who was dressed as a Christmas fairy — tiara, tutu, ballet slippers, wand topped with glittery gold star — pirouetted our way and waved her wand over us. We spun in place as if being animated for the first time. Then Tchaikovsky's "March of the Toy Soldiers" was played on a precariously tuned piano as we marched, first to the left and then to the right. Not knowing my left from my right, I kept colliding with James Jenkins. The death-dealing scowl from Sister Miriam Veronica ensured that from this day forward, I would never again mistake my left for my right.

On the last day of school before the week-long holiday, Father Conlon would come to every classroom and hand out our Christmas present. Each child in Grades 1 through 8 received a small, unwrapped, unmarked, white-cardboard box of hard candy. The lid was held in place by an inch-long piece of tape. Within the box were assorted hard candies the consistency of candy canes, but in several colors (white, red, green, yellow), flavors (lemon was my favorite) and shapes. It wasn't Whitman's or See's, but it *did* qualify as candy, and we were happy. Well, we were sugared up. We downed at least a third of the box before getting home.

You know who *else* was happy? Dentists.

GROWING UP IN AN 85-PERCENT JEWISH NEIGH-

borhood added another twist to my understanding of Christmas.

I was raised in a development known as Woodcrest, which was sometimes called "Little Israel," even by Jewish residents. So when I say, "Some of my best friends are Jewish," it's not in the Archie Bunker sense. I grew up playing in the rec rooms of a half-dozen Jewish households.

In December, you could easily spot the Christian households in Woodcrest by the colorful lights on their homes. On average, a given block would be air-raid dark except for one or two houses. My Aunt Peggy from Long Island called it "depressing."

This split made me feel sorry for my Jewish friends. In my thinking, how could they possibly enjoy watching the TV special "Rudolph the Red-Nosed Reindeer" if they didn't "believe" in Christmas? How could they enjoy Christmas decorations ... Christmas carols ... Christmas cookies ... even candy canes? Wasn't the very presence of these things a torture to them? It was as if the world was having a gigantic party, but they weren't invited.

I remember I once told Mrs. Sidewater that I felt sorry for her son Howard, because he didn't get Christmas toys. She informed me, "Howard gets Chanukah toys *and* Christmas toys." That twisted my brain a little. I knew what Christmas toys were — shiny, colorful, well-advertised marvels of manufacturing like Stick Shift Racerific and Barbie's Country Camper and the Great Garloo. But what were *Chanukah* toys? I pictured weird, unpainted, wooden toys from, like, the 19th century.

Despite being a very Jewish town, Woodcrest had a Christmas Eve tradition: Santa Claus rode down every street atop a fire truck, illuminated by a spotlight. A clanging bell announced his imminent arrival from a block away. It was magical. But why did they do this in a mostly Jewish development? I still don't know, but I'm very grateful. Half the time, Santa Claus was played by Mr. Goldberg, a family friend. He wore the costume well. But I wondered: Why would a Jewish man play Santa Claus?

LATER IN LIFE, I FOUND OUT THAT, FOR ALL THE

decrying of the commercial Christmas, it has one outcome even the most Jesus-y person might approve of: Many non-Christians celebrate Christmas. They don't believe Jesus Christ is the son of God, but they've adopted Christmas. (FYI, I identify as a "kind-of-secular-humanist-devout-lapsed-Catholic-with-agnostic leanings," a contradictory category all my own.) Many non-Christians think of it as, yes, a big party with cookies and twinkling lights, but also a time to take stock of your behavior toward your fellow man.

The most secular of TV specials emphasized charity and good will toward men, from the Grinch carving the roast beast to the Bumble putting a star atop the tree to Ralph telling Alice how people bumping into each other on the bustling streets of Bensonhurst laugh it off as it gets closer to Christmas Eve.

Hey, this aspect of commercial Christmas even happened for us Catholic school kids. Every December, we little squirts contemplated our behavior over the previous 11 months, as in: Were we naughty or nice? We would never admit to the nuns that this contemplation was inspired less by Baby Jesus in the manger than by greed for gifts under the tree.

When we were *very* young, we actually fretted over this. Does Santa know of the times I said cuss words, or was mean to my little brother? Would this translate into fewer toys?

Even as we got older and were less inclined to believe in Santa, this year-end assessment continued. It's a universal urge. At this festive time of year, one's propensity for charity increases. Toy drives ... coat drives ... food drives ... dropping a few bucks in the Salvation Army lady's bucket as she rings the bell.

The trick would be to, as Dickens wrote, make mankind your business throughout the year, not just in December. That would *really* be a Christmas miracle.

During Sunday Mass, we Catholic school kids didn't sing any of the "fun" Christmas songs — just the "holy" ones.

Christmas crystalizes

The patron saint of sailors, pawnbrokers, brewers, and repentant thieves. Sounds like a saint who didn't mind getting his hands dirty.

But St. Nicholas was also the patron saint of children. And one constant in Nicholas' life view is shared by the "Santa Claus" we often call "Old St. Nick": giving gifts anonymously.

Santa makes his Christmas Eve deliveries under cloak of darkness, when children are asleep. He doesn't hang around until morning to bask in their gratitude. *The act itself* is reward enough.

(This idea shows up in Dickens also. When the redeemed Scrooge sends a prize turkey to the Cratchits on Christmas morning, he delights in the fact that they won't know the benefactor.)

St. Nicholas — born in 270 A.D., died in 342, as far as is known — was a Christian monk who lived in what is now Turkey, and at age 30 became the bishop of Myra. It is believed his parents were well-off do-gooders who died while administering to diseased people, having contracted disease themselves. Nicholas used his inheritance to fund his anonymous — and nocturnal (just like Santa) — gift-giving.

One story has him tossing three bags of gold, on consecutive nights, into the home of a destitute man who was on the verge of selling his daughters into prostitution.

But wild legends were assigned to Nicholas also. One sounds like it could have been written by Stephen King (proposed title: "The Pickled Children"). In it, Nicholas resurrects three children who were murdered by a butcher and pickled in brine to be sold as — gross-out warning — pork.

Another legend in this vein has Nicholas chopping down a tree possessed by a demon. (Suddenly, the 1959 Mexican film "Santa Claus," in which Santa matches wits with a devil, doesn't seem so weird.)

Nicholas' legend traveled, inspiring copycat philanthropy. In the Middles Ages, needy families awoke on Dec. 6, the feast of St. Nicholas, to find money, food and clothing left in their homes. Wrote John Pronechen for the *National Catholic Register:* "St. Nicholas' popularity

The real St. Nicholas wasn't necessarily jolly, but he did have a knack for gift-giving.

eventually spread to northern Europe, where stories of the monk mingled with Teutonic folktales of elves and sky-chariots."

Elves? Sky-chariots? The modern Santa Claus was taking shape. In the Netherlands, St. Nicholas was called "Sinterklaas." In the 1620s, Dutch settlers carried this moniker to Manhattan, where English speakers massaged the pronunciation into "Santa Claus."

MUCH WAS ADDED TO THE LEGEND IN THE 19TH century, but in ways that were less religious, more fanciful. In 1822, Santa Claus was linked with Christmas in the poem "A Visit From St. Nicholas," better known as "The Night Before Christmas." (The poem was published anonymously; Clement Clarke Moore later claimed authorship.)

In 1862, political cartoonist Thomas Nast created a visual ideal of Santa — smiling, bearded, red suit, pipe — that yet endures (further modernized by such illustrators as J.C. Leyendecker, Norman Rockwell and Haddon Sundblom).

To introduce another twist to an already twisty origin story, Santa Claus isn't the same entity as "Father Christmas," necessarily. Both have the white beard, all right, but Father Christmas (who debuted in the 17th century) often wore green, a color representing the coming spring. Later, the characters coalesced, kind of.

Santa Claus aside, much that we associate with the Christmas holiday was introduced as early as the 16th century. The first Christmas trees, lit with candles, are believed to have originated in Germany in the 1500s, and the first known Christmas card was sent in 1611.

But the holiday as we know it really came together in the 19th century, in a time and place we wistfully call "Victorian England" — named for Queen Victoria (1819-1901), whose German husband, Prince Albert, installed a Christmas tree in Windsor Castle in the 1840s.

Left: The first commercially printed and marketed Christmas card, from 1843, bids "A Merry Christmas and a Happy New Year to You." In oval below: The card's illustrator, John Callcott Horsley. Below right: A card from 1850.

Cards © current copyright holders. Horsely photo by Henry Maull and George Henry Polyblank, the Wellcome Collection, London

TECHNOLOGY NUDGED THE HOLIDAY ALONG VIA the Victorian era's industrial revolution. Manufacturing made toys accessible to folks outside of the wealthy class. Advancements in printing brought about two key events in 1843: the publication of "A Christmas Carol" (a book which cemented many tenets of the period), and the marketing of Christmas cards.

The latter event occurred when a British museum founder spearheaded the first printing and mailing of Christmas cards for a mundane reason: his own convenience.

In Victorian England, you see, another tradition that yet survives was in full swing: sending year-end correspondence to family and associates. This presented a quandary for Sir Henry Cole (1808-1882), founder of London's Victoria and Albert Museum. How could he satisfy the social requirement of the year-end letter, but not be swallowed up by the enormity of the task?

Cole conceived the idea to print illustrated cards. He sketched a prototype and gave it to a friend, artist John Callcott Horsley (1817-1903), to execute. Horsley's illustration shows smiling, well-dressed Brits clutching glasses of wine. A turkey is carved, a little girl is given a taste of wine. This scene is flanked by images of poor folks receiving comfort. The greeting "A Merry Christmas and a Happy New Year to You" is preceded and followed by fill-in-the-blank dotted lines wherein Cole — or anyone — could personalize the card. An inscription at the bottom provides a further clue to the card's origin: "Published at Summerly's Home Treasury Office, 12 Old Bond Street, London." Accounts differ on the amount printed — 1,000? 2,050? — and some were said to have been sold by Cole for a shilling apiece.

(There is a competing narrative from the same decade. Thomas Shorrock of Scotland printed Christmas cards some time in the 1840s, which show a smiling, red-nosed man — he looks drunk — holding a bottle and standing in snow, with the greeting *"A Guid New Year Tae Ye."*)

In the ensuing decades, the practice crossed the pond to the United States. The first Christmas cards in America were printed in 1875 by Louis Prang (1824-1909), a German immigrant then based in Massachusetts, using his chromolithographic process. (Don't ask.) Prang is called the "father of the American Christmas Card."

But these were still *postcards.* Around 1912, the Norfolk Post Card Company, then in Missouri, printed its first Christmas cards, later introducing the innovation that the cards be folded and inserted into an envelope. In 1928, the company changed its name to Hallmark. Oh, and that company also invented wrapping paper.

Christmas as we know it was *on,* baby.

God bless us, every one

Charles Dickens' 1843 ghost story still haunts us

DID CHARLES DICKENS FEAR HE HAD GONE A BIT too far with his tale of death and regret; the poor, the rich, the infirm, the indifferent; repentance, forgiveness and second chances; redemption and the immortal soul?

In a prologue to the 1931 film "Frankenstein," the actor Edward Van Sloan hints at the horrors to follow and says with a shrug, "Well, we've warned you." Dickens, in a brief preface to "A Christmas Carol," likewise seemed to fret over what effect his 1843 novella might have on its readers.

"I have endeavored in this Ghostly little book to raise the Ghost of an Idea which shall not put any readers out of humor with themselves, with each other, with the season, or with me," he wrote.

What was Dickens getting at? The book is quite bleak at times, and not a little political. (Modern audiences are accustomed to these aspects, as this sometimes deadly serious material has been interpreted by Jim Carrey, the Muppets and Mr. Magoo.)

Was Dickens worried that the rich ruling class might take offense at his unblinking examination of classism and the tragic consequences of the wealth gap? Or that the ghosts in the story might give children nightmares?

IT REMAINS THAT "A CHRISTMAS CAROL," WHICH sold 6,000 copies on its first day of publication, is the most influential Christmas story since the New Testament. At least 15 movie and television adaptations have been made from it, with Scrooge played by Seymour Hicks, Reginald Owen, Alastair Sim, Fredric March, Basil Rathbone, Albert Finney, George C. Scott, Michael Caine, Patrick Stewart, Christopher Plummer and, in the silent movie days, Daniel Smith and Marc McDermott. The piece is performed live on hundreds of stages and on radio every year.

And Ebenezer Scrooge has dozens of descendants in popular culture, from the Grinch to the Abominable Snowmonster to Old Man Potter from Frank Capra's "It's a Wonderful Life" — even if Potter never gets his moment of redemption.

Dickens' story is so familiar, a synopsis seems like unnecessary folly, so naturally, I'll supply one, albeit a quickie.

It's Christmas Eve in old London ... Ebenezer Scrooge is the surviving partner of Scrooge & Marley, a cut-throat bank-and-loan ... Marley died seven years ago this very night, but cheapskate Scrooge never bothered to paint Marley's name off the sign (and now answers to either name) ... this merciless creditor is outright vicious to his nephew, Fred, and his clerk, Bob Cratchit, and calls Christmas a "humbug" ... that night, Scrooge is visited by Marley's ghost, a mournful phantom weighted down with chains who tells Scrooge, "You have a chance and hope of escaping my fate" ... Scrooge is visited by the Ghost of Christmas Past, who replays his life ... Christmas Present, who reveals the lives of those around him ... and Christmas Yet to Come, who unveils a dark future ... but is it "the" future? ... and will it teach Scrooge to keep Christmas in his heart and be good to his fellow man?

Spoiler alert: I think you know the answer.

Charles Dickens (1812-1870) championed the "lower classes."
1858 photograph

THE TALE'S EXPLORATION OF POVERTY IS HARDLY unfamiliar territory in Dickens' canon. These themes are present in "Oliver Twist" (1839), "Bleak House" (1852), "Hard Times" (1854), and "Great Expectations" (1861), for a few famous examples. Dickens seemed intent on calling on people of means to consider the plight of those less fortunate. These many years hence, the need for reiteration of same has never let up, unfortunately.

Dickens (1812-1870) was born in Portsmouth, England. His father, John Dickens, did time in a debtors' prison (a theme in "A Christmas Carol"). As a youth, Dickens labored in a rat-infested warehouse above the Thames. In his 15 novels and five novellas, the writer often gave voice to the working class and poor of Victorian England. His own name would enter the vernacular. The adjective "Dickensian" is used to describe situations in which the wealth gap makes itself felt in terrible, powerful ways.

The story in "A Christmas Carol" is deceptively simplistic — like I said, even Mr. Magoo had a crack at it — but the original is always singular, and always worth revisiting for its rich language.

Wrote Dickens of Scrooge: *"Oh! but he was a tight-fisted hand at the grindstone, Scrooge! a squeezing, wrenching, grasping, scraping, clutching, covetous old sinner! Hard and sharp as flint, from which no steel had ever struck out generous fire, secret, and self-contained, and solitary as an oyster. ... Even the blind men's dogs appeared to know him; and, when they saw him coming on, would tug their owners into doorways and up courts; and then would wag their tails as though they said, 'No eye at all is better than an evil eye, dark master!'"*

Take it easy, Fido.

He described the ghost of Marley as wearing *"his pigtail, usual waistcoat, tights and boots; the tassels on the latter bristling like his pigtail, and his coat-skirts, and the hair upon his head. The chain he drew was clasped about his middle. It was long, and wound about him like a tail; and it was made (for Scrooge observed it closely) of cash-boxes, keys, padlocks, ledgers, deeds, and heavy purses wrought in steel. His body was transparent; so that Scrooge, observing him, and looking through his waistcoat, could see the two buttons on his coat behind."*

Makeup artists, costumers and FX wizards by the hundreds have had a field day bringing these descriptions to life over the decades.

this it would have been difficult to detach its figure from the night, and separate it from the darkness by which it was surrounded."

In the second of the mere two sentences of his preface, Dickens hoped out loud that "A Christmas Carol" might be useful to readers beyond its initial publication: "May it haunt their house pleasantly, and no one wish to lay it."

Mission accomplished. Dickens' book has been haunting our houses pleasantly for going on two centuries.

A morality play, a ghost story and, I daresay, the best Christmas tale ever written, Dickens' "A Christmas Carol" will endure for as long as there is a human race.

It reminds us that Christmas is a time to take stock of our lives and contemplate our legacies. And to put ourselves in the next man's shoes, even if those shoes are shabby and worn.

Especially if they are.

Left: Old Fezziwig's ball by Punch cartoonist John Leech (1817-1864), illustrator of the first edition. Below: Marley haunts Scrooge in artwork by another renowned interpreter, Arthur Rackham (1867-1939).

DICKENS' VISION OF THE ROOM TRANSFORMED
by the Ghost of Christmas Present comes off like the best holiday party you could imagine: *"The walls and ceiling were so hung with living green that it looked like a perfect grove; from every part of which bright, gleaming berries glistened. The crisp leaves of holly, mistletoe and ivy reflected back the light ... Heaped up on the floor, to form a kind of throne, were turkeys, geese, game, poultry, brawn, great joints of meat, sucking-pigs, long wreaths of sausages, mince-pies, plum-puddings, barrels of oysters, red-hot chestnuts, cherry-cheeked apples, juicy oranges, luscious pears, immense twelfth-cakes, and seething bowls of punch ..."*

Bring on the barrels of oysters and immense twelfth-cakes!

A character that comes to represent the poor and infirm is Tim, the young son of Bob Cratchit who suffers from an undisclosed illness, uses a crutch and, whatever his ailment, is apparently in danger of dying. Says Bob of Tiny Tim: *"Somehow, he gets thoughtful, sitting by himself so much, and thinks the strangest things you ever heard. He told me, coming home, that he hoped the people saw him in the church, because he was a cripple, and it might be pleasant to them to remember, upon Christmas Day, who made lame beggars walk and blind men see."*

The description of the Ghost of Christmas Yet to Come is scarier than a dozen Freddy Krueger movies: *"The phantom slowly, gravely, silently approached ... in the very air through which this spirit moved it seemed to scatter gloom and mystery. It was shrouded in a deep black garment, which concealed its head, its face, its form, and left nothing of it visible save one outstretched hand. But for*

Wishing you a happy Christmas

FATHER CHRISTMAS'
ABC

LONDON.
F. WARNE & Cº
AND NEW YORK.
[ALL RIGHTS RESERVED]

There's nothing Santa
more enjoys
Than making toys for
girls and boys,
And in his way he's
wondrous wise,
For he knows just
what'll please
your eyes.

CHRISTMAS JOYS

A Joyful
Christmas

Ellen H. Clapsaddle

A merry Christmas to you

A happy Christmas

"THINE OWN WISH WISH I THEE"

Old-timey greetings

Christmas cards from the Victorian and early post-Victorian eras have a charm all their own, and the evolution of Santa Claus can be charted therein. The cards above and at left are by Ellen Hattie Clapsaddle (1865-1934), whose illustrations of children made her one of the most prolific greeting-card artists of her time. The top-right card on the opposite page was printed by Frederick Warne & Co., publisher of many books by Beatrix Potter.

A JOYFUL CHRISTMAS.

A simple token . . . . .
. . . . . . sent to say,
I think of you . . . .
this Christmas Day.

The great outdoors: From above, angels, poinsettias and candles make for a great holiday combination; Victorian carolers were once a prevalent theme in Christmas cards, right down to the top hats and hoop skirts; a horse-drawn sleigh is the only way to travel through a snowy downtown. Opposite page, from top: Snowbound churches beckon worshippers in a pair of cards; imagine the shock and horror of finding frozen babies in your mailbox on Christmas Eve.

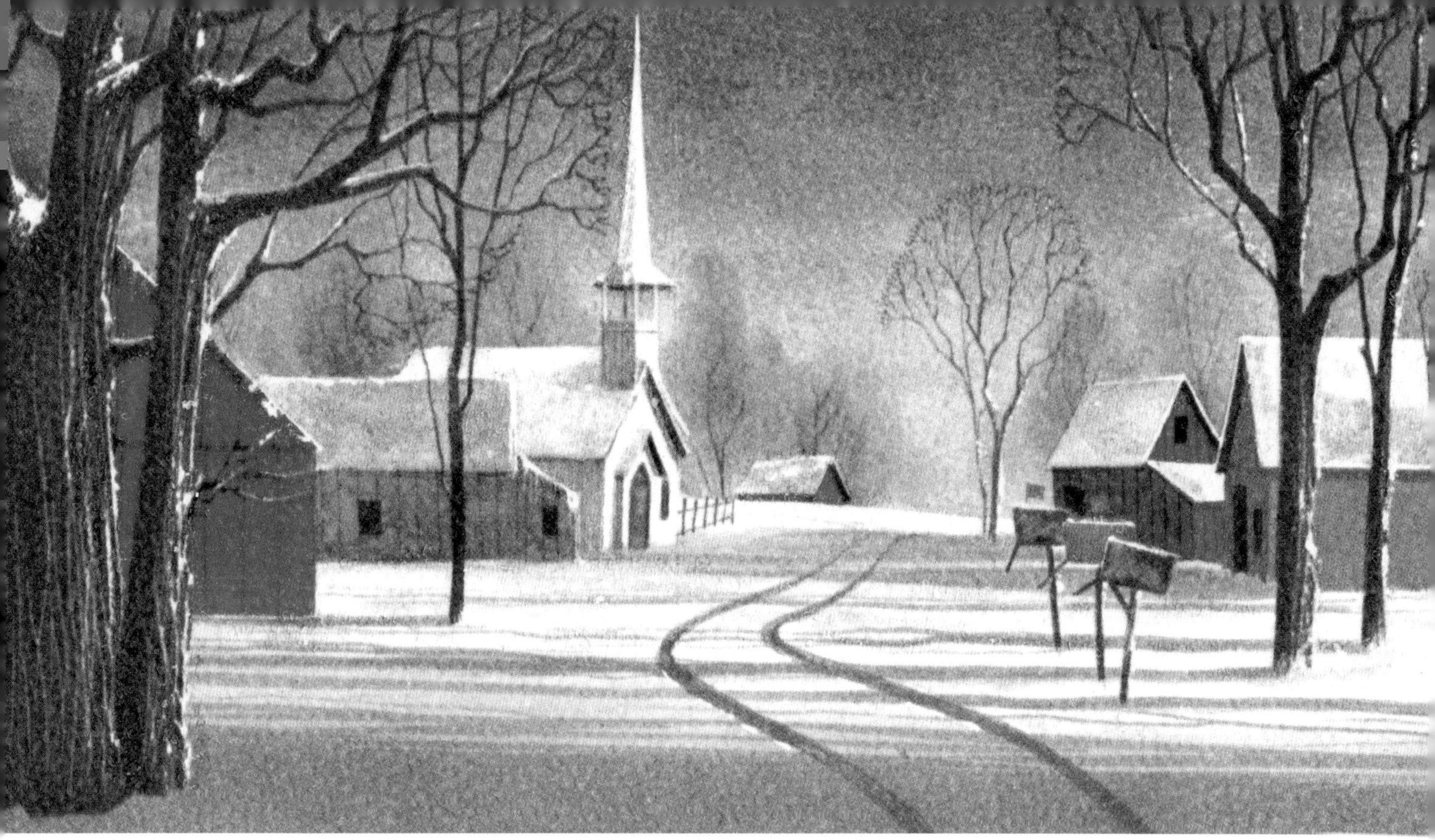

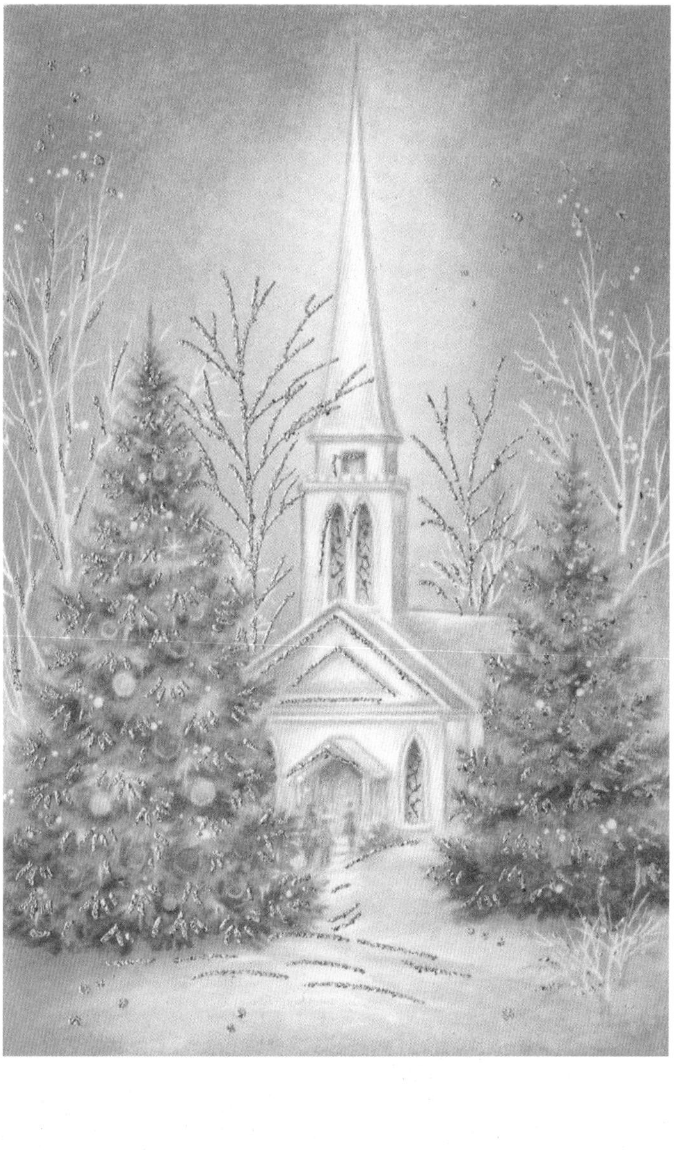

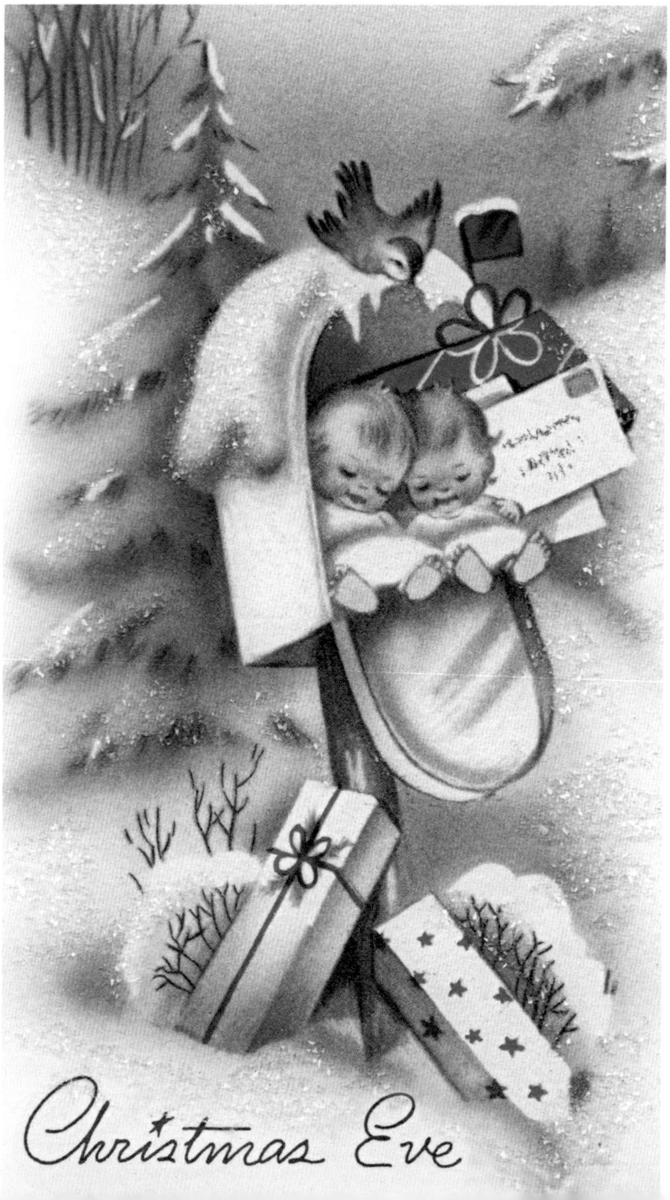
Christmas Eve

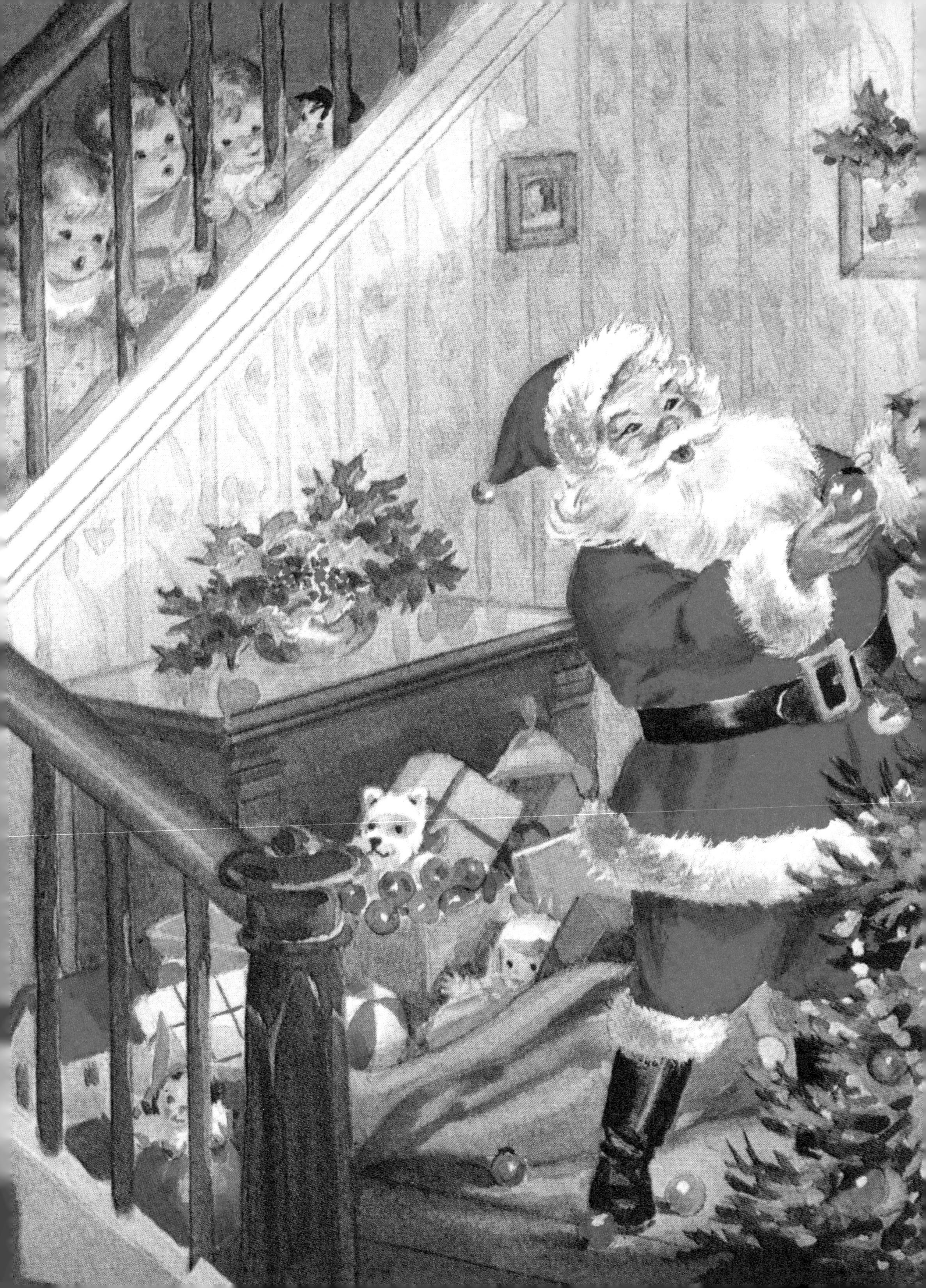

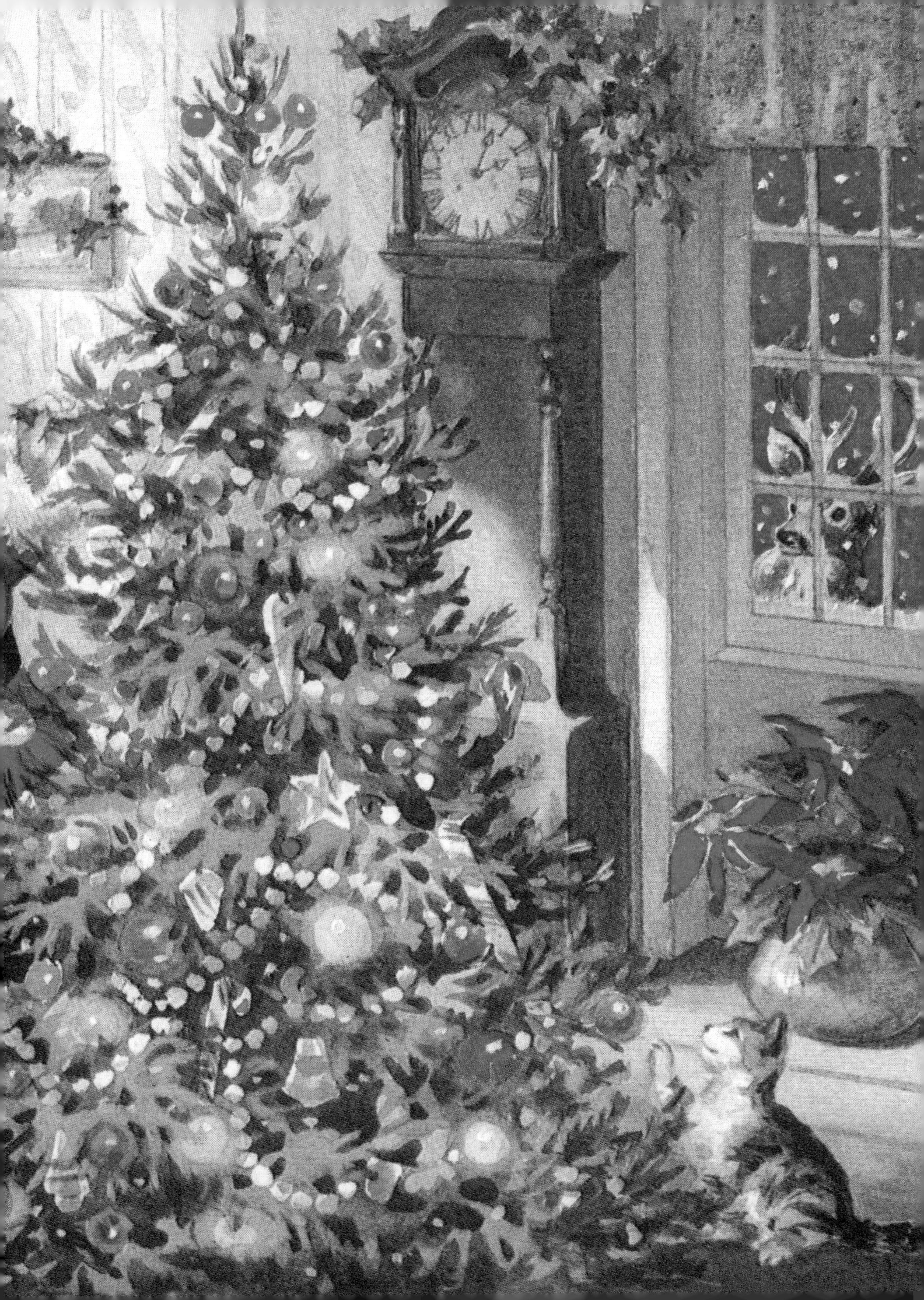

MERRY CHRISTMAS

A Christmas-time greeting

Merrie, Merrie Christmas

Merry Christmas to All!

The night
before Christmas—

Kris being Kris

In this selection of Christmas cards from the 1950s and '60s, Santa Claus is shown doing what he does best, checking his list, packing his sleigh, making deliveries, eating cookies, dancing with elves, and generally being his jolly self. (Printing buffs, please take note of the "popcorn embossing" on the top card of the opposite page.) Following page: Cards of Santa Claus merely saying "Hi!" or "Hello!" were, looking back, a curious trend of the period. There were dozens of them!

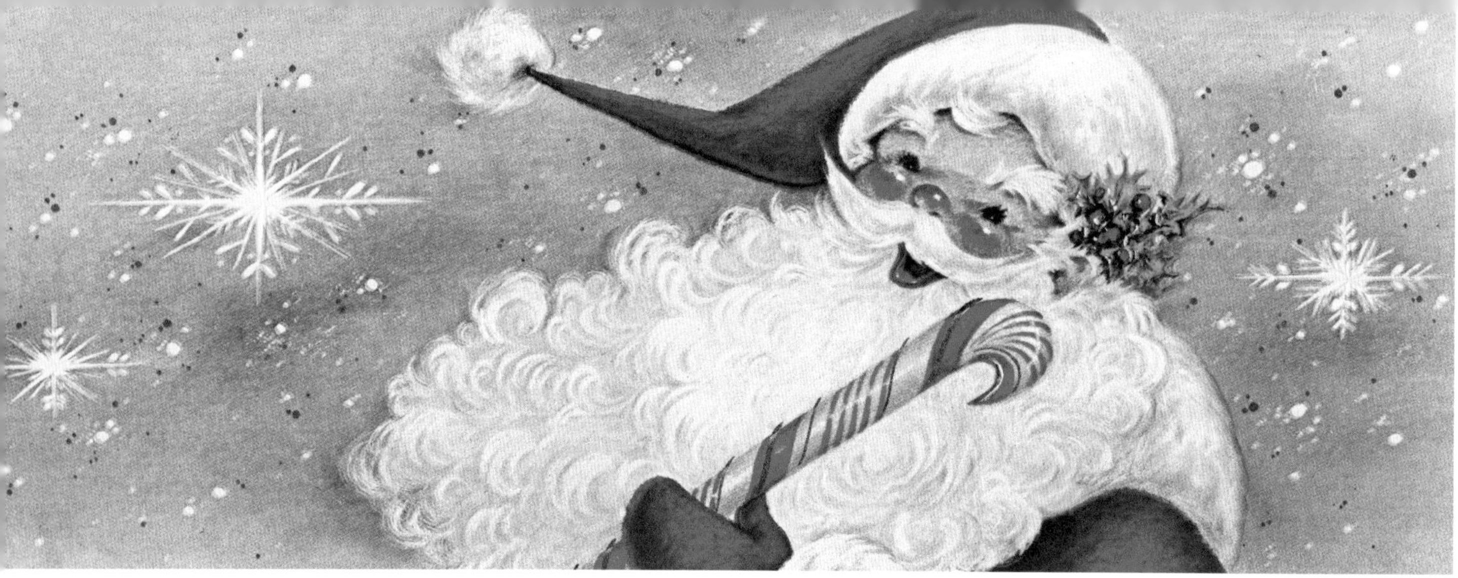

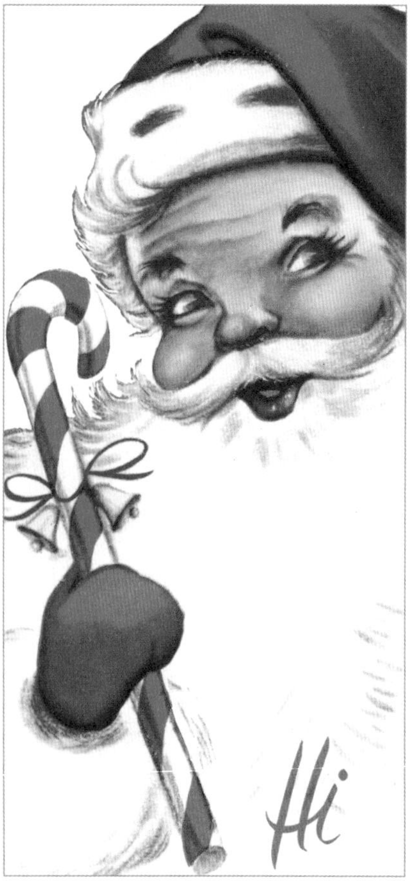
Hi

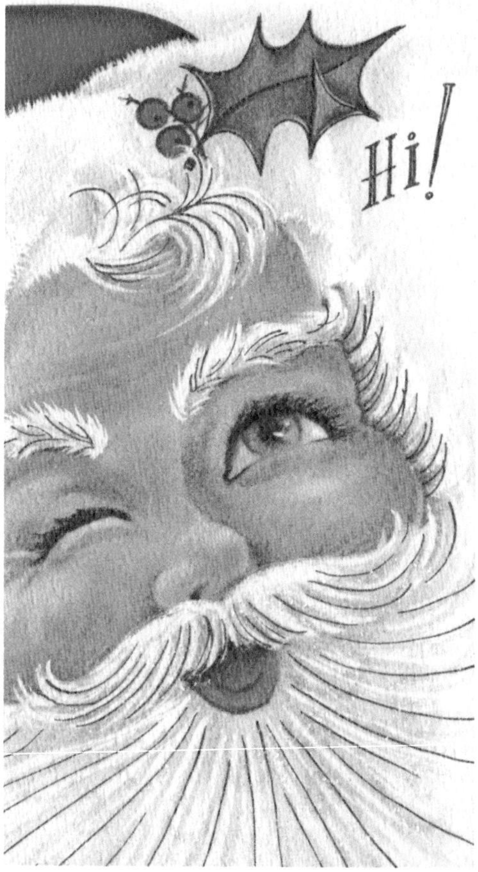
Hi!

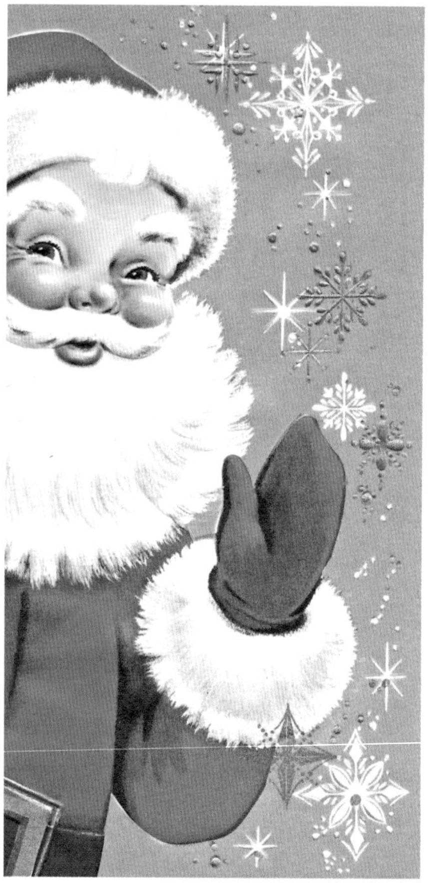

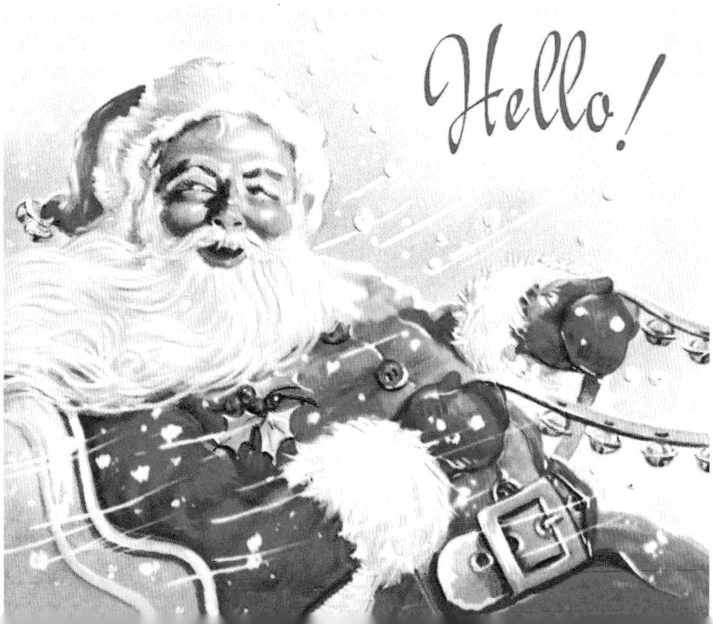
Hello!

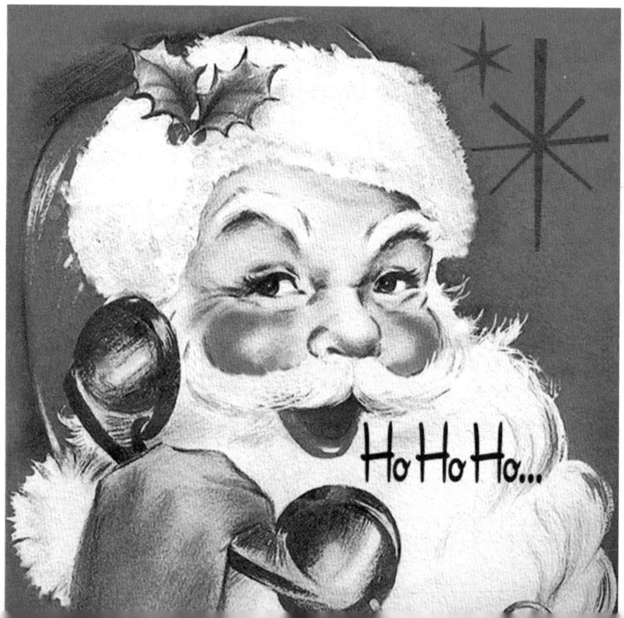
Ho Ho Ho...

St. Nick, soldier boy

Everybody was expected to do their bit for the war effort during the years of World War II. Even Santa Claus was pressed into service, selling war bonds and appearing on posters, Christmas cards, comic books, and covers of *Yank* magazine in the fight against the Axis powers. From top left: Hitler, Tojo and Mussolini are on Santa's "bad" list; Santa dons a helmet and picks up a rifle; two Christmas cards showing St. Nick as a soldier boy. Bottom right card: KP duty during the holiday.

Lil' page turners

In his earliest known depiction in a book, Santa is a vengeful fella.

This Santa from 1821 — then called "Santeclaus" — believes in corporal punishment. Bad children don't get presents; rather, their parents receive a rod with which to administer beatings:

"But where I found the children naughty / In manners crude, in temper haughty / Thankless to parents, liars, swearers / Boxers, or cheats, or base tale-bearers / I left a long, black, birchen rod / Such as the dread command of GOD / Directs a Parent's hand to use / When virtue's path his sons refuse."

Take that, you swearers and base tale-bearers.

The influential, uncredited poem, "Old Santeclaus With Much Delight" — aren't you lovin' this old-timey language? — was published in a book with the wordy title "The Children's Friend: A New-Year's Present, to the Little Ones from Five to Twelve" (1821, William B. Gilley). It introduced vital aspects of the Santa Claus character that survive to this day, in the form of likewise uncredited illustrations reproduced via early use of lithography.

For the first time, Santeclaus is shown in a sleigh pulled by a reindeer. (The sleigh is marked, in large letters, "REWARDS.") Though this Sante is bearded and wearing red, he bears little physical resemblance to the later popular ideal of the character. Santeclaus' beard is brown, and he wears a tall "cossack"-style hat. The poem also places Santeclaus' activities on Christmas Eve (as opposed to Dec. 6, the feast of St. Nicholas) for the first time.

ANOTHER EARLY BOOK WITH LASTING EFFECTS
was "Santa Claus, & His Works" (circa 1860s, McLoughlin Bros.), written by George P. Webster with illustrations by Thomas Nast or Howard Del, presumably depending on the edition.

The book opens with a charming rhyme: *"His nice little story for Girls and for Boys / Is all about Santa Claus, Christmas and toys ... In a nice little city called Santa-Clausville / With its houses and church at the foot of the hill."*

It's interesting to note that Webster's name for Santa's home base — Santa-Clausville — has not stood the harsh test of time. (Although, Webster wrote that Santa-Clauseville was "near the North Pole.") Webster's allusion to the church in Santa-Clausville is counter to an unwritten rule that followed concerning depictions of the character: to not mix the holy with the ho, ho, ho.

Detailed color illustrations depict Santa in his woodshop perfecting a toy horse; sewing a doll's dress amid dolls in various stages of manufacture; peering through a telescope (*"He looks for good children all over the land"*) accompanied by his dog; paging through giant volumes in which are listed the names of good boys and girls; and standing on a ladder gathering toys from a tree.

The final illustration shows Santa delivering toys in a private home on Christmas Eve. Standing on a chair by the fireplace, Santa appears to be proportionately smaller than the household's inhabitants, which explains how he squeezed down those chimneys all those years. Webster's closing rhyme pays Santa a back-

Santa is as busy as ever in "Santa Claus, & His Works" (circa 1860s). Opposite: The Chatterwells have "Holiday Fun" (1900).

handed compliment: *"Now, three cheers for Christmas! give them, boys, with a will! / Three more for the hero of Santa-Clauseville / We know he is old, and bald-headed and fat / But the cleverest chap in the world for all that / And a jollier codger no man ever saw / But good-bye, merry Christmas, Hip, Hip, Hip Hurrah!"*

So-called "series" books sometimes published Christmas episodes, such as "Holiday Fun" (1900) starring those irrepressible Little Chatterwells; "The Mystery of Cabin Island" (1929) by "Franklin W. Dixon" (actually Leslie McFarlane) starring teen sleuths the Hardy Boys; "The Bobbsey Twins' Wonderful Winter Secret" (1931) by "Laura Lee Hope"; "Babar and Father Christmas" (1941) by Jean de Brunhoff; and "Madeline's Christmas" (1956) by Ludwig Bemelmans.

Christmas-themed children's books soon became a niche, yielding scores of titles such as "Baby's First Christmas," "The Littlest Christmas Tree" and "The Christmas Puppy" from Wonder Books, Little Golden Books, Whitman Publishing and others.

HOLIDAY FUN

LITTLE CHATTERWELL SERIES

2179

Santa's big helper

The origin of French writer-artist Jean de Brunhoff's charming children's book character Babar the elephant is itself worthy of a storybook.

De Brunhoff's wife Cécile concocted the character in a bedtime story she told her sons, Mathieu and Laurent. The boys asked their father to illustrate her story, and in 1931, Babar's first adventure "Histoire de Babar" (English title: "Story of Babar") was published. It's the tale of an elephant forced to flee from his home country to a city not unlike Paris. There, Babar adopts fine dress and civilized ways, and brings them back to his home country, where he is crowned king. (Yes, de Brunhoff has been accused of touting French colonialism.)

De Brunhoff (1899-1937) died three years before the publication of his final book, "Babar et le Père Noël" ("Babar and Father Christmas"). De Brunhoff illustrated the book in black-and-white for newspaper reproduction; color was added posthumously.

In the story, Babar asks Father Christmas to bring toys to the elephant children of his country. Overworked Father Christmas instead deputizes Babar by giving him a Santa costume with the power of flight, plus a bottomless bag of toys.

De Brunhoff's final journey to the Babar-verse is like a Christmas miracle. Laurent later carried on the series in a style faithful to that of his father.

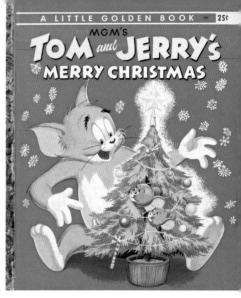

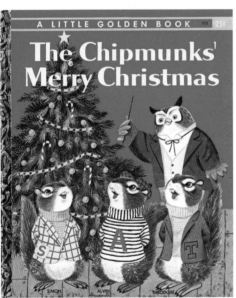

Character favorites: Christmas-themed children's books featured familiar characters such as, from top left, Richard Scarry's Animals (1950), Frosty the Snowman (1951), Tom and Jerry (1954), Mighty Mouse (1955), Howdy Doody (1955), Rudolph the Red-Nosed Reindeer (1958), Ross Bagdasarian Sr.'s Chipmunks (1959), and Hanna-Barbera's Huckleberry Hound (1960) and Yogi Bear (1961).

Interactivity

Christmas-themed "pop-up," connect-the-dot, coloring and otherwise activity-centric books demanded a bit more participation from little ones on the Big Day. From top left: "Merry Christmas Fun" (circa 1960s), which included red and green yarn, and artwork by children's book illustrator Daisy Mager; coloring books fashioned after "The Night Before Christmas" (1951), Rudolph the Red-Nosed Reindeer (1963), and Frosty the Snowman (1952); and "The Charlie Brown Christmas Activity Book" (1979).

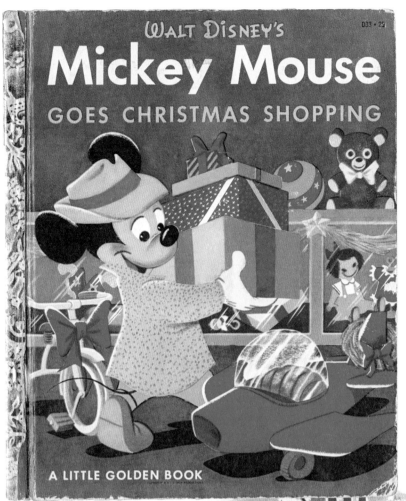

Disney on ice

In the 1950s, Walt Disney Studios branched out with TV's "The Mickey Mouse Club" and "The Magical World of Disney," and its theme park Disneyland. Simon & Schuster's Little Golden Books imprint piled on with many Disney adaptations, some Christmas-themed. "Santa's Toy Shop" (1950) was based on the 1932 short, but presented a more modern look. In it, Mrs. Santa bakes gingerbread-man cookies while Santa goes through his mail, and elves cheerfully assemble toys in the doll, train, and game departments. "Mickey Mouse Goes Christmas Shopping" (1953) was a "Mickey Mouse Club Book," an imprint within an imprint. In it, Mickey and Minnie take their nephews Mortie and Ferdie (remember them?) to a department store in the city. The little guys fall asleep on a 10-cent "Quick Trip to the Moon" ride piloted by Goofy, causing them to be locked in the store after hours. No worries — Santa comes to their rescue. Not to be outdone, Mickey's pal Donald Duck headlined at least three Little Golden Book editions: "Donald Duck and Santa Claus" (1952), "Donald Duck's Christmas Tree" (1954) with guest stars Chip 'n' Dale, and "Donald Duck and the Christmas Carol" (1960).

Un Noël Français

"In an old house in Paris / That was covered in vines / Lived twelve little girls / In two straight lines / They left the house at half-past nine / In two straight lines, in rain or shine / The smallest one was MADELINE."

These lines, by writer-artist Ludwig Bemelmans (1898-1962), opened "Madeline" (1939), the first in a series of six enchanting Madeline books published during Bemelmans' lifetime. He reused these opening lines in the subsequent books, almost like a TV series "recap." This includes "Madeline's Christmas," first published as a book insert in *McCalls* magazine in 1956, and in stand-alone form in 1985.

If ever there was a citizen of the world, it was Bemelmans. He was born in Austria-Hungary (now Italy) of a Belgian father and a Bavarian mother, and emigrated to New York City at age 16 in 1914, spending Christmas Eve on Ellis Island.

He recounted his heroine's origin in an essay: "I remembered the stories my mother had told me of life in the convent school at Altötting and the little girl, the hospital, the room, the crank on the bed, the nurse ... I thought about where Madeline and her friends should live and decided on Paris."

In true Bemelmansian fashion, he wrote the opening text about the old house covered in vines on the back of a menu in a New York City tavern.

(FYI, "Madeline's Christmas" wasn't the character's first brush with the holiday. In 1955, Bemelmans produced "Madeline's Texas Christmas" for the Neiman Marcus store chain.)

In "Madeline's Christmas," Bemelmans borrows, and tweaks, the opening stanzas from "Twas the Night Before Christmas." Christmas Eve finds everyone in the house — including headmistress Miss Clavel — sick except for Madeline, who makes soup for all and totes a hot-water bottle to Clavel.

A knock at the door brings a rug merchant who, in his white beard and red coat, is kind of a Santa Claus surrogate. Also a magician, the man sells Madeline 12 rugs — one for each girl, it happens — that possess the power of flight. The girls fly the rugs to their respective homes for Christmas.

"Madeline's Christmas" was akin to a first draft of Bemelmans' pet project, his unfinished book "Madeline and the Magician" — *and* a Christmas present for Madeline's generations of fans.

Babies and furry friends: From top left, "The Snowman's Christmas Present" (1951), "Christmas Favorites" (1951), "Christmas is Coming" (1952), "The Christmas Puppy" (1953), "Polly's Christmas Present" (1953), "The Littlest Christmas Tree" (1954), "Baby's First Christmas" (1959, in two editions) and "How the Rabbits Found Christmas" (1961).

Santa the cover boy: From top left, "The Golden Christmas Book" (1947), "Santa Claus in Storyland" (1950), "A Little Cowboy's Christmas" (1951), "The Wonder Book of Christmas" (1951), another edition of "The Snowman's Christmas Present" (1951), "Santa's Busy Day" (1953), "Uncle Mistletoe" (1953), "Santa's Surprise Book" (1966) and "The Night Before Christmas" (1976).

It came without ribbons

"The Grinch hated Christmas! The whole Christmas season! Now, please don't ask why. No one quite knows the reason."

THERE'S NO DENYING IT: THE GRINCH IS SCROOGE. But "A Christmas Carol" can get pretty morbid — all that death, all those ghosts, all that talk of boiling people in pudding.

For little ones, a children's book like Dr. Seuss' "How the Grinch Stole Christmas!" is less likely to inflict trauma. It has a hissable villain with a monster-ish visage, but no inhabitants of Who-ville are killed. Nor is their Christmas spirit.

"How the Grinch Stole Christmas!" — published by Random House in December 1957 — was written and illustrated by Theodor Geisel (1904-1991), better known by his pen name, Dr. Seuss. "The Grinch" was the 19th of more than 60 books published by Geisel, which include "The Cat in the Hat," "Horton Hears a Who!" and "One Fish, Two Fish, Red Fish, Blue Fish."

In Geisel's trademark sing-song verse and fluid cartooning, he tells the story of a holiday-hating sociopath isolated in the snowbound mountains above the village of Who-ville, where inhabitants gleefully immerse themselves in the holiday. The Grinch plots to "steal" Christmas from the Whos by disguising himself as Santa Claus and absconding with their decorations, gifts and food during their Christmas Eve slumber.

But — spoiler alert — the Grinch is disappointed when the Whos, rather than gnashing their teeth upon finding no goodies on Christmas morning, instead join hands and sing in celebration. The Grinch, you see, equated Christmas only with material trappings. Exclaimed the confused baddie: "It came without ribbons! It came without tags! It came without packages, boxes or bags!"

GOING HAND-IN-HAND WITH GEISEL'S WHIMSICAL, rhythmic stanzas are his deceptively sophisticated pen-and-ink drawings. You can almost see his hand moving across the page in his delicate cross-hatching, his expert control of white space, and his judiciously used "blacks" — artist-ese for black areas — as he depicts the evil-for-evil's-sake Grinch; the cozy, snow-topped huts of Who-ville; the imperturbably joyful Whos; and childish innocence personified in bug-like Little Cindy-Lou Who.

"The Grinch" was Geisel's followup to "The Cat in the Hat," his flagship book. He began "The Grinch" early in 1957 with an editing assist from his wife, Helen Palmer Geisel (1927-1967), a behind-the-scenes force on many of his books.

The writing went quickly — that is, until the time came for Geisel to figure out an ending, according to his longtime friends, journalists Judith and Neal Morgan (in their 1996 biography "Dr. Seuss & Mr. Geisel"). "I got hung up on how to get the Grinch out of the mess," said Geisel. "I got into a situation where I sounded like a second-rate preacher or some bible thumper."

Geisel ultimately settled on the simple image of the redeemed Grinch carving the roast beast. "I had gone through thousands of religious choices," he said, "and then after three months, it came out like that."

Theodor Geisel's cover for "How the Grinch Stole Christmas!" Below: Cindy-Lou Who is childish innocence personified.

So who *was* the Grinch, really — aside from Scrooge, of course? Said Geisel: "I was brushing my teeth on the 26th of last December, when I noticed a very Grinch-ish countenance in the mirror. ... I wrote about my sour friend the Grinch to see if I could rediscover something about Christmas that obviously I'd lost."

In addition to Geisel's own testimony, there's further evidence that he *was* the Grinch. In the book, the titular villain says of the Whos' noisy revelry: "Why, for fifty-three years I've put up with it now!" One guess how old Geisel was when he wrote that line.

And here's a fun fact: Geisel's car vanity license plates read, not "CATHAT" or "HORTON" or "1FISH2," but "GRINCH."

41

Caroling books

Believe it or not, Virginia, there was a time before radios and record players — and electricity itself — were affordable enough to be in every household. But even in the most modest and remote of domiciles, music could still be heard. In those olden days, sheet music was a thing. Pianos, and people who could play them, were another thing.

Sheet music led to bound compilations of holiday-themed songs. Christmas music, both the "holy" and the "commercial," was a perennial seller from the late 19th century through at least the 1970s. Today, caroling books survive as quaint memorabilia from a simpler time.

THE BOOK OF
CHRISTMAS
CAROLS

MUSICAL ARRANGEMENTS BY MARY NANCY GRAHAM

Christmas
Carols

Beginners CAROL BOOK

SEVENTY CENTS
THOMAS MUSIC COMPANY, Publisher -:- Detroit 1, Michigan

Fa la-la la-la, la-la la la!
From top left: "The Book of Christmas Carols" (1928), "Christmas Carols," and "Beginners Carol Book" (1953). Opposite page, from top left: "Treasure Chest of Christmas Songs and Carols" (1936), "Christmas Carols" (1900s), "Jolly Christmas Melodies" (1947), "Ye Christmas Piano Book: Christmas Carols Made Easy to Play or Sing" (1931), and "Christmas Melodies Arranged for Piano by Ada Richter" (1943). Richter (1900-1990) was a piano teacher who taught under-privileged children and published piano tutorials.

Light up

Is there anything Thomas Edison didn't *innovate?*

As if the light bulb, the phonograph and the movie camera weren't enough, Edison (1847-1931) invented electric stringed lights, which eventually became known and used as "Christmas lights."

In December 1880, the first electric stringed lights were hung outside of Edison's laboratory in Menlo Park, New Jersey. "These were his original incandescent lights, about 40 of them," said Leonard DeGraaf, archivist for Thomas Edison National Historical Park in New Jersey, in 2019. "Some were strung on poles outside the lab complex, some in windows. The initial public demonstration Edison put on was for reporters and important financial people. He was under pressure to show these lamps and how they worked."

However, Edison's intention regarding the stringed lights wasn't necessarily as Christmas lights *per se*. "I haven't seen any sources that say it was an exclusive Christmas display, so to speak," DeGraaf said.

Two years later, an Edison business associate, Edward Hibberd Johnson (1846-1917), assembled the first string of electric Christmas *tree* lights. He wired the 80-bulb strand by hand using red, white and blue bulbs — placing it on a rotating tree, yet. Johnson first displayed the lighted tree on Dec. 22, 1882, in the parlor window of his home at 136 East 36th Street in New York City.

At first, electric Christmas lights were prohibitively expensive and required the services of electricians. But the lights were popularized by two U.S. presidents. In 1895, Grover Cleveland introduced a White House Christmas tree decorated with electric lights — more than 100 multi-colored light bulbs in all. In 1923, Calvin Coolidge upped that total considerably to 3,000 electric lights.

The mass-marketing of Christmas lights began in earnest in 1903, when Edison's company, General Electric, started promoting and selling affordable pre-assembled Christmas light kits.

Varieties followed such as Satin Bright lights ("They shine even when they're off!"); Tinsel Lights (lights encased in sparkle-y tinsel); Mazda Lamps (with scalloped edges); Lighted Ice (round lights with a crackly finish); Merry Midget lights; Lighted Bells; floodlamps in many colors; color-changing LED lights; and unconvincing (but charming) "window candles." Though GE remained a leading purveyor of outdoor and indoor Christmas lighting for decades, it was once outsold by an all-but-forgotten competitor.

Many developments in the realm of Christmas lighting were spearheaded by NOMA (National Outfit Manufacturers Association), an organization founded in 1925 as a consortium of around 15 businesses.

the night

Among NOMA's founders were the Sadacca brothers, of which Albert Sadacca (1901-1980) was the chief cheerleader for Christmas lights. In 1926, the group incorporated as the NOMA Electric Corporation (later NOMA Lites, Inc.), and began marketing Christmas light sets the following year.

NOMA continued this specialty through the 1960s, introducing innovations that were useful beyond holiday lighting, such as parallel-wired lights; all-rubber cords; and fused safety plugs.

But NOMA's commercial innovations are what aficionados remember best, such as Bubble-Lites ("Watch them bubble"); character "bell" lights (with the likenesses of Mickey Mouse, Pinocchio and other Disney characters); illuminated tree-top angels and stars; and "halo-effect" window candelabras.

Lighting companies were forced to suspend the production of Christmas lights during World War II, and NOMA manufactured bombs within a special division, according to OldChristmasTreeLights.com. NOMA's bombs damaged Japanese factories, some of them manufacturers of Christmas lights, according to the website. It noted with irony that those factories rebuilt after the war, and the cheap export of their products to the U.S. contributed to NOMA's filing for bankruptcy in 1967. The following year, NOMA ceased as a manufacturer, continuing instead as a trademark. (At least the *name* still had juice.)

TIME, AND TECHNOLOGY, WERE MARCHING ON LIKE TOY SOLDIERS.

B.F. Goodrich introduced Christmas lights with wiring made from Geon polyvinyl materials — whatever *they* were — in 1949. Westinghouse introduced Permacote, which discouraged outdoor bulbs from chipping, in 1952. Once a year, these products transformed the common dad into an exterior designer.

Ever-evolving options include candy canes lining a walkway ... a giant Santa face hanging over the garage ... front-lawn Nativity scenes ... plastic figures of Santa Claus, Mrs. Santa, snowmen, Baby Jesus, Mary, Joseph and the Wise Men, lit from within ... grazing animatronic reindeer and other figures in motion ... giant inflatable "snow globes" (which deflate into crumples overnight) ... lighted "icicles" hanging from gutters that appear to "drip" ... tie-in figures of characters from "Peanuts," "Rudolph," "The Grinch" and others ... the projection of multicolored dots, stars and holiday icons on house fronts ... bells, stars and "Seasons Greetings" signage hanging from lightposts along bustling downtown thoroughfares ...

And the most low-tech decoration of all: a simple, green wreath hanging on the front door, as if to say, "Come on in for a cup of hot chocolate and a cookie!" (Yeah, that was corny. *And* a recipe for diabetes.)

Founded in 1925, National Outfit Manufacturers Association, or NOMA, was once the leading maker of Christmas lights. Above: NOMA's Outdoor Christmas Lights with Mazda Lamps. Left: NOMA's Safety Plug for outdoor lights had practical applications that were useful beyond the realm of holiday lighting. Below: NOMA's Bubble-Lites (1946).

Above: Vintage outdoor plastic lawn figures lit from within — cutting edge technology.
Below left: Westinghouse touts the miracle of Permacote.
Below right: General Electric promises customers the "Brightest Christmas Ever!"

From top left: Queen Victoria and family in The London News (1846); Edward Hibberd Johnson's first lighted tree (1882); a 1950s aluminum tree; Alcoa's ad for same; iconic floor lamp.

1882 photo courtesy of
Thomas Edison National
Historical Park

Sparkle plenty

POLITICS, SHMOLITICS. IF YOU WANNA IGNITE
a heated conversation, just ask people their Christmas tree preferences. You start with: Real or fake? (Some folks wouldn't dream of sacrificing the outdoors-y scent of a fresh-cut evergreen for something that looks like a toilet brush; others don't like to vacuum brittle branch needles.)

Then you get into: Tinsel or garland? (Painstakingly hung tinsel looks magical; but garland goes on and off in a jiffy.)

From there, you talk about lighting, decorations, tradition, technology, and before you know it, you're no longer *speaking*.

Some history: Evergreen trees represented eternal life to some pre-Christianity civilizations ... Christmas trees are believed to have originated in 16th-century Germany ... the first such trees were adorned with fruit, nuts, paper decorations and "sweetmeats" ... illumination via candlelight was added in the 18th century ... artificial trees first appeared in 19th-century Germany, a response to deforestation and made with goose feathers painted green ... the first known Christmas tree in America was erected in the 1830s in Pennsylvania by German settlers ... in 1846, England's Queen Victoria and her family were depicted around a Christmas tree in an illustration in *The London News* (Victoria grew up with trees decorated by her mother, German princess Victoria of Saxe-Coburg-Saalfeld) ...

In 1882, when Edward Hibberd Johnson displayed the first Christmas tree decorated with electric lights in New York City, William Augustus Croffut gushed in *The Detroit Post and Tribune*: "It was brilliantly lighted with many colored globes about as large as an English walnut, and was turning some six times a minute on a little pine box. There were 80 lights in all encased in these dainty glass eggs, and about equally divided between white, red and blue. As the tree turned, the colors alternated, the lamps going out and being re-lit at every revolution. The result was a continuous twinkling of dancing colors ... One can hardly imagine anything prettier."

The growing popularity of Christmas trees coincided with the rise of mass production. The mid 1950s saw the fakest fake trees of all: aluminum Christmas trees, with rigid, tinsel-y "branches" stuck into a wooden pole painted silver, accompanied by rotating floor lamps that bathed the trees in orange, blue, red and green light. Their drop in popularity about 10 years later happened to coincide with the 1965 TV special "A Charlie Brown Christmas," in which Lucy instructs Charlie Brown: "Get the biggest aluminum tree you can find!" Instead, he gets a scrawny *natural* one.

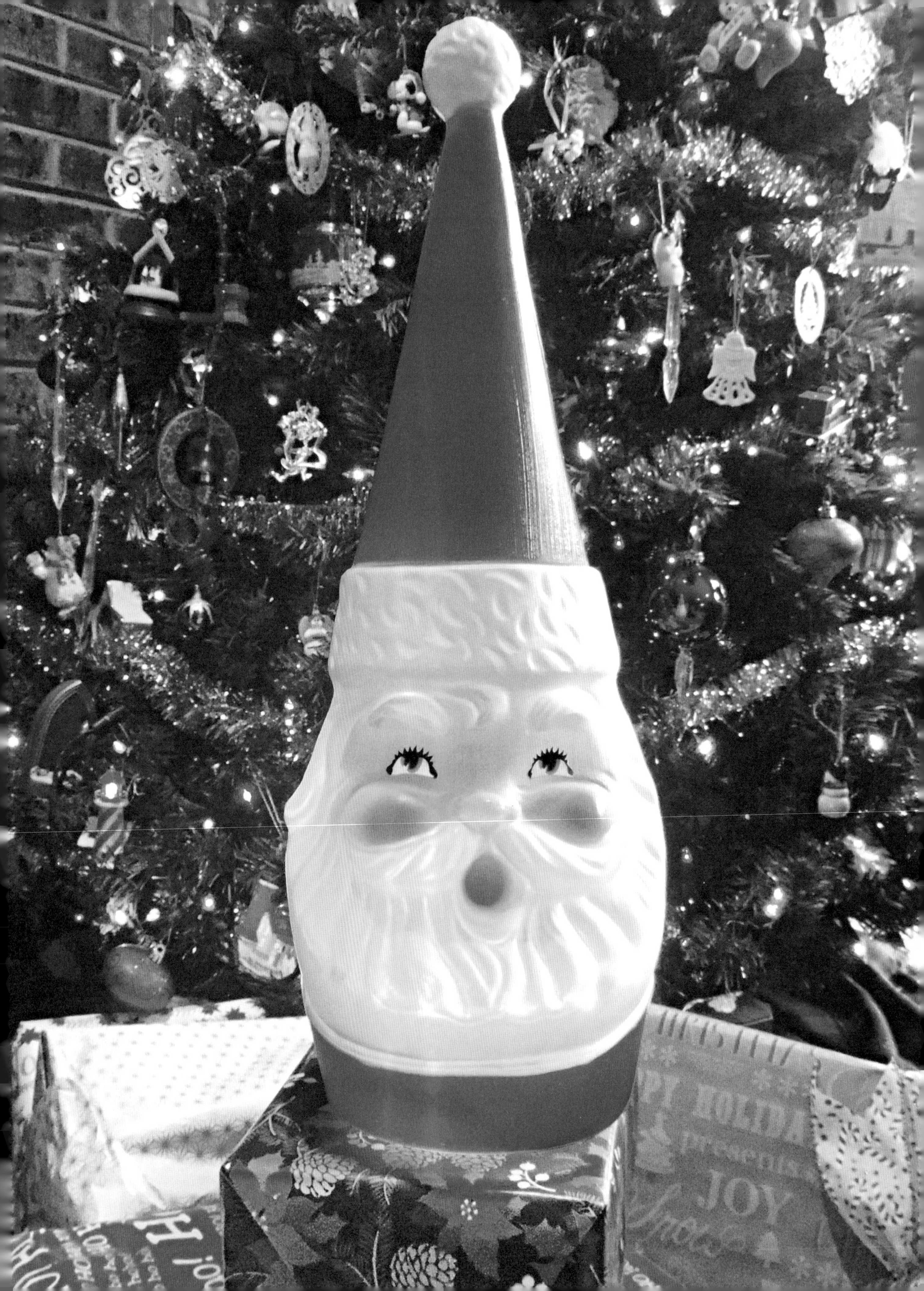
JOY

Jolly old St. Nick

Bijou's adorable Santa plush dolls with "beards" and rubber faces were ubiquitous from the 1940s through the '70s.
▶

◀
This 4-foot-high outdoor Santa face light is ideal for large areas on house exteriors such as below roof peaks.

◀
Santa Claus remains the most popular of PEZ candy dispensers.

▶
Mr. and Mrs. Santa Claus dance in this festive tree ornament from the 1950s.

Opposite: A warm glow emanates from a 21-inch-high indoor Santa head light from the 1960s.

Photos by Mark Voger

Vintage elf figures had a penchant for cradling their knees, the better to hang on a tree without gobbling up much vertical space. Opposite: Humpty Dumpty, complete with brick wall.

Of pointy ears

EVERY CHILD KNOWS THAT SANTA IS the boss, but elves get the job done. These mythic figures (which originated in German folklore) had all manners of powers and connotations before being usurped by Christmas Culture in degrees prior to the turn of the 20th century. (Check out Johnny Marks' song "We Are Santa's Elves" from the 1964 "Rudolph" special — which shows a happy chorus of pointy-eared, curly-shoed elves — to see how irrevocably elves are entrenched.)

Elves were popular Christmas-tree decorations in the 1950s and '60s, often with loose bells attached that jingled at the slightest provocation.

An odd cousin to the elf tree decoration was the Humpty Dumpty ornament, which was charming, a little bit weird — is that drag queen makeup? — and came sitting atop its own little brick wall.

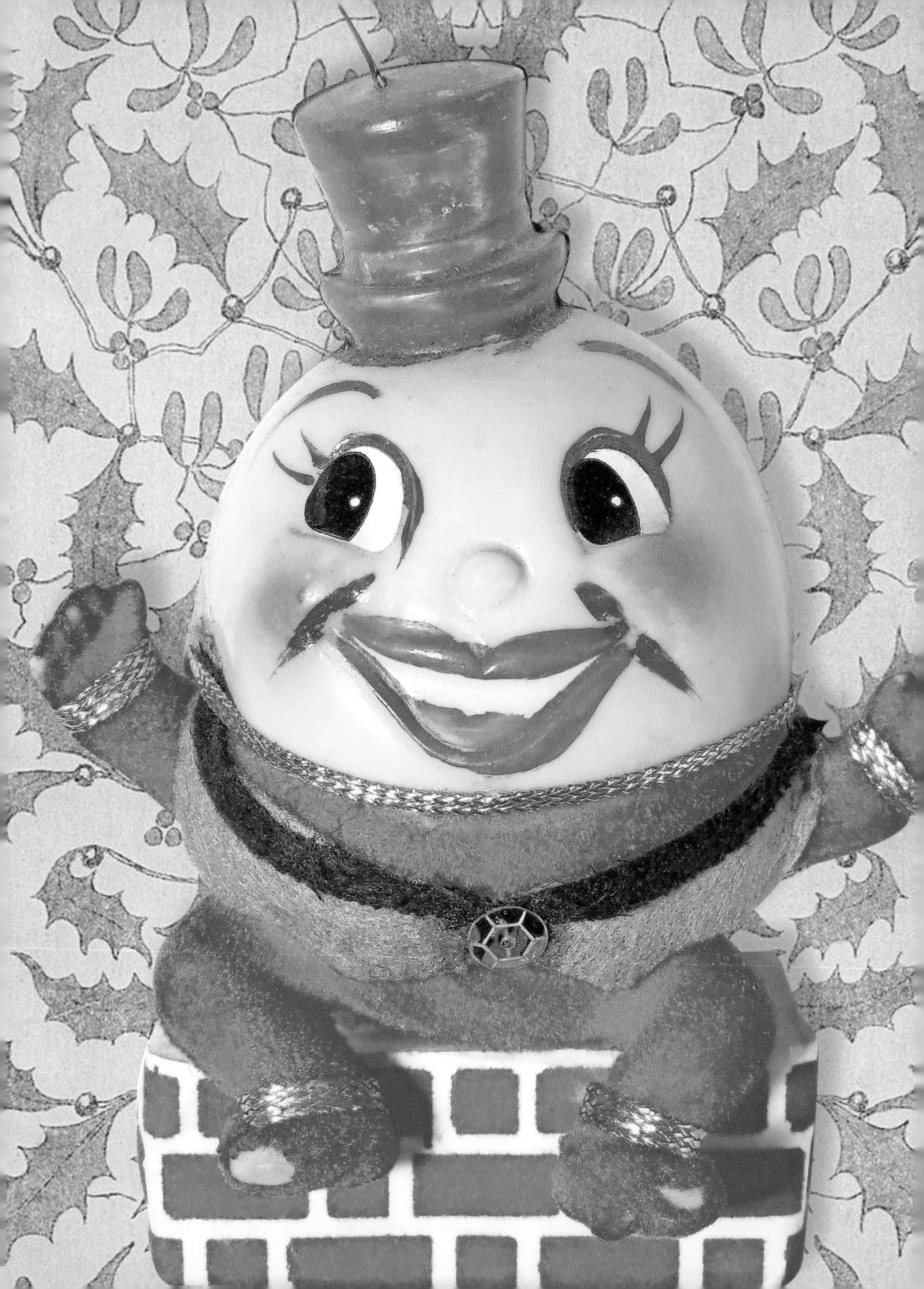

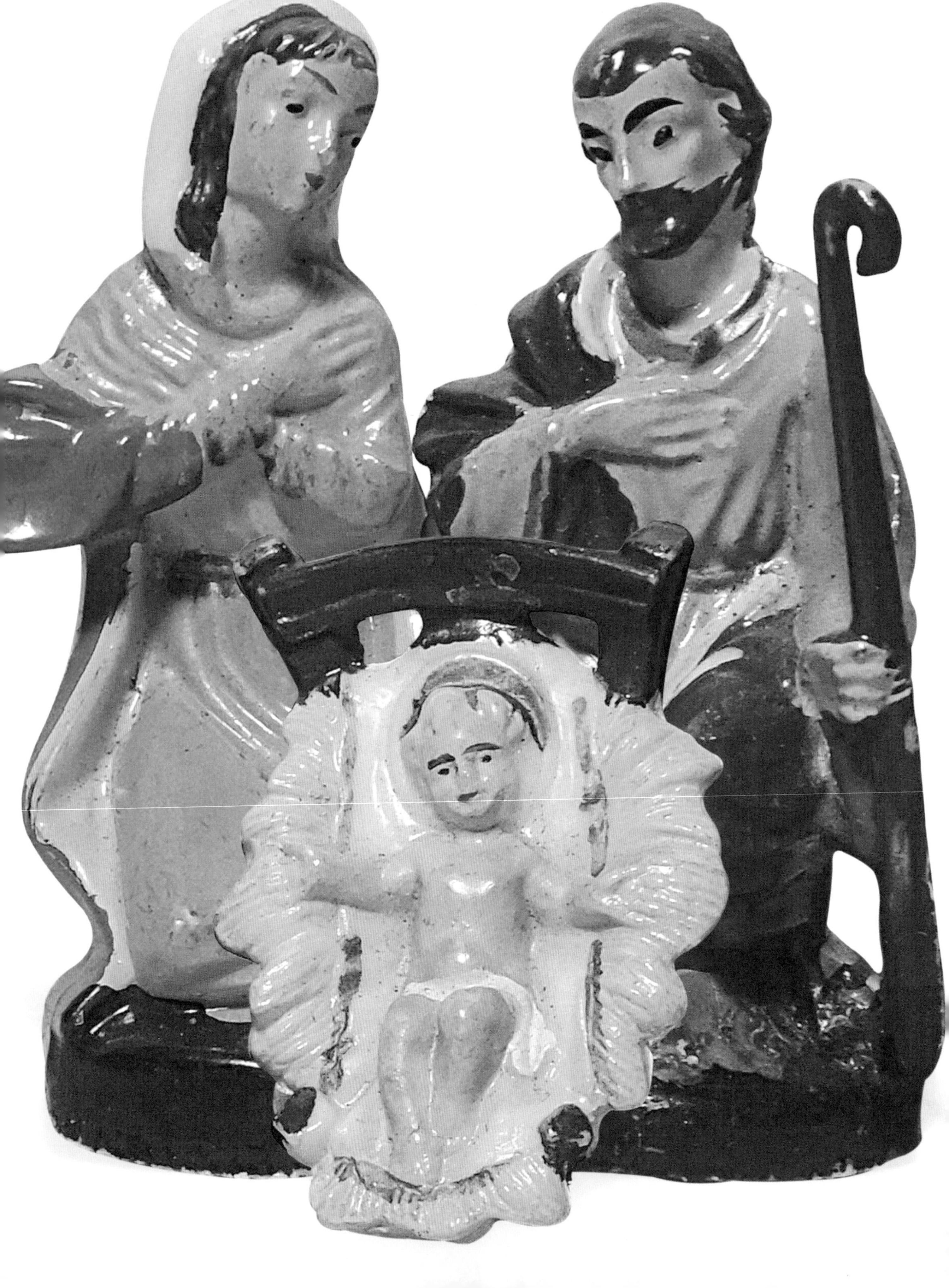

Away in a manger

FOR THE REVERENT, MINIATURE NATIVITY sets are a way to acknowledge your faith within your holiday home decor. For little kids who don't know any better, Nativity sets can be — unintended sacrilege warning — *play* sets. The "cast" of Nativity sets (Baby Jesus, Mary, Joseph, the Wise Men, et al.) is as well known to many children as the casts of "Rudolph" or "The Grinch."

And like it or not, the First Noël was popularized in kid-targeted media. "The Little Drummer Boy," "Nestor the Long-Eared Donkey" and others depicted the Nativity in animation. So don't blame us kids for actually playing with Nativity sets — albeit, in more of a "holy" way, as opposed to a Barbie or a Captain Action way.

The mass-produced Nativity set on these pages was ubiquitous in Christian households at Christmas from the 1950s into the '70s. It was likely purchased from Sears, which marketed the easily recognizable set during the period. The tallest figure is 2.5 inches high.

Fancier households (with fancier money) sometimes opted for larger imported sets in those days, with Italy being a popular supplier.

Nativity sets were often themselves decorated, augmented with snipped hay, evergreen sprigs, cotton (for "snow"), and animal figures from other types of sets such as zoo and train sets.

State of play

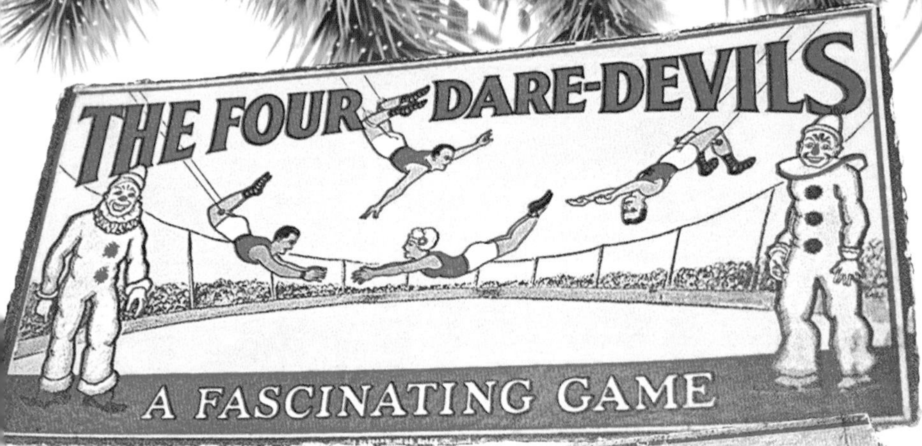
THE FOUR DARE-DEVILS
A FASCINATING GAME

Just imagine Christmas toys in the olden days.

Well, you'd *have* to imagine. In the time before battery-operated toys, a great deal of imagination was required. Still, even at the dawn of the 20th century, some toys featured automation (the Tri-Ang Gyro Cycle, Schoenhut's Cracker-Jack the clown, Sherwood's Whirling Wilmer) with a bit of assembly, and ingenuity, on the consumer's part.

Once the industrial revolution took hold, toy-making became a serious operation that advanced way beyond Santa's North Pole shop. Chief manufacturers of toys and games during this golden age included Milton Bradley (founded 1860); Parker Bros. (founded 1883); Lionel (founded 1900); Ideal (founded 1907); Trans-O-Gram (founded 1915); Marx (founded 1919); Hasbro (founded 1923); Fisher-Price (founded 1930); Mattel (founded 1945); Kenner (founded 1946); Wham-O (founded 1948); Remco (founded 1949); and Deluxe Reading (founded in the '50s).

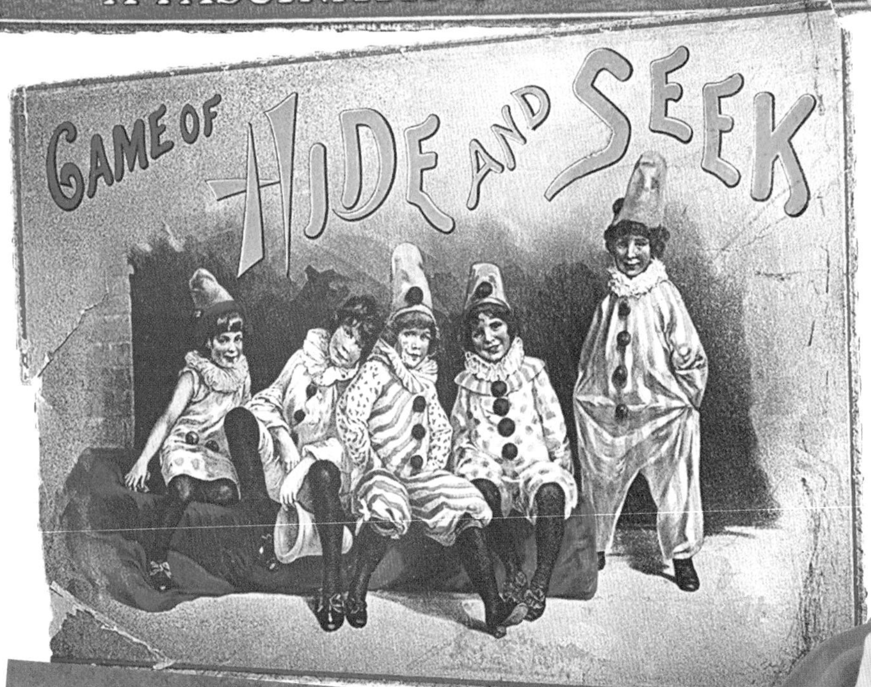
GAME OF HIDE AND SEEK

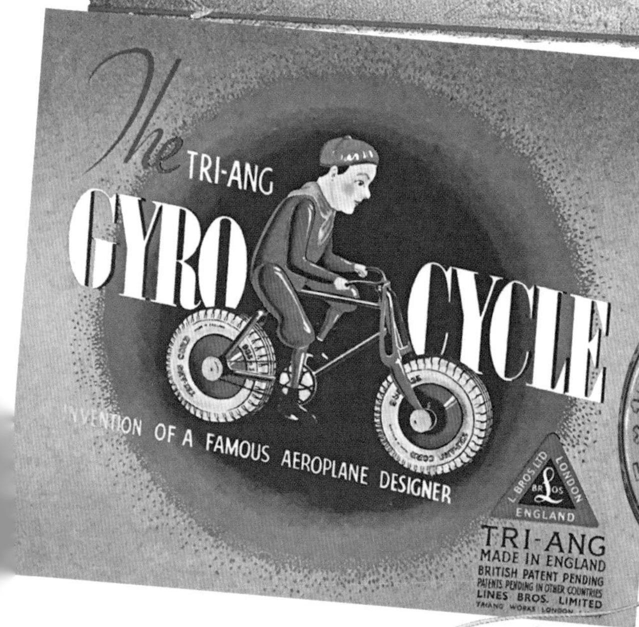
The TRI-ANG
GYRO CYCLE
INVENTION OF A FAMOUS AEROPLANE DESIGNER
L. BROS LTD LONDON ENGLAND
TRI-ANG
MADE IN ENGLAND
BRITISH PATENT PENDING
PATENTS PENDING IN OTHER COUNTRIES
LINES BROS. LIMITED

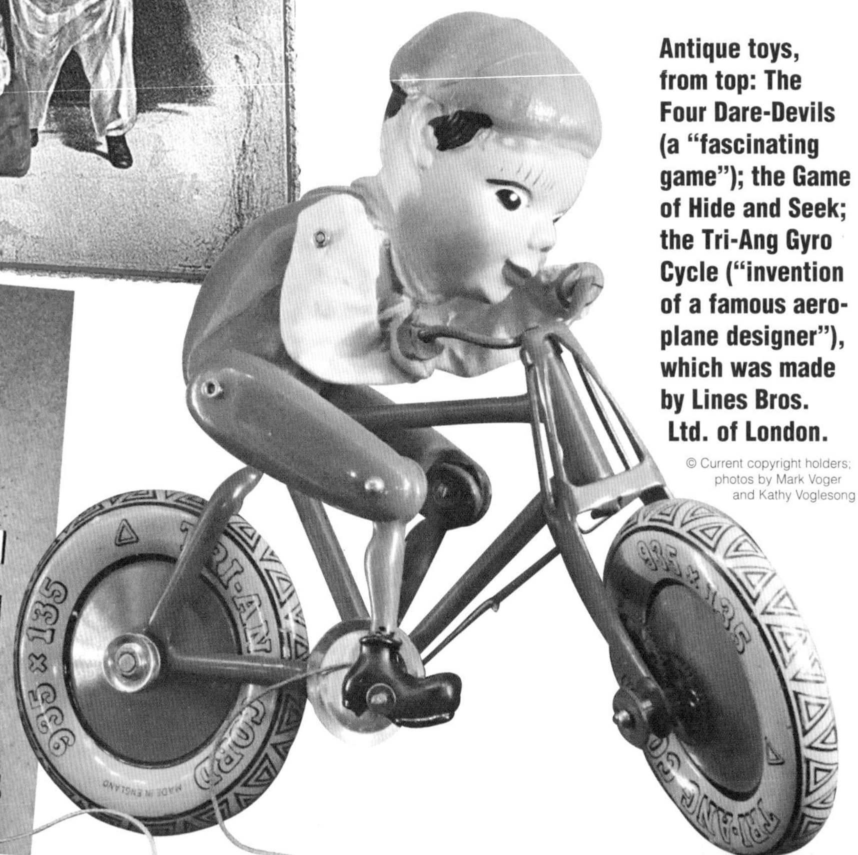
TRI-ANG
935 × 135

Antique toys, from top: The Four Dare-Devils (a "fascinating game"); the Game of Hide and Seek; the Tri-Ang Gyro Cycle ("invention of a famous aeroplane designer"), which was made by Lines Bros. Ltd. of London.

Top row, from left: The Wonderful Game of Oz (1921); Cracker-Jack the Clever Clown (1903); the Peter Rabbit Talking Storybook Game.

Bottom left: Lionel's Donald Duck Rail Car. Above: Sherwood's Whirling Wilmer.

'Actual' Christmas toys

Yes, Virginia, there *were* toys and games found under the tree on Christmas morning that were literally Christmas-centric, that one could inarguably call "Christmas toys." From top are Parker Brothers' The Night Before Christmas Game (1896); the Parkers' Santa Claus Game (circa 1900s), with the Jolly One wearing yellow tights in a (thankfully) rare instance; the Parkers' Rudolph the Red-Nosed Reindeer game (1948, the year before the song's release); and Noel Decorations' coin- and battery-operated "animated" Santa Bank (1960).

© Parker Brothers except Santa Bank © Noel Decorations

What is a "Christmas toy"? Must Santa Claus be on the box cover? Au contraire, mon ami.

Sure, a kid can receive a toy any old time of year — your birthday, when you get an A, when a generous relative visits. But we greedy American children always associated Christmas morning with "Christmas toys." When you snagged a toy on Christmas, it was thereafter remembered as a "Christmas toy."

Media enabled this with saturation advertising on TV and in print beginning in fall. The toy section of the Sears-Roebuck catalog was an annual phantasmagoria. Store displays worked their magic as well. In December in the 1950s and '60s, supermarkets would display toys on shelves high above the produce aisle — too high for a child to touch, but not to dream about.

The whole Santa myth involves a North Pole toy factory at which elves sing happily in an assembly line, despite the absence of salary, benefits and opportunities for advancement.

So the question of whether a toy is a "Christmas toy" is in the eye of the beholder, or more so, in the heart of the child.

THERE IS ALSO THE SMALL MATTER OF

expectation vs. reality. My brother desperately wanted something called a Kookie Kamera (1968). Ideal's toy camera was a Rube Goldberg-esque device requiring careful assembly. Two of my Irish-side uncles — one a plumber, the other a rental truck agency boss — put in overtime in assembling the complicated contraption. Alas, this was a glorified Polaroid camera — one that, to boot, didn't work. Every photo came out pure black. What my brother got for Christmas wasn't the wacky, innovative toy advertised, but a lesson in dealing with disappointment.

For my sister, the most coveted item one year was the Easy-Bake Oven from Kenner. It was a miniature "oven" powered by heat from a light bulb. It came with little plastic envelopes of cake mixes and frostings. My brother and I envisioned an endless supply of cakes. This never happened, of course. The "cakes" were tiny round things about 3 inches wide and 3/4-inch high. We didn't even get to sample the first cake issued from our sister's Easy-Bake. After carefully icing the miniature chocolate "cake" under our watchful eyes, our sister awarded it to our visiting Cousin Alfie. To this day, my brother and I still remember the slight with acute bitterness.

My folks knew I loved TV's "The Munsters," and on Christmas 1964, they gave me something I didn't know existed: Remco's 6-inch plastic dolls of Herman, Lily and Grandpa Munster. Kudos to the sculptor — the likeness of Al Lewis was amazing! (Remco made Beatles dolls that same year.) I remember grabbing a handful of chocolate "coins" (the kind wrapped in gold foil) and repairing to my bedroom, where I consumed the chocolate like medication and just stared at Herman, Lily and Grandpa for an hour straight.

But I knew all about Stick Shift Racerific (1968) from Ideal's Motorific imprint. There were ads for it in comic books, and maybe even a TV spot. It was a sprawling racetrack that took up most of the rec-room floor, on which a pair of two-speed cars raced against a wind-up clock. It had "terrific" features like the "Hairpin Turns," the "Oil Slick" and the "Terror Turn," which the cars had about a 50-50 chance of negotiating without "crashing" into a plastic tree and careening over a "mountain." This

mountain contained a bulky device that played the sounds of tires squealing and a crash — very high tech for 1968. Me and Cousin Alfie had the genius idea to put Vaseline on the Oil Slick for authenticity. It gummed up the cars to the point of ruination.

More classic toys from back in the day: Ideal's balancing game Tip-It (1965), with its acrobat perched precariously on his nose atop a swaying vertical beam ... Mattel's Thingmaker, which made "Creepy Crawlers," fake bugs that inevitably made you feel like a creepy kid ... Marx's Rock 'Em Sock 'Em Robots, with their soul-pleasing *"Zisssss"* sound whenever a boxing "robot" got its block knocked off ... Hasbro's Sno-Cone Machine, a rare toy based on Frosty (kind of) ... Milton Bradley's Battleship, which even your dad would play ... and Marx's ugly, mobile "target" toy Bop a Bear, which seemed to have a thing for my Aunt Peggy, once chasing her clear into the kitchen.

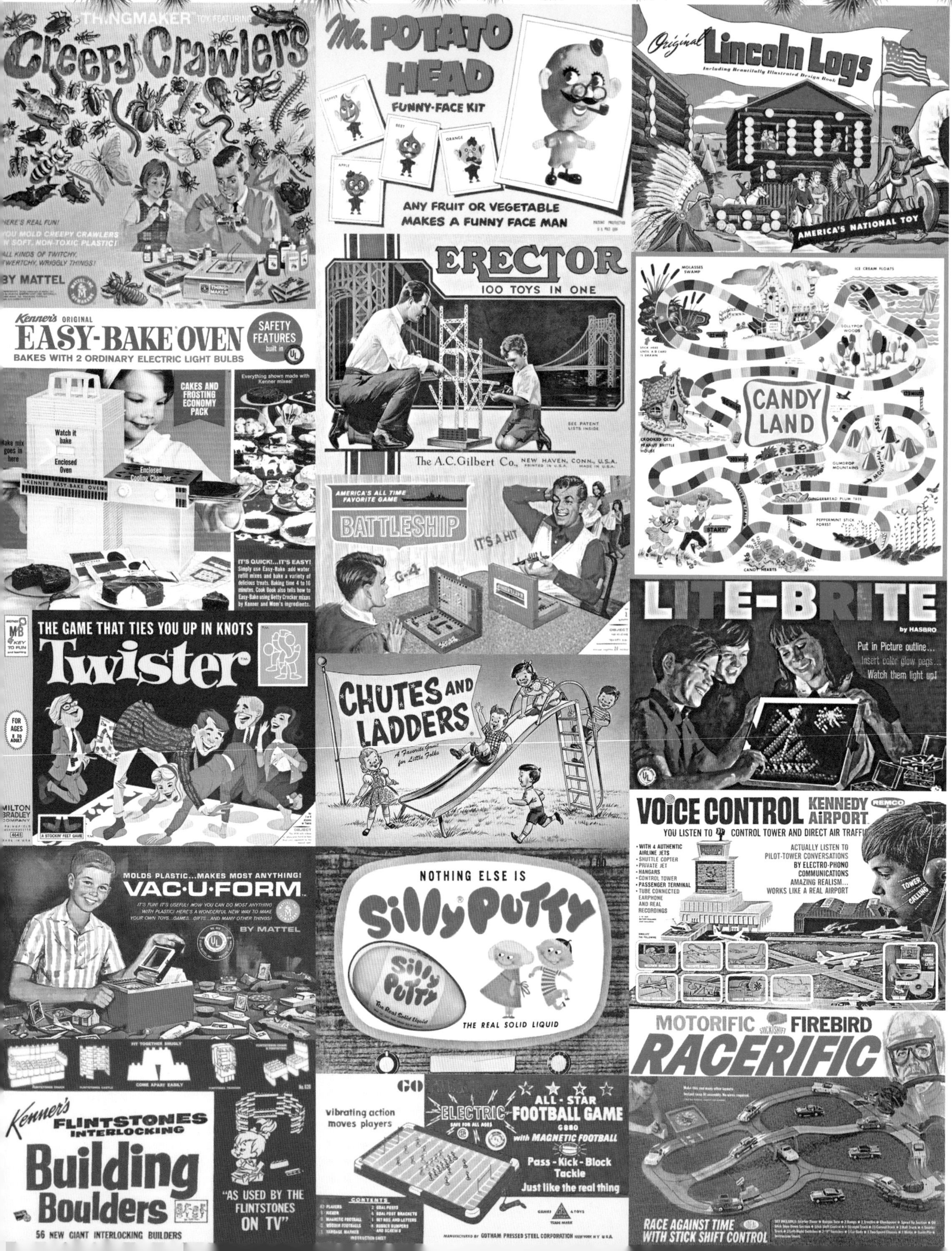
THINGMAKER TOY FEATURING
Creepy Crawlers
HERE'S REAL FUN!
YOU MOLD CREEPY CRAWLERS IN SOFT, NON-TOXIC PLASTIC!
ALL KINDS OF TWITCHY, SQWERTCHY, WRIGGLY THINGS!
BY MATTEL
Mr. POTATO HEAD
FUNNY-FACE KIT
ANY FRUIT OR VEGETABLE MAKES A FUNNY FACE MAN
Original Lincoln Logs
Including Beautifully Illustrated Design Book
AMERICA'S NATIONAL TOY
Kenner's ORIGINAL
EASY-BAKE OVEN
SAFETY FEATURES built in
BAKES WITH 2 ORDINARY ELECTRIC LIGHT BULBS
CAKES AND FROSTING ECONOMY PACK
Everything shown made with Kenner mixes!
Watch it bake
Make mix goes in here
Enclosed Oven
Enclosed Cooling Chamber
IT'S QUICK!...IT'S EASY!
ERECTOR
100 TOYS IN ONE
SEE PATENT LISTS INSIDE
The A.C.Gilbert Co. NEW HAVEN, CONN., U.S.A.
CANDY LAND
MOLASSES SWAMP
ICE CREAM FLOATS
LOLLYPOP WOODS
GUMDROP MOUNTAINS
PEPPERMINT STICK FOREST
START
AMERICA'S ALL TIME FAVORITE GAME
BATTLESHIP
IT'S A HIT
LITE-BRITE
by HASBRO
Put in Picture outline...
Insert color glow pegs...
Watch them light up!
THE GAME THAT TIES YOU UP IN KNOTS
Twister
FOR AGES 6 TO ADULT
MILTON BRADLEY COMPANY
A STOCKIN' FEET GAME
CHUTES AND LADDERS
A Favorite Game for Little Folks
VOICE CONTROL KENNEDY AIRPORT
REMCO
YOU LISTEN TO CONTROL TOWER AND DIRECT AIR TRAFFIC
ACTUALLY LISTEN TO PILOT-TOWER CONVERSATIONS BY ELECTRO-PHONO COMMUNICATIONS
AMAZING REALISM...
WORKS LIKE A REAL AIRPORT
• WITH 4 AUTHENTIC AIRLINE JETS
• SHUTTLE COPTER
• PRIVATE JET
• HANGARS
• CONTROL TOWER
• PASSENGER TERMINAL
• TUBE CONNECTED EARPHONE AND REAL RECORDINGS
TOWER CALLING
MOLDS PLASTIC...MAKES MOST ANYTHING!
VAC-U-FORM
BY MATTEL
NOTHING ELSE IS
Silly Putty
THE REAL SOLID LIQUID
MOTORIFIC STICKSHIFT FIREBIRD
RACERIFIC
RACE AGAINST TIME WITH STICK SHIFT CONTROL
Kenner's FLINTSTONES INTERLOCKING
Building Boulders
"AS USED BY THE FLINTSTONES ON TV"
56 NEW GIANT INTERLOCKING BUILDERS
vibrating action moves players
ELECTRIC
ALL-STAR FOOTBALL GAME
G880
with MAGNETIC FOOTBALL
Pass - Kick - Block Tackle
Just like the real thing
MANUFACTURED BY GOTHAM PRESSED STEEL CORPORATION

Christmas classics

Corgi's 007 Aston Martin: Based on James Bond's pimped-out car from "Goldfinger" (1964), the Aston Martin had pop-out machine guns, a pop-up bulletproof shield and a villain-vanquishing ejector seat.

Wham-O's Air Blaster: Many a bratty kid used this toy to mess up his big sister's hairstyle.

Marx's Bop a Bear: Hit it with a suction-cup dart, and this self-propelled "bear" on hidden wheels would shriek and change direction (1963).

Ohio Art's Etch A Sketch: With a little talent and coordination, you could draw nasty things on an Etch A Sketch in, say, a store.

Wham-O's Monster Magnet: This (relatively) powerful magnetic toy was the namesake of the rock band formed in 1989.

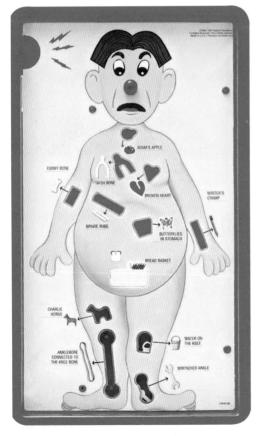

Slinky: Which trick was better, walking it down stairs or stretching it between two people, then letting go for a face wallop?

Hasbro's Operation: Don't set off the buzzer when removing his "Spare Ribs" or "Charlie Horse." Thank God his belly covers his "Twig and Berries."

Rainbow Craft's Play-Doh: You could play sculptor with this non-toxic "modeling compound," but some kids just ate it.

Hasbro's Frosty Sno-Man Sno-Cone Machine: A twist on ye olde lemonade stand. Grind up Kool-Aid ice cubes, instant water ice salesman!

From top left: Marx's Geronimo and Jane West figures (1965);
Ideal's Mr. Machine (1960); Marx's Big Loo robot (1963); Lakeside's
Gumby and Pokey (1965); Gilbert's 007 figures Emilio Largo, Dr. No,
Goldfinger, Miss Moneypenny and Bond ... James Bond (1965).

"Best of the West" figures and Big Loo © Louis Marx and Company; Mr. Machine ©
Ideal Toy Company; Gumby and Pokey © Art Clokey; James Bond © Eon Productions

GI JOE
ACTION SOLDIER T.M.
by HASBRO®

From left: Hasbro's
GI Joe (1964); Mattel's
Barbie (1959, reissue
shown); Ideal's
Captain Action (1966,
reissue shown); Bozo
Punch-Me; Knicker-
bocker's Boo Boo
(1959); Marx's Rock
'Em Sock 'Em Robots
(1964); Flintstones
bowling game "pin."

GI Joe © Hasbro; Barbie © Mattel;
Captain Action © Captain Action
Enterprises; Bozo the Clown ©
Larry Harmon; Boo Boo Bear and
Fred Flintstone © Hanna-Barbera
Productions; Rock 'Em Sock 'Em
Robots © Louis Marx and Co.

America's
movable
fighting man ™

MOVE G.I. JOE™ INTO
ACTION POSITIONS

BOZO

Off the air: Board games inspired by broadcast programs included, from top left, Uncle Jim's Question Bee, based on the 1936-41 radio quiz show; Trans-O-Gram's Angela Cartwright's Buttons 'n Bows Game, a "Make Room for Daddy" TV tie-in; Lisbeth Whiting's Spanky and His Rascals in the Fun Game (1956); Whitman's Zorro game based on the TV show starring Guy Williams; Ideal's The Soupy Sales Game; and Trans-O-Gram's The Flintstones Stone Age Game.

Goldberg-esque

It's a good bet that cartoonist Rube Goldberg, who was known for drawing wacky contraptions, inspired Ideal Toy Co.'s "Mouse Trap Game" (1963) and its "Kooky Kamera" (1968).
© Ideal Toy Co.

Anatomy of a game: Kreskin's ESP by Milton Bradley

KINDA SPOOKY, KINDA COOL, KRESKIN'S ESP WAS the Ouija board of 1967, with a pendulum instead of a planchette.

"I must tell you what happened," said The Amazing Kreskin (the entertainer's official moniker) when we spoke in 2004.

"For me to put out a game, the expectation is that I'm going to tell you how to read people's thoughts. Well, that's kind of double-talk. Some people are more sensitive than others. That's a lifetime of intuitive work. It wouldn't be very effective. So I thought of using the pendulum and some tests. Remember there were cards in it, where you would test each other? So I had an idea.

"This was at the beginning of my career. I was appearing on TV with Johnny Carson and Merv Griffin and Mike Douglas. We called Milton Bradley. They said, 'Well, come on in.'"

As it happened, Kreskin met Milton Bradley executives at Toy Fair, the industry convention held annually in New York City.

"It was madness," he recalled. "All the games for the year were being demonstrated and sold. They weren't thinking about new games. They were thinking of what they were selling.

"It was the worst time I could walk in. I didn't have any elaborate board game. I just had some cardboards and a chain and a weight. There were 10 or 12 salesman. They said to one salesman, 'Chet, go over and check it out.' He comes in the room. Instead of leaving four minutes later, he's there 20 minutes. He comes out and the other guy says, 'Well, let *me* go in.' Before you know it,

I'd spent a half a day there. The chairman of the board comes in and sits down and says, 'Kreskin, come and see us in two weeks.'"

A contract was later signed to go forward with Kreskin's ESP.

"They made the decision right then and there," he said.

"The game wasn't even written up yet. They said, 'It's going to be our No. 1 projected game this following year.'

"And then one year later, the television commercial was done. And here, I'm a guest on the Carson show, and what's the commercial? *My* commercial. And of course, it became a hit. Then, it was sold in Australia and England and everywhere."

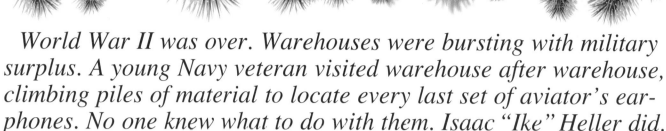

World War II was over. Warehouses were bursting with military surplus. A young Navy veteran visited warehouse after warehouse, climbing piles of material to locate every last set of aviator's earphones. No one knew what to do with them. Isaac "Ike" Heller did.

Heller was repurposing the earphones to make walkie-talkie toys of his own invention, which were fast becoming a big seller in the fledgling one-man toy business he named Remco (for "remote control").

That early toil yielded a toy empire. As Remco grew, it migrated from a New York City basement to Newark, New Jersey, to a specially-built factory in nearby Harrison, where thousands were employed.

In 2014, I asked Heller (1926-2015) if there was a particular toy he loved as a kid. "That I loved? A toy?" Heller said. "No. I grew up on a farm. We were very poor. And they didn't give poor kids toys."

So how did he know what kind of toy a child might like?

"Well, I said, 'Would *I* enjoy it?' And if I would say 'yes,' then I'd say a child would enjoy it. I tried making a toy that I would like."

Founded in 1949, Remco manufactured such toys as the Johnny Reb Civil War Cannon, the Firebird 99 dashboard, Voice Control Kennedy Airport and the "Lost In Space" Robot (for boys); the Heidi, Snugglebun, Finger Ding and Judy Littlechap dolls (for girls); and the company's most popular item, the Beatles figures (for both).

Heller was born of Russian immigrant parents and grew up in upstate New York, where he attended a one-room schoolhouse. He later was accepted to Brooklyn Technical High School, where this farm boy was exposed to a whole new world. "They taught me technical things," Heller said. "It came pretty naturally."

THIS EDUCATION CAME IN HANDY DURING THE years of World War II. Heller served in the Navy from 1944 to '46, attaining the rank of enlisted radar operator. While stationed on the USS Meredith and the USS O'Hare, he did trouble-shooting and repairs. "Mostly radar," Heller said. "That was a long time ago."

(Heller's radar experience would later influence Remco, whose toys often involved battery-operated communication.)

After the war, Heller landed a job as a toy designer before going solo. Over the next two decades, Heller and his cousin, Saul Robbins, built Remco into a robust toy manufacturer.

"Remco made a wide range of toys, of which some were good sellers, and were always competing with Ideal and Deluxe Reading," said Bill Bruegman, author of "Toys of the Sixties" (1996, Toy Scouts).

"For example, they would take a Deluxe Reading toy and make a less sophisticated copy of it for a younger age. Remco made a concerted attempt on licensed characters in the early '60s."

When "Beatlemania" exploded in America in 1964, Heller traveled to England to secure marketing rights from the Beatles' management. Remco's 4.5-inch figures had hard-plastic bodies, detachable instru-

Top: Isaac "Ike" Heller, standing, and his cousin Saul Robbins test a toy at the Remco factory in the 1960s. Left: Heller holds up a Judy Littlechap doll in 2014.

1960s photo courtesy of Hollie Heller; 2014 photo by Mark Voger

ments and moveable soft-plastic heads with comb-able fake hair.

Bruegman said the Beatles caricature dolls became Remco's signature toy, and kicked off many more character dolls, including Lyndon Johnson and Barry Goldwater (during the 1964 presidential election), "The Munsters," "The Addams Family," Daniel Boone and some original characters. "But none of these combined sold as well as the Beatles," Bruegman added.

Howard Bender — a memorabilia dealer and an artist who once drew Superman for DC Comics — agreed that Remco's Beatles figures remained the company's most desirable toys, though not necessarily its most rare. "The 'Munsters' and 'Addams Family' dolls are harder to come by," Bender said. "You don't see as many as you do the Beatles. The Beatles dolls are more in demand. They cycle up and cycle down. If the Beatles are in the news, (the toys) get more popularity."

Character toys are reliably popular among collectors. Remco's Dick Tracy 2-Way Wrist Radio, for one, never seems to go out of rotation on web auctions. Heller remembered developing it.

"Dick Tracy was an important comic strip, and he had a wrist radio," he said. "I thought that would make a good toy."

HELLER WAS REMINDED HOW, EARLY ON, REMCO favored boys in its toy development, until making a conscious push to develop a doll line, accompanied by the slogan: "Every boy wants a Remco toy ... and so do girls."

"I had figured out that girls would like toys — not the same toys that boys would like, but they would like them," he said.

Remco rolled out Judy Littlechap, the company's attempt to compete with Mattel's Barbie. Judy dolls were sold individually and in a Littlechap Family box set. (Mom sported a wild two-tone beehive hairdo.) An impetus at home may have inspired Heller to branch out into the "girl market."

"He had four daughters, so he started making dolls," said artist Hollie Heller, one of Heller's daughters, with a chuckle. "But these dolls were larger than Barbie, so they didn't do as well."

When she was a girl, Hollie would visit her father at the bustling Harrison factory. "My dad rode around the factory on a scooter," she recalled. "There were telephone operators just like on 'Mad Men.'"

Being the daughter of a toy manufacturer was not without its privileges.

"He would come home with this big brown box full of toys — the new ones that were just coming out, that might not be on the market yet," Hollie said. "We never had to go to the toy store. We always had toys in the house."

Heller and Robbins sold Remco in 1966, when Heller was 40. He reckoned he walked away with $1 million, and reinvented himself as a builder and philanthropist. Professionally, these roles overshadowed Heller's earlier career as a toy manufacturer — except in the hearts of those grown-up children who, from the '40s through the '60s, played with Remco toys.

Heller was asked if, in his Remco days, he ever received feedback from those children.

"Yeah," he said. "Kids said I was a good guy."

Remco's toys often involved battery-operated communication and automation. From top: Dick Tracy 2-Way Wrist Radios, Firebird 99 dashboard, Automatic Car Wash. Left: Ringo Starr was one of Remco's popular Beatles figures.

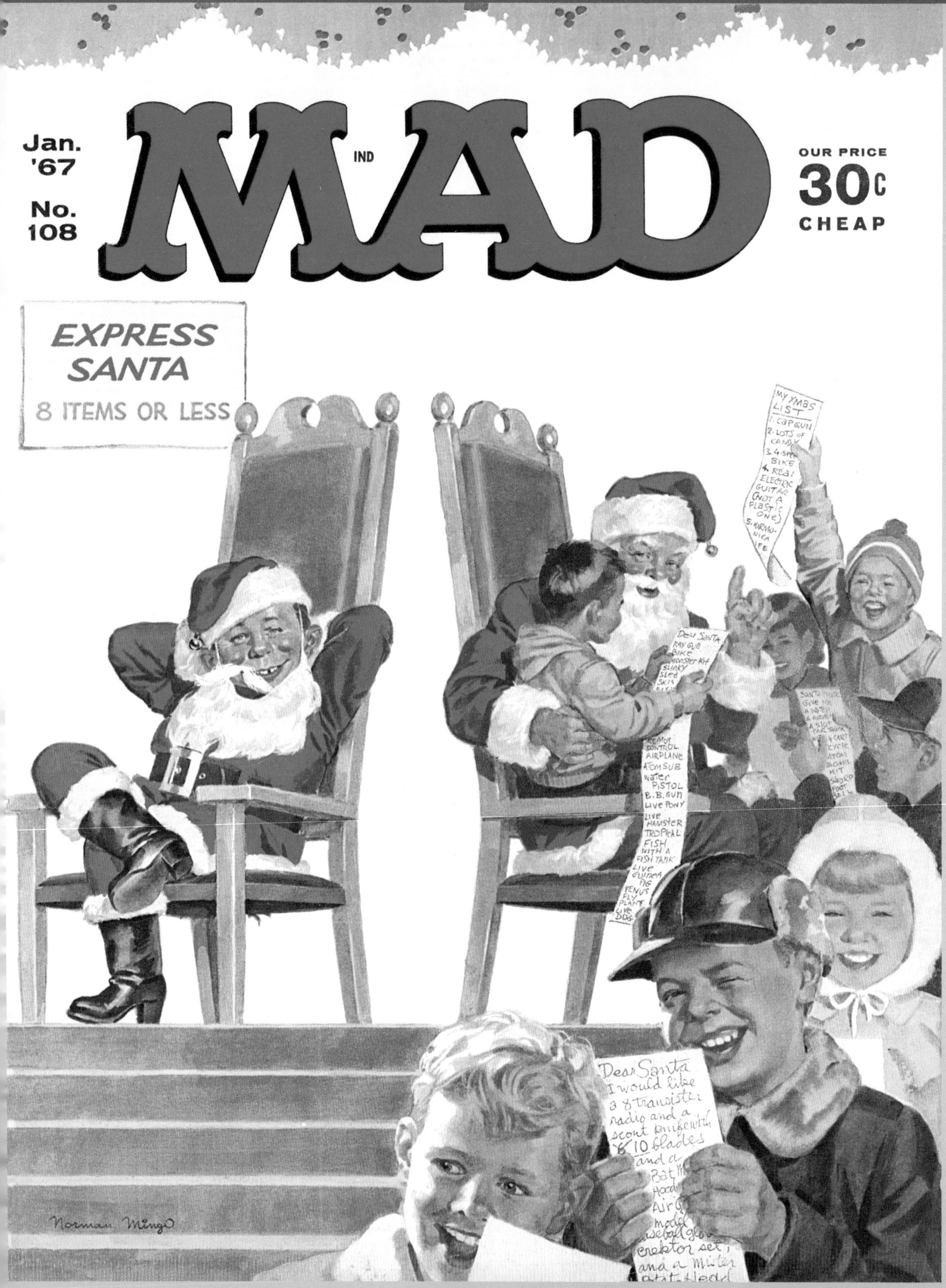
Jan. '67
No. 108
MAD
IND
OUR PRICE
30¢
CHEAP
EXPRESS SANTA
8 ITEMS OR LESS
MY XMAS LIST
Dear Santa
REMOT CONTROL AIRPLANE
ATOM SUB
water PISTOL
B.B. GUN
LIVE PONY
LIVE HAMSTER
TROPICAL FISH WITH A FISH TANK
LIVE GUINEA PIG
VENUS FLY PLANT
LIVE DOG
Dear Santa
I would like
a 8 transister
radio and a
scout knife with
10 blades
and a
Norman Mingo

Merry magazines

Droll, erudite, Christmas-y *New Yorker* covers ... Americana preserved by Norman Rockwell on *Saturday Evening Post* covers ... the "perfect" Christmas on women's magazine covers ... Santa pitching in for the war effort on *Yank* covers …

Print magazines are time capsules reflecting the ideals and interests of the society they are produced in. Holiday editions survive as a window to Christmases past.

From left: Up-to-the-minute 19th-century style in *Ladies Home Journal* (1890); Santa laughs, and rails, in two issues of the humor magazine *Puck* (1896 and 1901); mother and daughter by the toy shop in *Good Housekeeping* (1904); Janet Gaynor, star of the original "A Star is Born," encapsulates the spirit in *Photoplay* (1928); Santa gives new shoes to a young lady who is presumably on his "good" list in *Film Fun* (1931), in art by pinup master Enoch Bolles; perfume makes for a perfect gift in *Cosmopolitan* (1936). Opposite: As you might expect, Alfred E. Neuman is a lousy department-store Santa Claus in art by Norman Mingo — who was kind of a Rockwell in his own right — on the cover of *Mad* #108 (1967).

Times that try men's souls

Two distinct iterations of Santa by Norman Rockwell on *Saturday Evening Post* covers, 22 years apart: weighing expenses against gift recipients (1920) and a welcome interruption of World War II news (1942). Meanwhile, Walt Disney's mascot gets his skate on in *Mickey Mouse Magazine* (1935); Shirley Temple meets Santa in *Look* (1937); a Christmas-wrapping lesson in *Ladies Home Journal* (1939) by artist Al Parker, who did 50 *LHJ* covers; Santa the soldier in *Yank* (1943 and '44), the latter also depicting Sad Sack and drawn by Sack's creator, George Baker; and domestic perfection in the British magazine *My Home* (1952).

The times, they were a'changin'

The New Yorker presented urban tree-shopping by Ilonka Karasz (1935); Santa punching a clock by Constantin Alajalov (1937); mommy kissing Santa Claus by Perry Barlow (1939); Santa on the job by William Cotton (1948); and Central Park grooviness by Charles Saxon (1967). Sugar Ray Robinson plays Santa at home in *Our World* (1951); Alfred E. Neuman abuses mistletoe in *Mad #92* in Mingo art (1965); and a badass Santa by Jean Sole in *Heavy Metal* (1977).

Ah, giving the gift of smoking. From above: Ronald Reagan pushes Chesterfields (and his 1952 movie "Hong Kong"); Joan Crawford comes calling with Lucky Strikes; more celebs sell Chesterfields; Santa flogs Luckys, Camels and Pall Malls.

Chesterfield © Liggett & Myers; Lucky Strike © R.A. Patterson; Pall Mall and Camel © R.J. Reynolds Tobacco Co.

For Sparkling Holidays

Bring home the Coke

DRINK
Coca-Cola

DRINK
Coca-Cola

PURE WHOLESOME

Extra Bright Refreshment

STOCK UP FOR THE HOLIDAYS

DRINK
Coca-Cola

" Give and take"-say I

Michigan-born artist Haddon Sundblom (1899-1976) did more than sell Coca-Cola with heartwarming advertisements depicting Santa Claus beginning in 1931. Sundblom's often-imitated art solidified the culture's ideal of Santa.

© The Coca-Cola Company

It keeps his GINGER *up!*

Drink Canada Dry Ginger Ale

IT'S GINGERVATING!

Picks you up . . . aids digestion

-and all through the year!
CANADA DRY

Merry Christmas to all
FROM
The All-Family Drink!

So pure...so good...so wholesome for everyone...including the tiniest tots!

Santa and "gingervating" Canada Dry; more Canada Dry choices; caroling while jacked up on 7Up. © Canada Dry Bottling Co.; © The 7Up Company

73

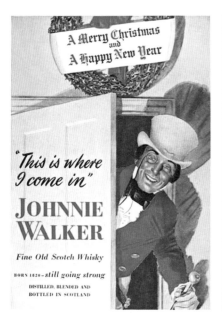

A Merry Christmas and A Happy New Year

"This is where I come in"

JOHNNIE WALKER
Fine Old Scotch Whisky

BORN 1820—still going strong

DISTILLED, BLENDED AND
BOTTLED IN SCOTLAND

make it
merry
make it
MOJUD

A word to every Santa from Portland to Atlanta!
To make the lady's Christmas Merry give her
Mojud stockings. The stockings with Magic-Motion
... extra "give" and spring-back in the knit.

★ Magic-Motion means longer wear, and more
fabulous fit from top to toe. Is your Christmas belle
tall, tiny or in-between? Ask for the Mojud stocking
length made especially for her!

stockings by

MOJUD

★ Remember, there's lovely
Christmas lingerie by Mojud, too

The Christmas They'll Never Forget!

Cadillac

New! Crisco's short cut to the merriest Christmas Cookies ever!

New, creamier Crisco makes the richest, tastiest cookies...
Crisco's homemade mix makes them double-quick!

use Crisco
IT'S DIGESTIBLE

Bless your Hearth!

Necco

Buy 'em by the box
for Holiday
handouts.

Mighty good stuffin'
for any stockin'

still only 5¢!

Necco Chocolate Peppermints–King size box 10¢

New England Confectionery Co., Cambridge 39, Mass.

From top left: A Victorian moment from Johnnie Walker; an "oops" moment from Mojud; classiness from Cadillac; cookie recipes from Crisco; sweets from Necco; and the gift of guns from Remington, Daisy Air Rifles and Colt.

© John Walker & Sons Ltd.; © Mojud Hosiery Co. Inc.; © Cadillac;
© Proctor & Gamble; © Necco; © Remington Arms Co.; © Daisy
Air Rifles; © Colt's Manufacturing Co.

Christmas lasts a lifetime
when it's a
REMINGTON 22

Remington DUPONT

The New
GOLDEN BANDED
1000-SHOT
RED RYDER
Saddle
CARBINE

I'll help You get a DAISY for CHRISTMAS
—Red Ryder

$2.95
DUTY
ADDED IN
CANADA

Send
Coupon For
FREE
CHRISTMAS
Reminder
KIT

The Popular 500 SHOT LIGHTNING-LOADER CARBINE
Only $2.50

DAISY AIR RIFLES

Isn't it time
you gave
yourself a
Christmas
Gift?

While you're making everybody happy . . . do a good job and include yourself!

COLT

From top left: Jack Lemmon sells Christmas Seals; Chatty Cathy doll; Rock 'Em Sock 'Em Robots; Coke's hippie choir; Santa's wild ride; Hershey's Kisses ring in the season; Elizabeth Montgomery sells savings bonds; CBS's touching spot; Ronald McDonald pushes gift certificates as stocking stuffers. © Christmas Seals; © Mattel Inc.; © Louis Marx and Company; © Coca-Cola Company; © Norelco; © The Hershey Company; © CBS; © McDonald's

When Santa traded his sleigh for an electric razor

"Christmas is a time for closeness — and closeness is what Norelco razors are all about."

Children in the 1960s really, really, really wanted there to be a Norelco Christmas special, thanks to the stop-motion animated commercial showing a jubilant Santa whizzing through snowy hills on Norelco's rechargeable Tripleheader model shaver.

Hey, the California Raisins — also Madison Avenue mascots — got their own Christmas special. Why not the Tripleheader?

Christmas-themed TV commercials (especially those about toys) helped get consumers psyched for the holiday.

In 1971, Coca-Cola scored buzz with its commercial featuring a choir of shiny, happy hippies from many lands holding bottles of Coke while crooning, "I'd Like to Teach the World to Sing." At Christmastime, the jingle was resung with added bells, while the hippies traded their Coke bottles for candles.

Hershey's Kisses also got musical, with the chocolate candy doubling as bells playing "We Wish You a Merry Christmas."

Celebs got their Christmas on by appearing in PSAs (public service announcements). Doris Day touted the Marine Corps' Toys for Tots campaign. Jack Webb and Jack Lemmon sold Christmas Seals. Elizabeth Montgomery pitched savings bonds as Christmas gifts — from the living-room set of "Bewitched," yet.

The most touching in CBS' series of animated PSAs by illustrator R.O. Blechman showed adorable birds happily chirping in a tree on a snowy morning, when a man approaches carrying a saw. Just as removal of the tree seems imminent, the man holds the saw to his chin like a violin, pulls out a bow, and plays "God Rest Ye Merry Gentlemen." The birds resume their chirping.

Festive funnies

At Christmastime, newspaper comic strips delivered what comic books could not: Timely greetings on the very day.

Century of celebration: Not every syndicated newspaper comic strip referenced the holiday when published on Dec. 25 of a given year. But when they did, it added special resonance to this old-school medium. From top: Christmas by the fireplace in Cliff Sterrett artwork in "Polly and Her Pals" (1917); Rudolph Dirks depicts holiday pandemonium in "The Katzenjammer Kids" (1902); Christmas-themed ad featuring Sunday funnies icon the Yellow Kid (1910); a Yokum yuletide in Al Capp art in "Li'l Abner" (1934); Beetle has a surprise for Sarge in Mort Walker art in "Beetle Bailey" (1960).

Crimefighters a'caroling: In Chester Gould art from top, Dick Tracy and Pat Patton visit Junior in the hospital, while gun moll Kitty implores dapper murderer Krome to suspend activities on Christmas Day (1940); Tracy and the gang spotlight Santa (1941); Sparkle Plenty sings along with Bing Crosby in a TV broadcast (1951); Gravel Gertie shuts down B.O. Plenty (1951); the gang harmonizes (1951). "Dick Tracy" © Chicago Tribune Syndicate

Tidings from 'Terry'

"Terry and the Pirates" writer-artist Milton Caniff often reminded his readers that not everyone got to spend Christmas at home. From left: Pat Ryan, Captain Blaze and April Kane have a makeshift celebration under watchful eyes (1939); April surprises Terry and Pat with an assist from Big Stoop (1941); Terry's and Tote's eyes mist up while listening to the American Mission School choir's rendition of "Silent Night" in China (1943).

"Terry and the Pirates"
© Chicago Tribune Syndicate

Christmas far and near: As he did with "Terry and the Pirates," Milton Caniff depicted characters celebrating Christmas overseas in the adventure strip "Steve Canyon," his likewise military-themed followup to "Terry." Caniff also marked the holiday with somber tributes to members of the Armed Forces who lost their lives in combat. Above: In "Steve Canyon" panels from 1947, old salt Happy Easter plays Santa in the Middle East. Meanwhile, on the home front, Charles M. Schulz could be relied upon to acknowledge the holiday in his long-running strip, "Peanuts." When the animated TV special "A Charlie Brown Christmas" premiered in 1965, keen-eyed fans identified echoes of earlier "Peanuts" strips. Right: Could that be an ancestor of the "Charlie Brown Christmas tree" in a 1954 panel? Below left: Snoopy's doghouse is electrically equipped for outdoor decorations in a 1963 panel, as on the television special. Below right: In 1964, Linus recites a passage from St. Luke, as he would the following year on the special.

Sequential Santas

Holiday entertainment for a thin dime (at first)

NOT TO SOUND CROTCHETY, BUT THERE WAS A time when a simple thing like some newsprint — with illustrations printed in cyan, magenta, yellow and black ink, held together by two staples — could create excitement on Christmas morning. (Back then, the old folks groused that all *they* ever got for Christmas was an apple and some nuts, so it's all relative.)

The comic books of yore sometimes featured Christmas-themed editions, many of which found their way into stockings or under the tree. For the most part, such books honored the separation of church and state; they were more about candy canes and reindeer than hay-strewn mangers and gift-bearing wise men.

Notable exceptions were Educational Comics' *Picture Stories From the Bible, New Testament Edition* #1 (1944) and *Complete Life of Christ Edition* (1945), published by Max C. Gaines, the acknowledged "father" of the comic book. Another was the *Classics Illustrated* special edition *The Story of Jesus* (1955).

CHRISTMAS EDITIONS WERE A MAINSTAY OF DELL Publishing, via its long-running *Four Color Comics*. (The title — a reference to the aforementioned cyan, magenta, etc. — was a "catch-all" for this anthology series.) The most visible of *Four Color Comics'* holiday editions was its annual *Santa Claus Funnies*, which ran for 20 years beginning in 1942.

Typical issues of *Santa Claus Funnies* featured stories about — surprise! — Santa, Mrs. Santa, the elves and the reindeer, set at the North Pole. Some stories focused on original characters such as Winky the Toymaker, Petey Polar Bear, Betsy Mouse or Hippity and Hoppity Rabbit. There were prose stories ("Christmas in Many Lands"), adaptations of Charles Dickens and Hans Christian Andersen, puzzles, connect-the-dots, how-to activities, Christmas carols and poems. A recurring back-cover feature was the Bright Twins (mischievous redheaded boy, precocious blond girl).

The interior art ranged in style from cartoony to semi-realistic. Artists who drew for *Santa Claus Funnies* include Mel Crawford, Dan Gormley, Arthur E. Jameson, and Walt Kelly. (Besides his work in *Santa Claus Comics,* "Pogo" artist Kelly was also behind *Four Color's Christmas With Mother Goose* series of 1945-49.)

More resources were dedicated to the all-important covers. Most *Santa Claus Funnies* covers depicted Santa in traditional settings, but modernity crept in. Santa rode an Army jeep (1942), a rocket-powered sleigh (1959), and a convertible (1960). The uncredited cover artists occasionally imitated Haddon Sundblom, whose painted incarnation of St. Nick sold a lot of Coca-Cola.

Carl Barks (1901-2000) — the revered Donald Duck artist — introduced Donald's wealthy uncle, Scrooge McDuck, in *Four Color* #178 (1947), in an unprecedented origin: a Disney character that debuted in a comic book and later crossed over into film.

"Uncle Scrooge was needed as part of the plot for Donald in (the story) 'Christmas on Bear Mountain' in 1947," Barks said in

Gifts galore in Roy Rogers Comics #61 (1952). Opposite: Santa Claus Funnies toplines Four Color Comics #867 (1957).

Roy Rogers Comics and Four Color Comics © Dell Publishing

my 1997 interview with him. "Everyone dreams of having a ridiculously rich uncle. I never gave a thought as to whether I would use Uncle Scrooge again. I was populating Duckberg with a cast of characters. These characters went on stage only as needed to suit a particular story. It was a surprise to me that a few months later, Uncle Scrooge fit right into another story."

In *Four Color*, Barks also produced *Donald Duck in the Golden Christmas Tree* (1948) and *A Christmas for Shacktown* (1952).

Four Color published its *Frosty the Snowman* series between 1951 and '62. Syndicated cartoonist Walt Scott had holiday-themed installments of his comic strip "The Little People" reprinted in *Christmas Stories* in 1958 and '59.

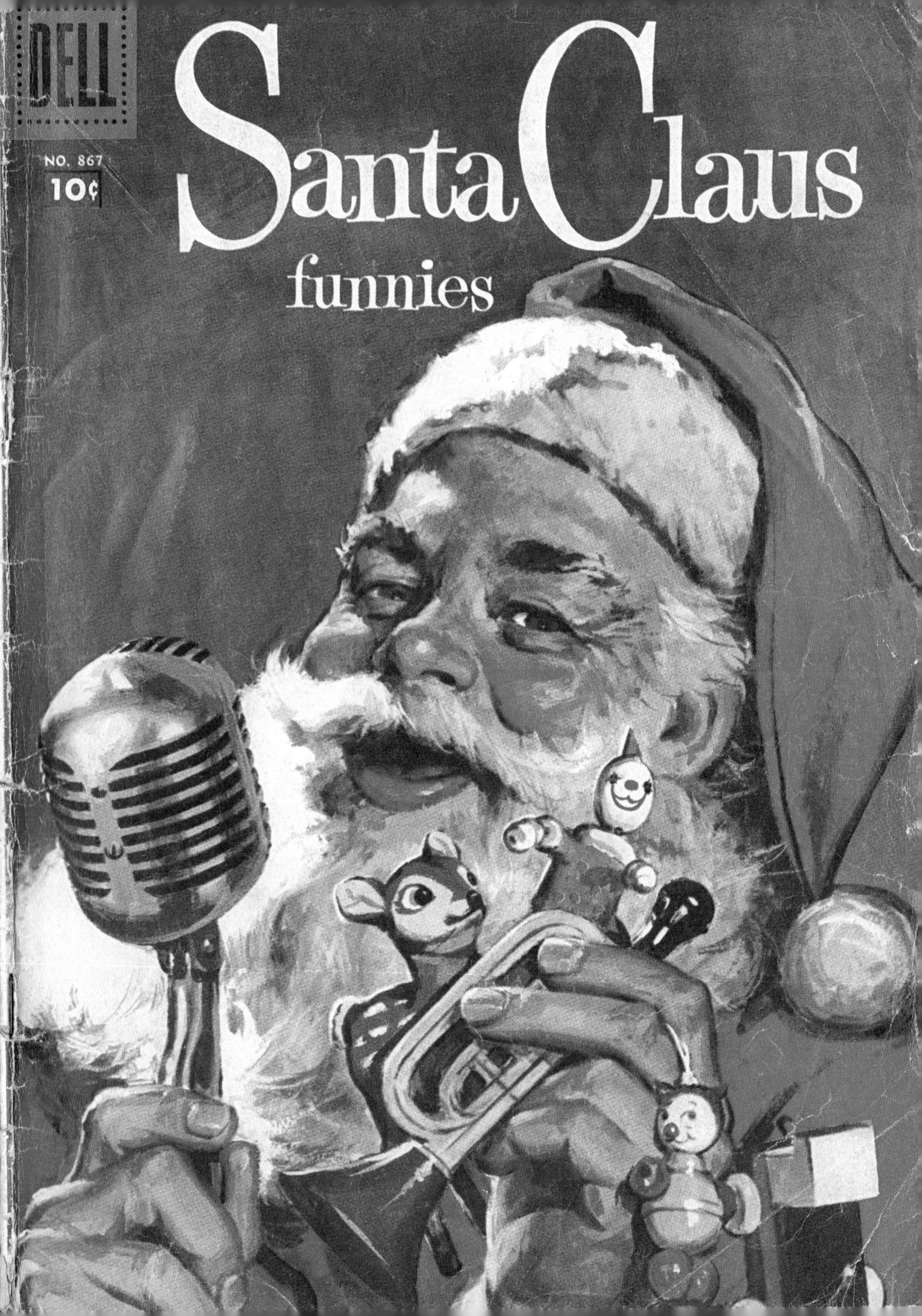
DELL
NO. 867
10¢
Santa Claus
funnies

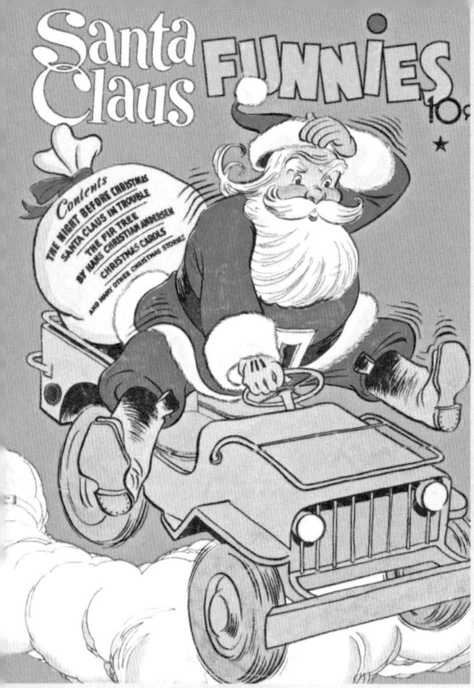
Santa Claus FUNNIES
10¢
Contents
THE NIGHT BEFORE CHRISTMAS
SANTA CLAUS IN TROUBLE
THE FIR TREE BY HANS CHRISTIAN ANDERSEN
CHRISTMAS CAROLS
AND MANY OTHER CHRISTMAS STORIES

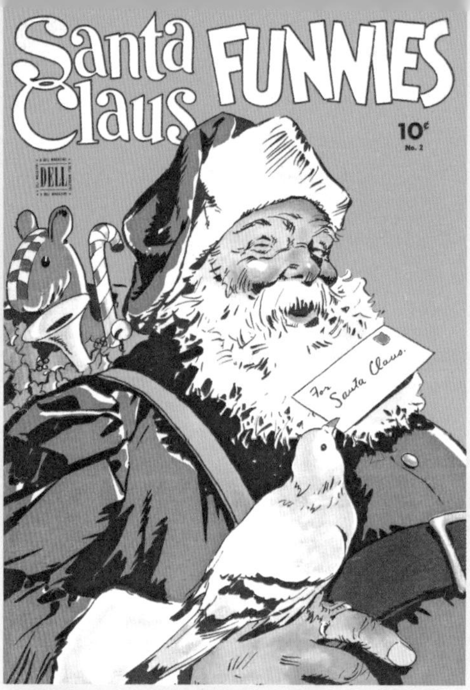
Santa Claus FUNNIES
10¢
No. 2
DELL
For Santa Claus

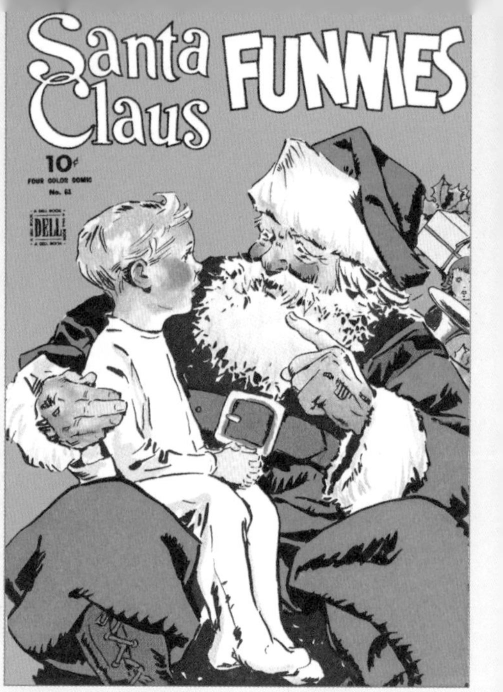
Santa Claus FUNNIES
10¢
FOUR COLOR COMIC
No. 61
DELL

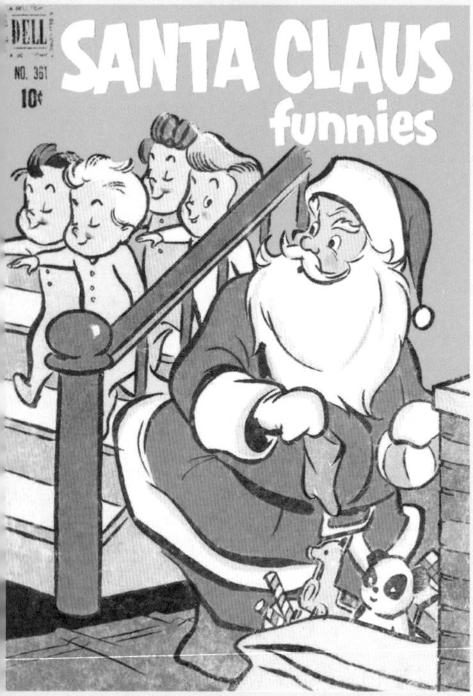
DELL
NO. 361
10¢
SANTA CLAUS
funnies

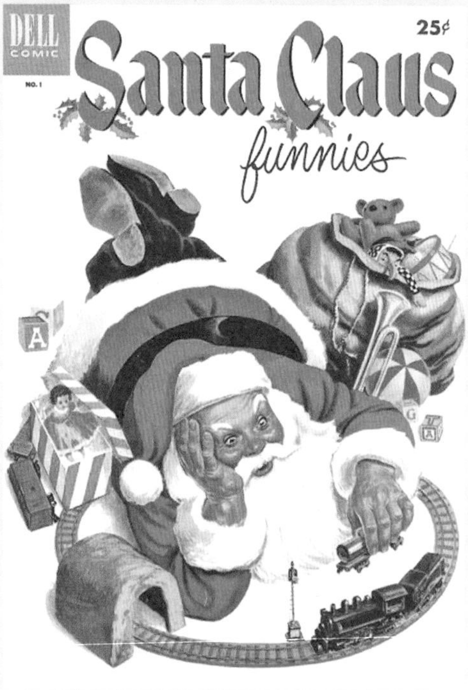
DELL COMIC
NO. 1
25¢
Santa Claus
funnies

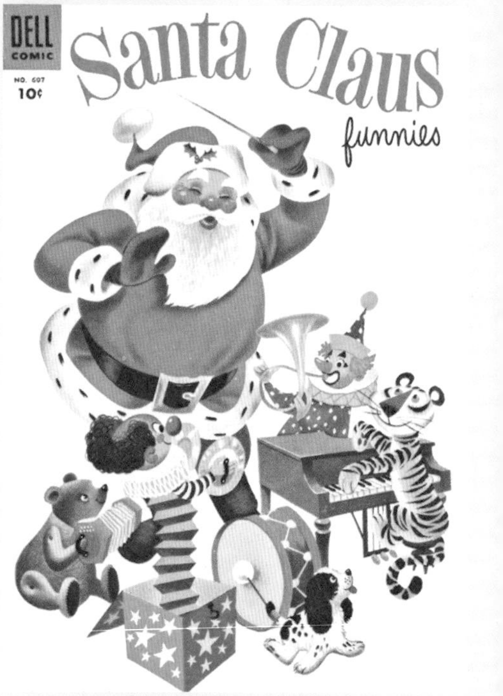
DELL COMIC
NO. 607
10¢
Santa Claus
funnies

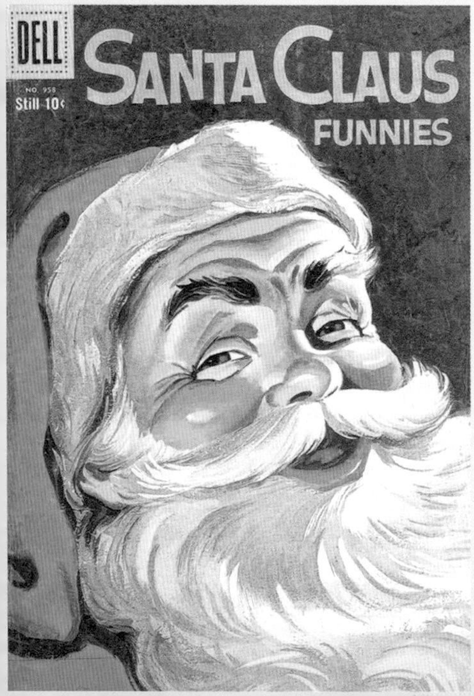
DELL
NO. 958
Still 10¢
SANTA CLAUS
FUNNIES

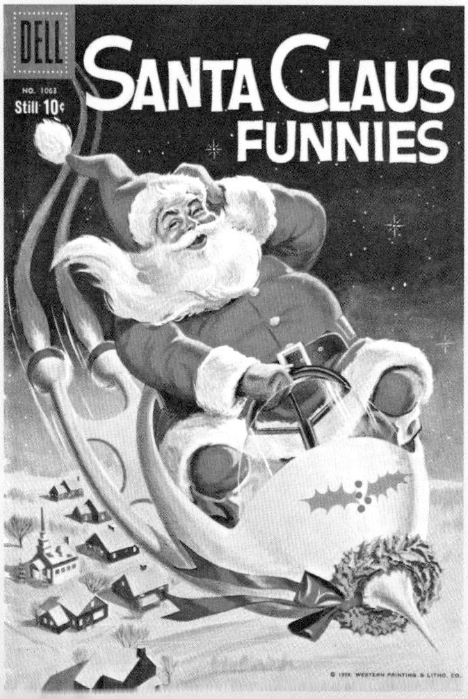
DELL
NO. 1063
Still 10¢
SANTA CLAUS
FUNNIES

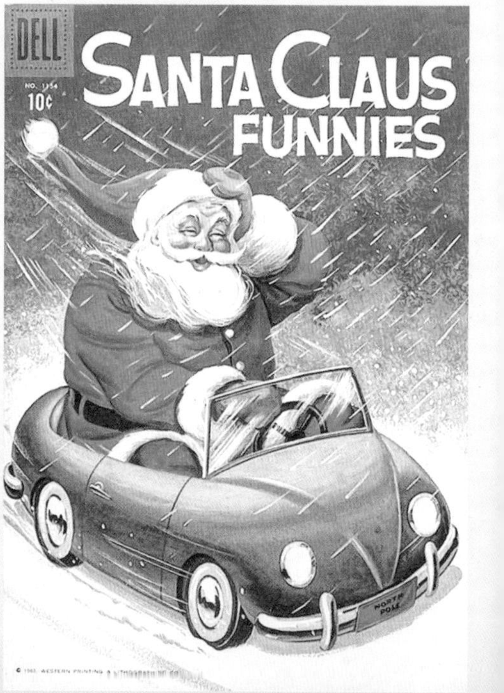
DELL
NO. 1154
10¢
SANTA CLAUS
FUNNIES
NORTH POLE

Santa panics in Santa Claus Funnies (1957). Opposite: SCF covers from 1942 through 1960. Below: Martian meetup. © Dell Publishing

SANTA CLAUS — NO STRANGER TO COLORFUL costumes and supernatural abilities — also interacted with the comic-book medium's superheroes.

In 1940, two years after Superman's debut in *Action Comics* #1, DC Comics produced the department-store giveaway *Superman's Christmas Adventure*. In the story, Superman trades lines with Santa, visits Santa's workshop and hoists Santa's sleigh above his head. The story was written by Superman co-creator Jerry Siegel and illustrated by early Superman artist Jack Burnley.

In illustrations by prolific Superman artist Wayne Boring, the Man of Steel brandishes a globe marked "Christmas 'Round the World" on the *Action* #93 cover (1946), and helps tubby ol' Santa squeeze into a chimney on the *Action* #105 cover (1947).

SANTA ALSO MET SUPERMAN'S BUDDY, BATMAN.
The Jolly One is flanked by Batman and Robin on the cover of *Batman* #27 (1945) in Burnley art. (Even a kiddie comic book at Christmastime was infiltrated by reality; type above the Batman logo commanded readers: "Back the 6th War Loan!") *Batman* #33 (1946) shows Robin tumbling while decorating a Christmas tree, to Batman's amusement (oh, those cutups) in Dick Sprang art. *Batman* #45 (1948) depicts the Dynamic Duo as gift-bearing Jack-in-the-boxes in art by Win Mortimer. (It's kinda weird.)

Sandman and Sandy met Santa in *Adventure Comics* #82 (1942), in art and story by Joe Simon and Jack Kirby. (Kirby drew another Santa-Sandman crossover that was published in 1982.)

Sensation Comics #38 (1945), with the tag "Wonder Woman Alias Miss Santa Claus," shows WW delivering toys while an unshaven hoodlum trains a tommy gun on her, in H.G. Peters art.

Comic Cavalcade's annual tradition placed Wonder Woman, Flash and Green Lantern — in their Golden Age iterations — in holiday settings via Frank Harry art. In *CC* #5 (1944), the trio yuks it up with Santa; in *CC* #13 (1946), they peer through a frosty

window; in *CC* #25 (1948), they assemble toys for an ailing Santa.

St. Nick was a supporting player in DC's annual series *Rudolph the Red-Nosed Reindeer* (1950-62). *Rudolph* artists include Rube Grossman and, in a '70s revival, Sheldon Mayer. (Mayer is a historic figure in comics, having been instrumental in greenlighting a then-oft-rejected character back in 1938 … Superman.)

One of Santa's strangest appearances in the comics was based on one of his strangest appearances in the movies: Dell's adaptation of *Santa Claus Conquers the Martians* (1964). But in true Santa fashion, he conquered them with good cheer.

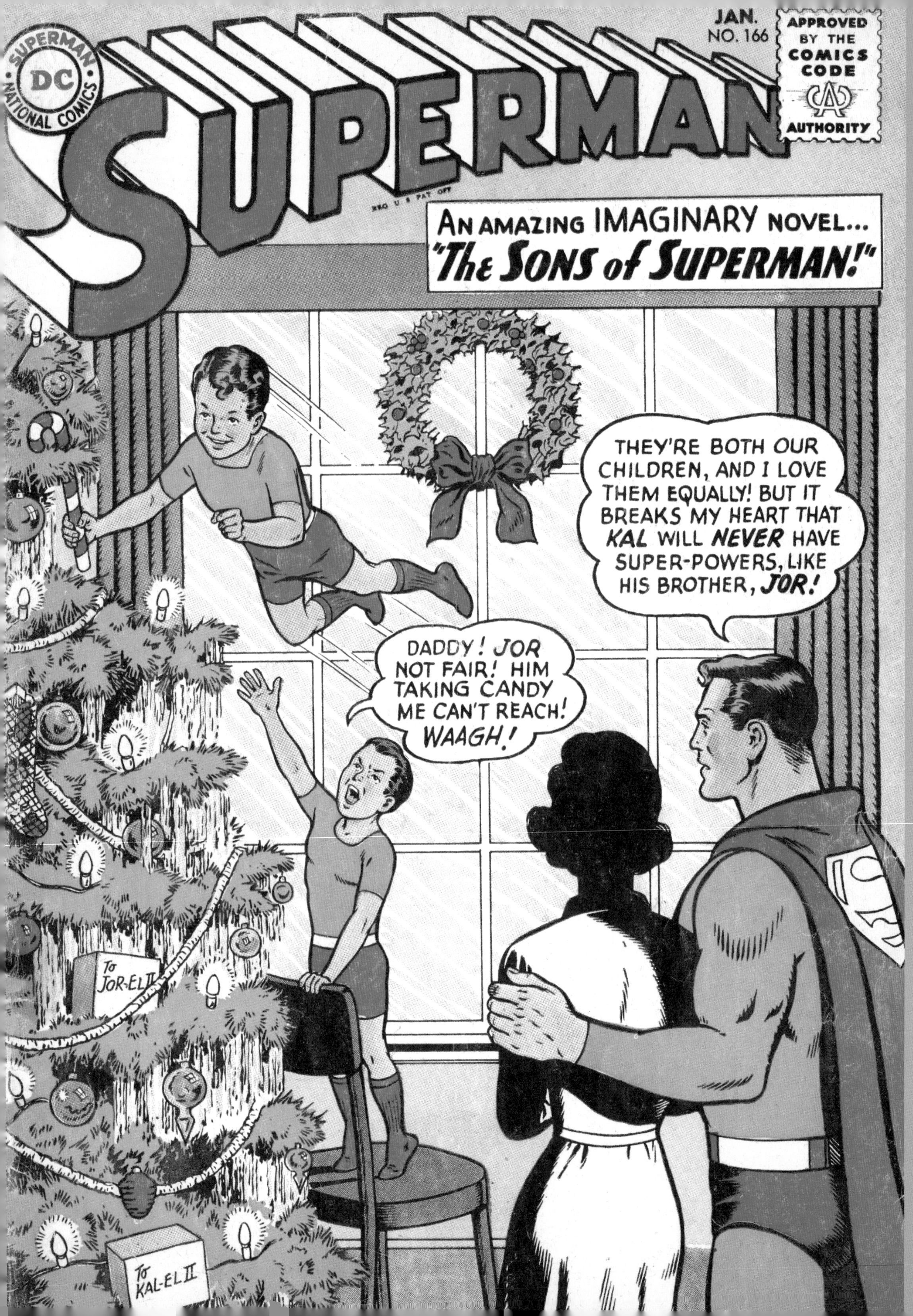

SUPERMAN DC NATIONAL COMICS
SUPERMAN
JAN. NO. 166
APPROVED BY THE COMICS CODE AUTHORITY
AN AMAZING IMAGINARY NOVEL... "The SONS of SUPERMAN!"
THEY'RE BOTH OUR CHILDREN, AND I LOVE THEM EQUALLY! BUT IT BREAKS MY HEART THAT KAL WILL NEVER HAVE SUPER-POWERS, LIKE HIS BROTHER, JOR!
DADDY! JOR NOT FAIR! HIM TAKING CANDY ME CAN'T REACH! WAAGH!
To JOR-EL II
To KAL-EL II

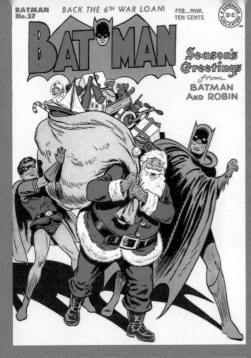

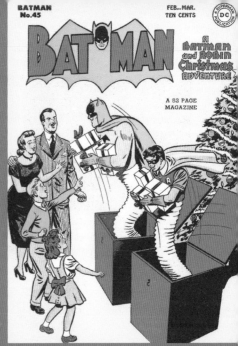

Holiday with the heroes: From top left, Golden Age Christmas covers for Batman #27 (1945), Batman #33 (1946), Batman #45 (1948), Action Comics #93 (1946), Action Comics #105 (1947), Sensation Comics #38 (1945), Comic Cavalcade #5 (1944) and Comic Cavalcade #25 (1948). Opposite: In a Silver Age "imaginary" story (as if all Superman stories weren't imaginary), the Man of Steel's twin sons, Jor-El II and Kal-El II, bicker by the tree in art by Curt Swan and George Klein on the cover of Superman #166 (1964). © DC Comics, Inc.

Santa in the DCU
Above, Superman descends on the North Pole in Jack Burnley art from the department-store giveaway *Superman's Christmas Adventure* (1940). At right, Wonder Woman plays Santa in H.G. Peters art (1942). Below, Rudolph to the rescue in Sheldon Mayer art from a *Rudolph the Red-Nosed Reindeer* special edition (1974).

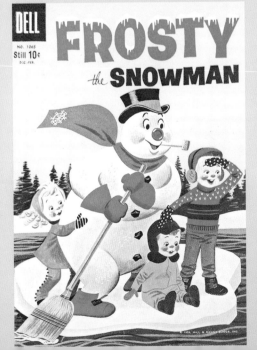

Familiar characters, new format
DC Comics' *Rudolph the Red-Nosed Reindeer* comic books from 1952 (top left), 1961 (second from top left) and 1959 (above). Far left: Dell's *Frosty the Snowman*, a.k.a. *Four Color Comics* #1065 (1959). Left: *Classics Illustrated* #53 (1948), an adaptation of Charles Dickens' "A Christmas Carol." The *Classics Illustrated* volume has interior art by Henry C. Kiefer (1890-1957), a pulp artist in the 1930s who became a popular *CI* artist, illustrating 34 editions of the title.

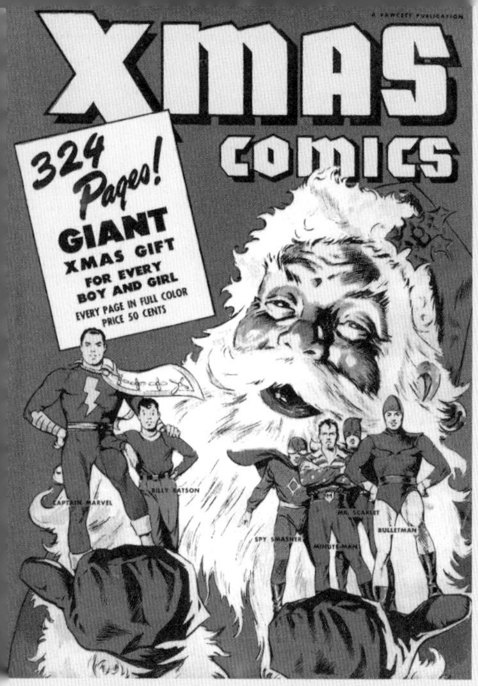
A FAWCETT PUBLICATION
XMAS
COMICS
324 Pages!
GIANT
XMAS GIFT
FOR EVERY
BOY AND GIRL
EVERY PAGE IN FULL COLOR
PRICE 50 CENTS
CAPTAIN MARVEL
BILLY BATSON
SPY SMASHER
MINUTE-MAN
MR. SCARLET
BULLETMAN

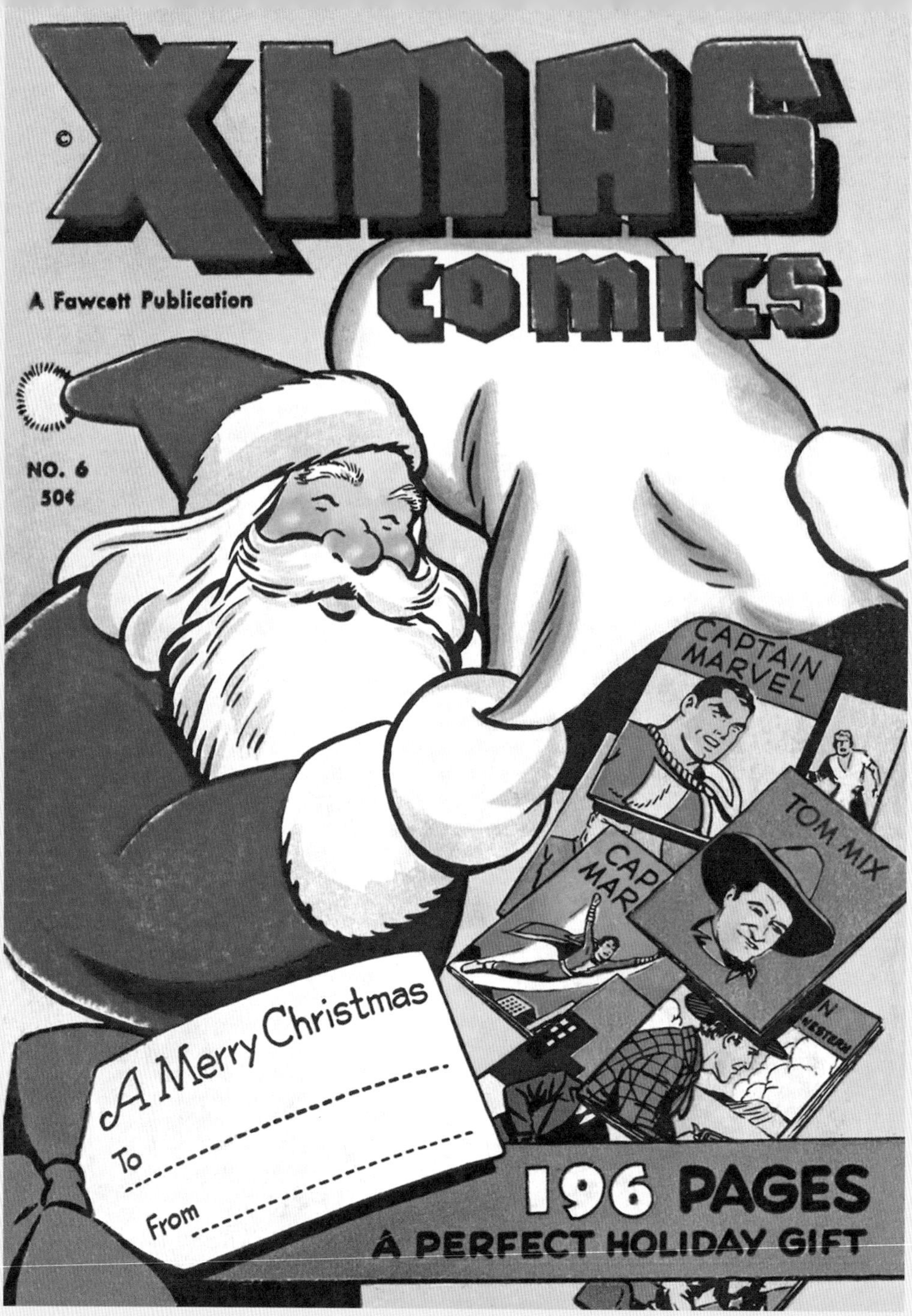
©
XMAS
COMICS
A Fawcett Publication
NO. 6
50¢
CAPTAIN MARVEL
TOM MIX
A Merry Christmas
To
From
196 PAGES
A PERFECT HOLIDAY GIFT

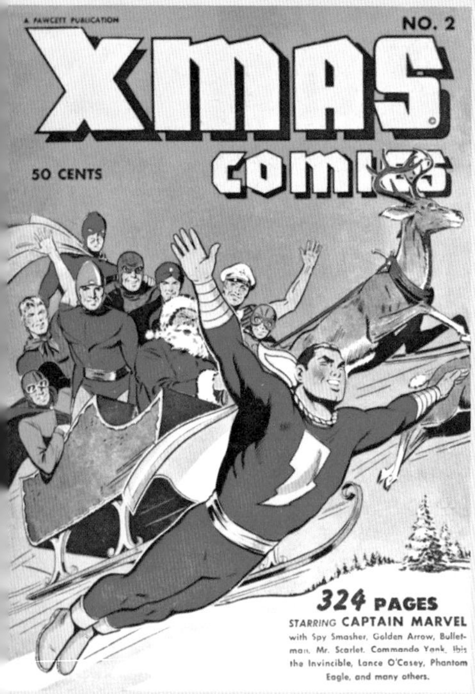
A FAWCETT PUBLICATION
NO. 2
XMAS
COMICS
50 CENTS
324 PAGES
STARRING CAPTAIN MARVEL
with Spy Smasher, Golden Arrow, Bulletman, Mr. Scarlet, Commando Yank, Ibis the Invincible, Lance O'Casey, Phantom Eagle, and many others.

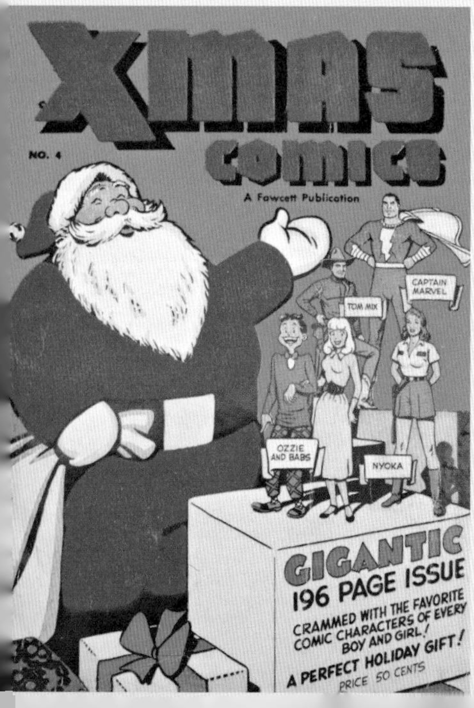
XMAS
COMICS
NO. 4
A Fawcett Publication
CAPTAIN MARVEL
TOM MIX
OZZIE AND BABS
NYOKA
GIGANTIC
196 PAGE ISSUE
CRAMMED WITH THE FAVORITE COMIC CHARACTERS OF EVERY BOY AND GIRL!
A PERFECT HOLIDAY GIFT!
PRICE 50 CENTS

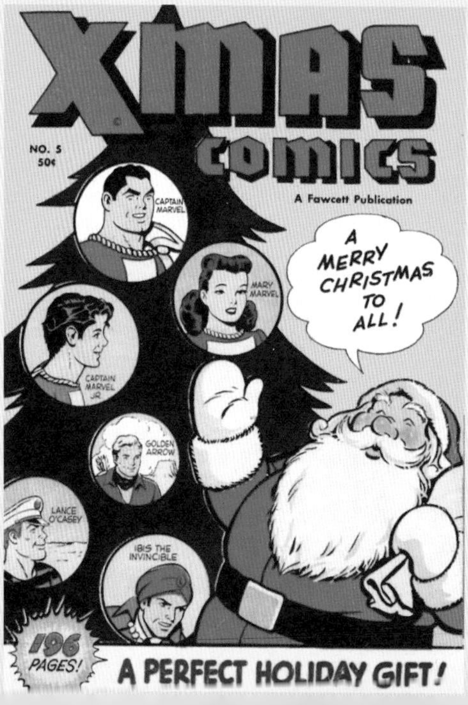
XMAS
COMICS
NO. 5
50¢
A Fawcett Publication
CAPTAIN MARVEL
MARY MARVEL
A MERRY CHRISTMAS TO ALL!
CAPTAIN MARVEL JR.
GOLDEN ARROW
LANCE O'CASEY
IBIS THE INVINCIBLE
196 PAGES!
A PERFECT HOLIDAY GIFT!

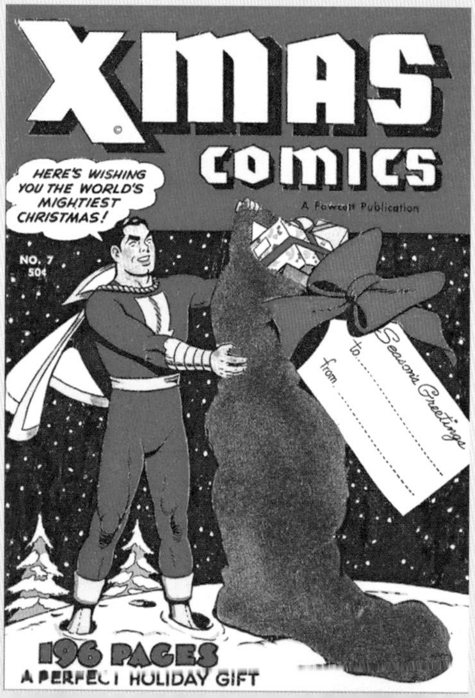
XMAS
COMICS
HERE'S WISHING YOU THE WORLD'S MIGHTIEST CHRISTMAS!
A Fawcett Publication
NO. 7
50¢
Season's Greetings
to:
from:
196 PAGES
A PERFECT HOLIDAY GIFT

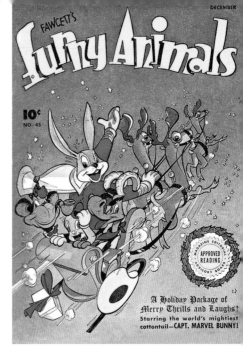

Holy (holiday) Moley! Fawcett Publishing, home of Captain Marvel, got in the spirit with covers for *Captain Marvel Adventures* #19 (1941) with Marc Swayze art; *Captain Marvel Jr.* #14 (1943) with Mac Raboy art; and *Funny Animals* #45 (1946). Opposite: Fawcett's giant rebound *Xmas Comics* editions shown are #1 (1941) with Raboy art; #2 (1942) with Dan Barry art; and, in C.C. Beck art, #4 (1949), #5 (1950), #6 (1951), and the title's final issue, #7 (1952). Below: A detail from *Captain Marvel* #42 (1944). © Fawcett Publications

SCROOGE HIMSELF WOULD HAVE ADMIRED THE business ingenuity on the part of Fawcett Publishing.

In 1941, the company behind the Captain Marvel line of comic books gave itself a Christmas present by removing the covers from unsold issues and binding them together, five at a pop, with a new Christmas-themed cover, essentially repurposing them as stocking stuffers. The result, *Xmas Comics* #1, must have seemed more like a phone book than a comic book at a whopping 324 pages.

But if you received (or bought at a price of 50 cents each) more than one copy, there's a good chance they weren't identical. Because, again, these were not mere reprints.

"The contents comprised of five rebound, totally random remainder (unsold) comics, sans covers," explained P.C. Hamerlinck, editor of *Fawcett Collectors of America,* in 2019. "One issue could have *Whiz Comics* #21, *Captain Marvel Adventures* #3, *Bulletman* #2, *Wow Comics* #3, and *Master Comics* #18 ... while another copy could consist of *Captain Marvel Adventures* #3, *Master Comics* #15, *Wow Comics* #2, *Bulletman* #1, and *Whiz* #18."

Wow, indeed. *Xmas Comics* #2 (1942) also contained a quintet of rebound remainders, but the title was discontinued after 1942 due to wartime paper conservation.

When *Xmas Comics* resurfaced in 1947, it retained the numbering, though not the ridiculously high page count. *Xmas Comics* #3 totaled 132 pages. Content-wise, there

was another significant change. Noted Hamerlinck: "Again, the contents were rebound comics, this time, four random issues of Fawcett's *Funny Animals.*"

After skipping another year, *Xmas Comics* returned for four more annual issues, from #4 in 1949 through #7 in 1952 (the final Christmas prior to Fawcett canceling its Captain Marvel line).

All were 196-page editions with tactile cover enhancements. Felt — red, green or both — was used on the covers drawn by artist C.C. Beck, co-creator of Captain Marvel.

More rebound-remainder editions were the one-shot *Holiday Comics* (1941) and four issues of *Gift Comics* beginning in 1942.

The rebound editions aside, Fawcett Publishing put out its share of Christmas-themed stories. Hamerlinck pointed to "Christmas With Half Man," an Ibis story in *Whiz Comics* #24 (1941); "The Phantom of the Department Store" in *Captain Marvel Adventures* #19 (1942); "The Night Before Christmas," a Mary Marvel story in *Wow Comics* #9 (1942); "The Case of the Christmas Crimes" in *Bulletman* #11 (1942); "Sgt. Twilight Writhes Again" in *Captain Midnight* #4 (1942); "Flash! The North Pole Has Been Bombed!" in *Funny Animals* #2 (1942); "The Plot Against Christmas" in *Captain Marvel Adventures* #42 (1944); "Billy Batson's Xmas" in *Captain Marvel Adventures* #69 (1946); and "Freddy Freeman's Christmas" in *Captain Marvel Jr.* #46 (1947).

Season's Greetings
Captain Marvel

Merry Meeska Mooska!
The first proper comic book to be based on Disney characters, *Walt Disney's Comics and Stories #1* (1940) was an offshoot of the larger-format *Mickey Mouse Magazine*. Western Printing and Lithographing produced the artwork and stories featuring Mickey Mouse, Donald Duck and gang, while Dell Publishing was the distributor. Christmas-themed editions soon followed, such as the comic books shown from top left, *Walt Disney's Christmas Parade* (in 1949-62 issues) and *Walt Disney's Donald Duck* (in 1952 and '61 issues). In 1962, Western parted ways with Dell to start its own imprint, Gold Key.

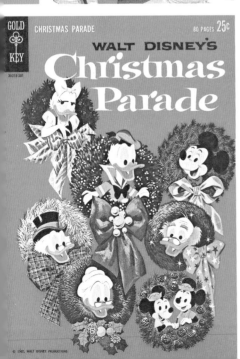

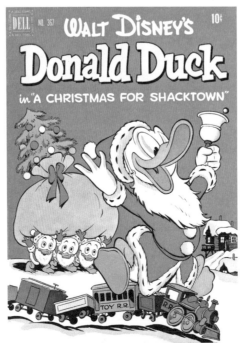

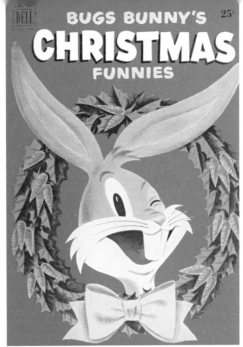

Eh-h-h, what's up, Santa?

With the success of *Walt Disney's Comics and Stories* and the ongoing popularity of the "funny animal" genre of comics, the door was opened for Warner Bros.' smart alecky Bugs Bunny to claim his place in the medium. Bugs made his comic-book debut in Dell Publishing's *Looney Tunes and Merry Melodies Comics* #1 (1941), joined by his pals Daffy Duck, Porky Pig, and Elmer Fudd. Bugs toplined Dell's *Bugs Bunny's Christmas Funnies* — under the *Dell Giant Comics* umbrella — for nine annual editions beginning in 1950 (though it was renamed *Bugs Bunny's Christmas Party* for issue #6 only). Shown from top left are issues #1 (1950), #2 (1951), #3 (1952), #4 (1953), #5 (1954), #6 (1955), #8 (1957), and #9 (1958).

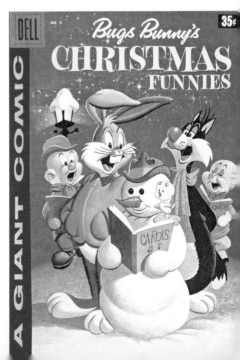

Kids' stuff: From top left, Dell Publishing's *Christmas With Mother Goose* (1949) was produced by "Pogo" writer-artist Walt Kelly; Marjorie Henderson Buell's character Little Lulu makes like a Christmas tree on the cover of Dell's *Little Lulu* #90 (1955) in art by Irving Tripp; a juvenile delinquent sets a trap for Santa in Al Feldstein art for EC's *Panic* #1 (1954), which was a "sister" title to the early comic-book iteration of *Mad;* the Flintstones and the Rubbles ride a rock sleigh pulled by dinosaurs in Gold Key's *The Flintstones: Christmas in Bedrock* (1960); Santa puts one over on "the tuff little ghost" in Harvey Comics' *Spooky* #72 (1962).

Everything's Archie: Archie Comics gave readers an annual Christmas present starting in 1954, when it began publishing "giant" editions titled *Archie's Christmas Stocking*, which spotlighted the holiday hijinx of the hormonally charged Riverdale gang: girl-crazy Archie, girl-next-door Betty, spoiled rich girl Veronica, goof-off Jughead and wise guy Reggie. Shown, from top left: *Archie's Christmas Stocking* #3 (1956), #4 (1957), #6 (1959), #10 (1961) and #137 (1966). Right: Dressed as a sexy Ms. Santa Claus, Veronica totes a sackful of Archie-themed toys in a 1961 pinup.

© Archie Comics

Merry monsters

Scary Santas: From top left, detail from a *Galaxy Science Fiction* cover by Ed Emshwiller (1956); Lurch plays Santa in "The Addams Family" (1965); detail from *Famous Monsters of Filmland* #48 (1967); "Monster's Holiday" by Bobby "Boris" Pickett (1962). Opposite: *Monster World* #6 (1965).

A WARREN MAGAZINE

MONSTER WORLD

JAN. NO. 6   35¢

PDC

HAVE A
COOL
YULE
WITH A
GHOUL
IN THIS
HORRIFIC
HOLIDAY
ISSUE!
PLUS
REVENGE of the
ZOMBIES
AND
RETURN of the
VAMPIRE

DECCA RECORDS
9-23778

WHITE CHRISTMAS

GOD REST YE MERRY GENTLEMEN

Printed in U.S.A.

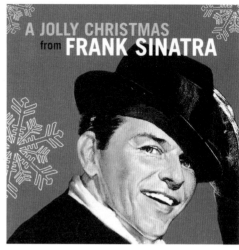

A JOLLY CHRISTMAS from FRANK SINATRA

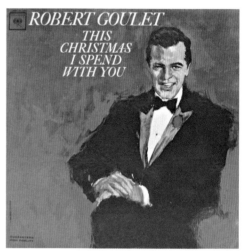

ROBERT GOULET
THIS CHRISTMAS I SPEND WITH YOU

The ones I used to Know

THINK OF THE DOZENS OF CHRISTMAS ALBUMS released every year, each with 10 or so songs vying to become "classics." And then think of "White Christmas." Bing Crosby first sang the Irving Berlin-penned song over the radio on Christmas Day 1941, just weeks after the attack on Pearl Harbor. Crosby soon recorded it for release, and wartime audiences found resonance in its themes of longing for home in an earlier time.

Many decades later, we are still captivated by the song (though the version we're most familiar with is the singer's faithful redo of 1947). Crosby's "White Christmas" is, by gum, old-fashioned — his Jiminy Cricket-style whistling solo alone drives this point home — but it never gets *old*.

And "White Christmas" isn't merely a holiday favorite. Back in the day, it was also a #1 hit. Yep, Christmas music could also be popular music — a novel concept in 1942.

Many vintage songs heard on radio, in stores and at parties during the season debuted as bona fide hits. Movie cowboy Gene Autry scored hits with "Here Comes Santa Claus" (#5, 1947) and "Rudolph the Red-Nosed Reindeer" (#1, 1949). Composer Johnny

Marks' "Rudolph" was conceived as a mascot commissioned by the Montgomery Ward chain — a metaphor about commercialization?

1949 also saw the release of "Sleigh Ride" — the instrumental with the "horse-y" neighing and clopping — by the Boston Pops Orchestra (covered in 1963 in a bouncy version by the Ronettes).

Also on vinyl through the years: "Have Yourself a Merry Little Christmas" by Judy Garland (#27 in 1944, the year she introduced the song in "Meet Me in St. Louis"); "Santa's Secret" by Johnny Guarnieri with Slam Stewart (1944, with the lyric *"He's got a reefer 100-feet-long / smokes it from end to end"*); "Silver Bells" by Crosby and Carol Richards (1950); "The Little Drummer Boy" by the Trapp Family Singers (1951); "It's Beginning to Look Like Christmas" by Perry Como and the Fontane Sisters (1951); "Santa Baby" by Eartha Kitt (#4, 1953); "Zat You, Santa Claus?" (1953) and "Christmas Night in Harlem" (1955) by Louis Armstrong; "Be-Bop Santa Claus" by Babs Gonzales (1954); "Home for the Holidays" by Como (#8, 1954); "Mistletoe and Holly" by Frank Sinatra, which Sinatra co-composed (1957); "Let it Snow" by Dean Martin (1959); "The Christmas Song" by Nat King Cole

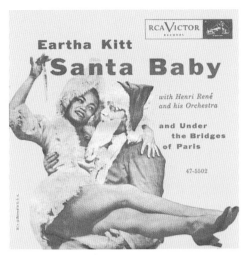

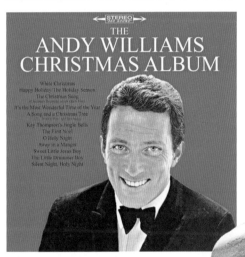

Classic crooners: Opposite from far left, Bing Crosby's "White Christmas" (1955), "A Jolly Christmas From Frank Sinatra" (1957) and Robert Goulet's "This Christmas I Spend With You" (1963). From top left: Eartha Kitt's "Santa Baby" (1953), "Christmas at Liberace's" (1954), Louis Armstrong's "Armstrong as Santa Claus" (1958), Nat King Cole's "The Christmas Song" (1961), "The Andy Williams Christmas Album" (1963) and "The Doris Day Christmas Album" (1964).

"White Christmas" © Decca Records; "A Jolly Christmas From Frank Sinatra" and "The Christmas Song" © Capitol Records; "This Christmas I Spend With You," "Christmas at Liberace's," "The Andy Williams Christmas Album" and "The Doris Day Christmas Album" © Columbia Records; "Santa Baby" © RCA Records; "Armstrong as Santa Claus" © Brunswick Records

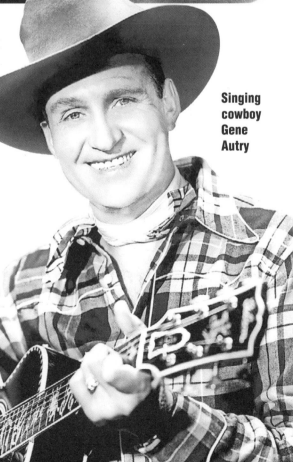

Singing cowboy Gene Autry

(1961, his fourth, most popular version); "It's the Most Wonderful Time of the Year" by Andy Williams (1963); "Holly Jolly Christmas" by Burl Ives (#10, 1964); and "Do You Hear What I Hear?" by Robert Goulet in his "Camelot"-level baritone (1968).

Novelty songs include "All I Want For Christmas (Is My Two Front Teeth)" by Spike Jones (1948); "I Saw Mommy Kissing Santa Claus" by Jimmy Boyd (#1, 1952); "The Chipmunk Song" by Ross Bagdasarian Sr. (#1, 1958); "Dominick the Donkey" by Lou Monte (1960); "Snoopy's Christmas" by the Royal Guardsmen (1967); and, *ugh,* "Grandma Got Run Over by a Reindeer" by Elmo and Patsy (1979).

An out-of-left-field trend was holiday music from ... tire companies. Compilation albums from Goodyear (1961-77) and Firestone (1962-68) were eagerly anticipated annual events. Goodyear's contributors included Crosby, Sinatra, Williams, Doris Day, Tony Bennett, Sammy Davis Jr. and Maurice Chevalier. Firestone's contributors included Julie Andrews, Gordon MacRae, André Previn and the, *ahem,* Firestone Orchestra and Chorus.

Rubber, synthetic polymers, antiozonants and Christmas. Now *that's* a sure-fire formula for holiday cheer.

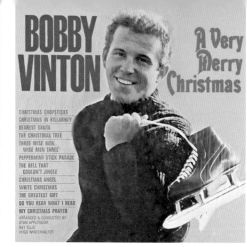

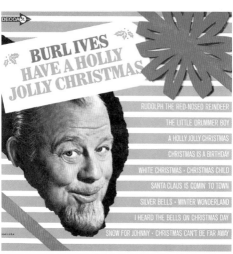

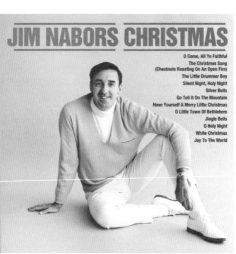

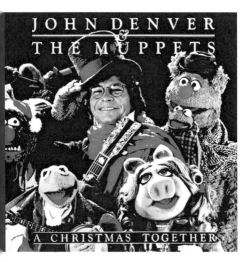

TV stars & hitmakers

Familiar boob-tube acts from Lawrence Welk to the Partridge Family, and chart successes from Bobby Vinton to the Carpenters, got in the spirit. From top left: TV musical-variety host Welk's "Jingle Bells" (1957) and "Merry Christmas From Lawrence Welk and His Champagne Music Makers" (1958); Vinton's "A Very Merry Christmas" (1964); Steve Lawrence and Eydie Gorme's "That Holiday Feeling!" (1964); Burl Ives' "Have a Holly Jolly Christmas" (1965), with its title song from the 1964 TV special "Rudolph the Red-Nosed Reindeer" (in which Ives voiced the snowman character); "The Perry Como Christmas Album" (1968); "Jim Nabors Christmas" (1970); "A Partridge Family Christmas Card" (1971); the Carpenters' "Christmas Portrait" (1978); and the John Denver/Muppets' crossover "A Christmas Together" (1979).

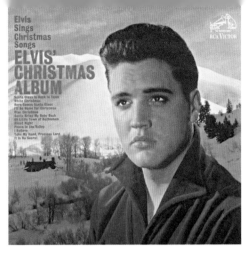

From left: Elvis Presley's "Elvis' Christmas Album" (1957); Chuck Berry's "Run Rudolph Run" (1958); and Vee-Jay Records' Christmas-themed Beatles' picture sleeve (1964). "Elvis' Christmas Album" © RCA Records; "Run Rudolph Run" © Chess Records; Beatles' picture sleeve © Vee-Jay Records

ROCKERS GOT THEIR CHRISTMAS ON NOT LONG after the rock 'n' roll genre was born in the middle 1950s.

Sounding very birth-of-rock were "Jingle Bell Rock" by Bobby Helms (#13 in 1957); "Blue Christmas" and "Santa Bring My Baby Back to Me" by Elvis Presley (both 1957); "Rockin' Around the Christmas Tree" by Brenda Lee (#3 in 1958); "Run Rudolph Run" by Chuck Berry (#20 in a holiday category in 1958), and "Christmas Day" by Detroit Junior (1961).

"Jingle Bell Rock" and "Rockin' Around the Christmas Tree" are like sister songs. Both give shout-outs to "rock" in their titles — a commercial plus in those days — though Helms and Lee identified as country singers.

The guitarist on "Jingle Bell Rock," Hank Garland, also played with Presley, Johnny Cash, Patsy Cline and Roy Orbison.

Despite what sounds like a world-weary rasp, Lee was 13 when she sang "Rockin' Around the Christmas Tree." The patently R&B sax solo is by Boots Randolph ("Yakety Sax"). Guitarist Grady Martin, another Presley session guy, does a cute tradeoff with Randolph as the closer.

The '60s brought us "Little Saint Nick" by the Beach Boys (#3 in a holiday category in 1963); "Christmas (Baby Please Come Home)" by Darlene Love (1963); "Santa Claus Go Straight to the Ghetto" by James Brown (1968); "Christmas Song" by Jethro Tull (1968); and "Christmas" by The Who (from "Tommy," 1969).

Mike Love of the Beach Boys recalled the genesis of "Little St. Nick" when we spoke in 2004. "You know, we played with that song," he said. "There were a couple of different versions,

---

Trimming the tree on the cover of "The Beach Boys' Christmas Album" (1963).
© Capitol Records

but the single version that everybody knows is what we ended up doing. I worked on that with Brian (Wilson, Love's cousin). I did the preponderance of the lyrics on 'Little St. Nick.' Brian did the track and the arrangement.

"When I first heard that back, it sounded like angels singing. The chorus backgrounds are so beautiful. It sounds like the Vienna Boys Choir in action," Love added with a laugh.

The same year, the Beatles recorded a Christmas greeting for their fan club. This rarity was pressed in the cost-efficient, lightweight "flexi disc" format. The greeting, which casually mixed music and humor, became an annual tradition through 1969.

Vee-Jay Records, the first to release Beatles singles in the U.S., gave *themselves* a Christmas present in 1964 with "The Beatles: We Wish You a Merry Christmas and a Happy New Year" — essentially cash-grab reissues with a new picture sleeve.

Leave it to John Lennon and Yoko Ono to come up with that improbable hybrid, a heartwarming Christmas song that doubles as a Vietnam War protest song: "Happy Xmas (War is Over)" (#4 in the U.K. in 1971). More from ex-Beatles: "Ding Dong, Ding Dong" by George Harrison (#36 in 1974) and "Simply Having a Wonderful Christmas Time" by Paul McCartney (#15 in a holiday category in 1979).

The warming-of-hearts continued with "Merry X-mas Everybody" by Slade (#1 in the U.K. in 1973); "Santa Claus is Comin' to Town" by Bruce Springsteen (recorded in 1975, a radio perennial thereafter); "I Believe in Father Christmas" by Greg Lake (#2 in the U.K. in 1975); "Father Christmas" by the Kinks (1977); "Run Rudolph Run" by Keith Richards (1978); "Christmas Wrapping" by the Waitresses (1981); "Do They Know It's Christmas" by Band Aid benefiting Ethiopian famine victims (#1 in the U.K. in 1984); and "Christmas in Hollis" by Run-DMC (1987).

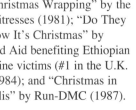

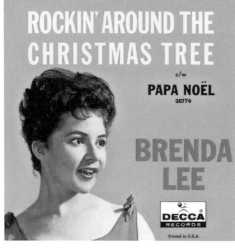

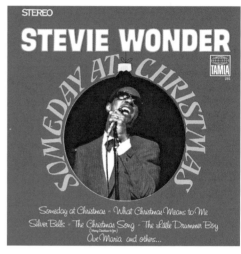

Rock, soul & Motown

As the upstart genre rock 'n' roll continued making contributions to the holiday pantheon, popular music continued its journey through soul and the Motown sound. From top left: Bobby Helms' "Jingle Bell Rock" (1957); Brenda Lee's "Rockin' Around the Christmas Tree" (1958); "The Ventures' Christmas Album" (1965); "The Supremes' Merry Christmas" (1965); "James Brown and His Famous Flames Sing Christmas Songs" (1966); Stevie Wonder's "Someday at Christmas" (1967); "Soul Christmas" by various artists (1969); "Jackson 5 Christmas Album" (1970); George Conedy's "Merry Soul Christmas" (1972); and Slade's "Merry X'mas Everybody" (1973).

Darlene Love, top, with Bob B. Soxx and the Blue Jeans, the Crystals and the Ronettes from "A Christmas Present for You" (1963). © Phil Spector Records

Darlene loves Christmas

THAT BOOMING VOICE ... SAILING OVER THAT WALL of sound. When pop fans think of Christmas, Darlene Love springs to mind, thanks to her enduring, Phil Spector-produced hit of 1963, "Christmas (Baby Please Come Home)." From 1992 to 2014, Love sang the song on "Late Show With David Letterman" each December.

But what comes to mind when *Love* thinks of Christmas?

"Christmas has always been a great time for me, a time of giving," the singer told me during a 2014 interview.

"It seems to be the time when everybody is in the mood for giving. That's what makes it special. I wish it could be like that all year long. Especially with everything that's going on around the country. People are in a giving mood. I don't think it'll slow down. People need help."

The Hawthorne, California, native — who was born Darlene Wright in 1941 — said the spirit of giving was instilled in her as a child.

"I grew up in a Christian home," Love recalled.

"So Christmas was always about the birth of Jesus Christ and the love Jesus Christ had for us. And that we should always be more in a giving mode than a receiving mode. I mean, we didn't have a lot. I had three brothers and a sister and a mother and a father — a very loving family. If we got one gift, that was wonderful.

"We didn't have a tree until we woke up on Christmas morning. We thought there really *was* a Santa Claus, because that's what we woke up to. The house was all decorated. There was plenty of food. It was the one time of year when you had more food than you needed," Love added with a laugh.

"And living in California, I was always around my grandparents and my aunt and uncle and cousins. We would always get together on that day."

She began singing as a young girl in the church choir.

"When we went to school in those days, there was the a cappella choir and the glee club," Love said. "We were always singing in some kind of assembly. I didn't think I had a great voice. But being part of the family, you were in the choir, and you were supposed to *sing*. That's what we did."

"We thought there really was a Santa Claus," said Darlene Love.

Photo courtesy of Darlene Love

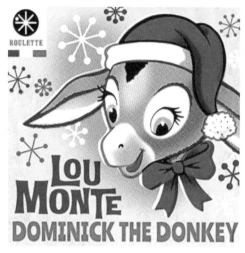

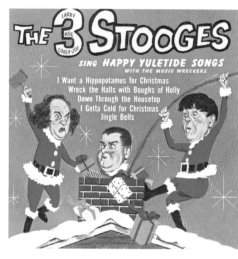

Novelty & kids' stuff

Timed correctly, novelty Christmas songs could top the charts. Three that hit #1 are "All I Want For Christmas (is My Two Front Teeth)" by Spike Jones (1948); "I Saw Mommy Kissing Santa Claus" by Jimmy Boyd (1952); and "The Chipmunk Song" by Ross Bagdasarian Sr. (1958). See also "Dominick the Donkey" by Lou Monte (1960); "The Three Stooges Sing Happy Yuletide Songs" and "The Three Stooges Sing Wreck the Halls With Boughs of Holly" (both 1960); "Merry Snoopy's Christmas" by the Royal Guardsmen (1967); "Christmas With Colonel Sanders" (1969); and "All I Want For Christmas Is My Two Front Teeth & Festive Favorites For Children" (circa 1970s).

Holiday music videos

'Little Drummer Boy/Peace on Earth' Bing Crosby/David Bowie (1977)

Backstory: The improbable teaming of old-school crooner Crosby and rock chameleon Bowie was taped for Crosby's final special in 1977. Bowie had planned to decline the offer to appear with Crosby, but his mother, Peggy Jones, insisted. No one knew this little song would be remembered beyond that TV special. It was finally released as a single in 1982 — another classic for Crosby, and one for Bowie.

Sample lyrics: "Every child must be made aware / Every child must be made to care / Care enough for his fellow man / To give all the love that he can / I pray my wish will come true / For my child and your child, too / He'll see the day of glory / See the day when men of good will / Live in peace, live in peace again / Peace on Earth / Can it be / Can it be?"

'Christmas is the Time to Say I Love You' Billy Squier (1981)

Backstory: Massachusetts-born rocker Billy Squier released "Christmas is the Time to Say I Love You" as the B-side of his 1981 hit "My Kinda Lover." But Squier's Christmas song really made noise when he taped a lip-synched "singalong" version at MTV in New York amid the station's crew and on-air talent, which included Martha Quinn, Nina Blackwood, J.J. Johnson, Mark Goodman and Alan Hunter.

Sample lyrics: "On the corner, carolers are singing / There's a touch of magic in the air / From grownup to minor, no one could be finer / Times are hard, but no one seems to care / Christmas Eve and all the world is watching / Santa guides his reindeer through the dark / From rooftop to chimney, from Harlem to Bimini / They will find their way into your heart"

'Do They Know it's Chrismas' Band Aid (1984)

Backstory: Bob Geldof of the Boomtown Rats spearheaded this all-star project to benefit famine victims in Ethiopia. Participants included Sting, Bono, Robert "Kool" Bell, Boy George, George Michael, Phil Collins, Duran Duran and Bananarama. The video documents the artists recording the song. In 1985, Geldof organized the multi-continent Live Aid concerts, which also benefited Ethiopian famine victims.

Sample lyrics: "Say a prayer, pray for the other ones / At Christmastime, it's hard, but when you're having fun / There's a world outside your window / And it's a world of dread and fear / Where the only water flowing / Is the bitter sting of tears / And the Christmas bells that ring there / Are the clanging chimes of doom / Well, tonight, thank God it's them instead of you"

'Christmas in Hollis' Run-DMC (1987)

Backstory: When a publicist suggested that Run-DMC record a track for the 1987 compilation "A Very Special Christmas" (with Bruce Springsteen, Bon Jovi, Madonna and other mainstream artists), the rap trio wanted nothing to do with it. But a horn lick borrowed from "Back Door Santa" by Clarence Carter enticed Run-DMC, and a Christmas classic was recorded, followed by a sweet, funny video.

Sample lyrics: "It's Christmastime in Hollis, Queens / Mom's cookin' chicken and collard greens / Rice and stuffing, macaroni and cheese / And Santa put gifts under Christmas trees / Decorate the house with lights at night / Snow's on the ground, snow white so bright / In the fireplace is the yule log / Beneath the mistletoe as we drink eggnog / The time is now, the place is here"

'Santa Claus Goes Straight to the Ghetto' Snoop Dogg (1996)

Backstory: The title of this track from the 1996 compilation "Christmas on Death Row" was inspired by the 1968 James Brown song. Guest rappers include Daz Dillinger, Big Tray Deee and Bad Azz. The sometimes bleak, sometimes hopeful video shows Snoop at a pulpit and riding high over L.A. streets in a flying convertible, transforming a wino's cheap booze into champagne. See also fine ladies in Santa hats.

Sample lyrics: "Santa Claus on the ceilin', Jack Frost chillin' / Pinch the Grinch for bein' a holiday villain / Season's greetings, all the proceedings / Are brought to you by the church house where we'll be eatin' / Chestnuts roastin' on an open fire / Singin' my jingle, where is Kris Kringle? / I didn't pop, I ain't even shouted ... Catch me givin' out turkeys at the church house"

Bing & Bowie

IT WAS THE UNLIKELIEST OF COLLABORATIONS. IN 1977, A CROONER FROM THE BIG BAND ERA HARMONIZED WITH A GENDER-BENDING BRITISH ROCKER. THE RESULT: A CHRISTMAS CLASSIC.

YOU THE NEW BUTLER?

IT'S BEEN A LONG TIME SINCE I'VE BEEN THE NEW *ANYTHING*.

I'M DAVID BOWIE. SIR PERCIVAL LETS ME USE HIS PIANO WHEN HE'S NOT AROUND.

COME ON IN!

YOU'RE NOT THE POOR RELATION FROM AMERICA, ARE YOU?

HA! NEWS SURE TRAVELS FAST.

I'M BING.

YOU'RE THE ONE THAT SINGS, RIGHT?

WELL, RIGHT OR WRONG, I SING EITHER WAY.

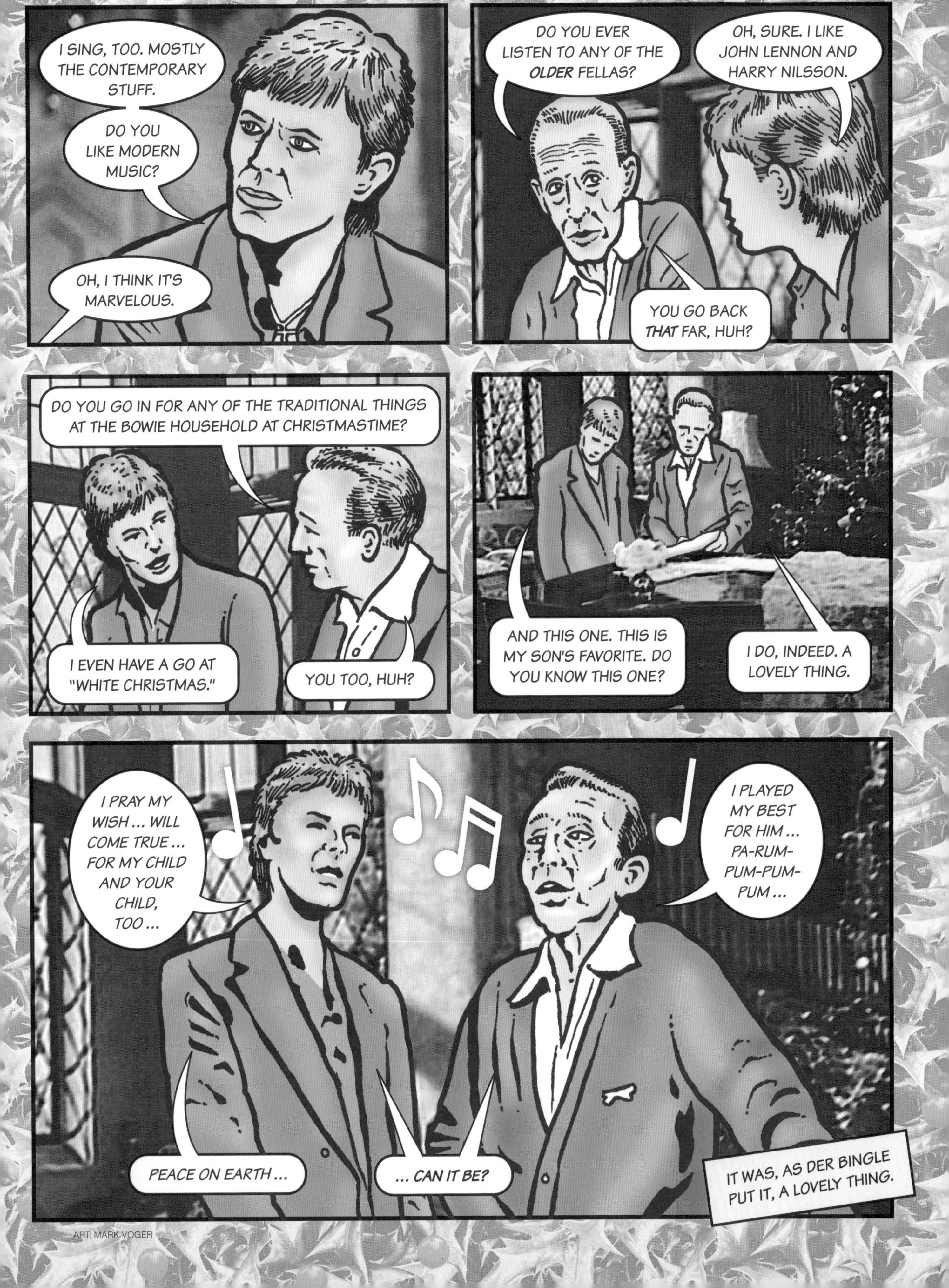
I SING, TOO. MOSTLY THE CONTEMPORARY STUFF.
DO YOU LIKE MODERN MUSIC?
OH, I THINK IT'S MARVELOUS.
DO YOU EVER LISTEN TO ANY OF THE OLDER FELLAS?
OH, SURE. I LIKE JOHN LENNON AND HARRY NILSSON.
YOU GO BACK THAT FAR, HUH?
DO YOU GO IN FOR ANY OF THE TRADITIONAL THINGS AT THE BOWIE HOUSEHOLD AT CHRISTMASTIME?
I EVEN HAVE A GO AT "WHITE CHRISTMAS."
YOU TOO, HUH?
AND THIS ONE. THIS IS MY SON'S FAVORITE. DO YOU KNOW THIS ONE?
I DO, INDEED. A LOVELY THING.
I PRAY MY WISH ... WILL COME TRUE ... FOR MY CHILD AND YOUR CHILD, TOO ...
I PLAYED MY BEST FOR HIM ... PA-RUM-PUM-PUM-PUM ...
PEACE ON EARTH ...
... CAN IT BE?
IT WAS, AS DER BINGLE PUT IT, A LOVELY THING.

ART: MARK VOGER

Celluloid cheer

THE "CHRISTMAS MOVIE" IS A GENRE UNTO
itself, like romantic comedy, film *noir* or the Dwayne Johnson
movie. As with any genre, the Christmas movie has its tropes. The
films all have a central problem — some seemingly unsolvable
quandary often related to the holiday. Like, will Jimmy Stewart
realize the world is better off with him in it? Will Bing Crosby
and Danny Kaye rescue their old Army general's struggling
resort? Will Santa Claus conquer the Martians?

Most of these have what the cliché gods have come to call a
"Christmas miracle." And usually, that miracle has a deadline.
And usually, that deadline is Dec. 25. (Blame it on Dickens.)

In the following pages, we'll examine "must-see" Christmas
movies — the "desert island" stuff, the best of the best. This is not
to disparage films like 1947's "It Happened on Fifth Avenue"
(millionaire Charles Ruggles spends the holiday with squatters in
his ritzy apartment); 1947's "The Bishop's Wife" (Cary Grant is
an angel with mad ice-skating skills); 1949's "Holiday Affair"
(Robert Mitchum wants Janet Leigh for Christmas, and who could
blame him?); or 1952's "The Holly and the Ivy" (a baggage-
plagued family reunites for the holiday). There are *so-o-o* many.

PONDERING THESE OLDIES-BUT-GOODIES YIELDS
a fun "office cooler" question: Who is the best Santa Claus in the
movies? Believe it or not, two very good Santas are in what can
confidently be called the two weirdest, and least recommendable,
Santa movies ever made: José Elías Moreno in the Mexican
import "Santa Claus" (1959) and John Call in the kiddie sci-fi
flick "Santa Claus Conquers the Martians" (1964).

Ferdinand Munier in "March of the Wooden Soldiers" (1934)
is a notable movie Santa as the first to follow commercial artist
Haddon Sundblom's influential vision of Santa Claus for Coca-
Cola, which solidified our collective notion of Santa's look.

But the best, best, best movie Santa has to be Edmund Gwenn
in "Miracle on 34th Street (1947). His eyes literally twinkle. Even
Oscar thought so; Gwenn snagged an Academy Award in the role.

Then again, do you believe Gwenn was *really* playing Santa
himself, or just a "nice old man with whiskers" who *thinks* he's
Santa? The film leaves room for doubt. It's one of those eternal
questions, like, Did Jimmy Cagney "turn yella" when he went to the
chair in "Angels With Dirty Faces"? Did Tony Soprano get
whacked, or finish his onion rings, in "The Sopranos" climax?

Which brings us to an important spin-off question: Who is the
best "fake Santa" in the movies? You know, guys who played regular guys *pretending* to be Santa. Contenders include Alvin

Greenman, the naive Brooklyn teen in "Miracle on 34th Street" (1947); William Frawley, one of Bob Hope's henchmen in "The Lemon Drop Kid" (1951); and Jeff Gillen, the maniacal Santa who delivers a taunting "ho, ho, ho" before dispatching Peter Billingsley in "A Christmas Story" (1983).

The winner could very well be Hal Smith in "The Apartment" (1960). Smith — Mayberry's town drunk Otis on "The Andy Griffith Show" — was practically *playing* Otis opposite Jack Lemmon in a wild barroom sequence. (Smith also donned the suit on TV, making an undeliverable promise to Cindy in a memorable "Brady Bunch" episode.)

Another vital office-cooler topic: Who is the best movie Scrooge? I am anything but objective on the matter — it's Alastair Sim or the highway — but there are many contenders. God blessed us, every one, with lotsa movie Scrooges.

OF COURSE, YOU DON'T HAVE TO GO BACK
to the olden days for a good Christmas movie; filmmakers continue to produce work deserving of a place in the pantheon. Some such films even have authentic "hankie" moments.

In Chris Columbus' "Home Alone" (1990), Macaulay Culkin's family departs on a holiday trip unknowingly leaving him, well, home alone. There, Culkin must thwart scary, ruthless burglars from robbing his family's McMansion. (Doesn't *everyone* in producer John Hughes' movies live in a McMansion?) Hankie moment: Culkin's church encounter with a mysterious elderly neighbor (Roberts Blossom).

In Jon Favreau's "Elf" (2003), Will Ferrell leaves the North Pole on a journey of self-discovery, and learns why he is so much taller than other elves. There's even a nod to Rankin/Bass via animated characters. Hankie moment: When James Caan unreservedly acknowledges Ferrell as his son.

In Terry Zwigoff's crude "Bad Santa" (2003), Billy Bob Thornton plays a fowl-mouthed, drunken Santa who wets himself in his costume. (It's the least of his offenses). Hankie moment: Any scene with Brett Kelly as the roly-poly, curly-haired boy whose belief in Christmas is unshaken. Warning: Make sure the kiddies are in bed before watching *this* one.

Janet Leigh and Robert Mitchum have a "Holiday Affair" (1949).
© Warner Bros. Pictures

Left: Charles Ruggles is mystified in "It Happened On Fifth Avenue" (1947). Right: Ralph Richardson and Denholm Elliott have a showdown in the British drama "The Holly and the Ivy" (1952). "It Happened On Fifth Avenue" © Allied Artists; "The Holly and the Ivy" © London Film Productions

Shhh! Santa Claus in the silent era

YOU MIGHT EXPECT 100-PLUS-YEAR-OLD films to be old-fashioned in tone with primitive FX.

Well, they *are* old-fashioned in tone with primitive FX. But — as any movie buff knows — the silent film is an art form unto itself. If you can see past the occasional scratchiness, blurriness and wonky contrast, and appreciate the storytelling language created by turn-of-the-20th-century filmmakers, rewards await. FX wise, many Christmas-themed films from cinema's silent era have surprisingly effective special effects that interpolate tech and stagecraft.

Three pioneer filmmakers — one English, one French, and one American — left behind Christmas-themed silent films with imaginative FX: George Albert Smith, Georges Méliès and Thomas Edison.

The earliest known film depiction of Santa is from 1898: "Santa Claus," directed by Smith (1864-1959).

In what remains of the film, a woman distracts her children from the fireplace and puts them to bed. They dream of Santa coming down their chimney, and then the *real* Santa appears bearing gifts, wearing a floor-length hooded robe trimmed in white fur.

The "dream" Santa is superimposed onto a black curtain; the "real" Santa emerges from behind the curtain — a neat trick from someone who began his career as a stage hypnotist, and once patented a method for double-exposures.

"By 1898, with 'Santa Claus,' (Smith) was using superimposition to effect the arrival of Santa," explained Frank Gray in "Who's Who of Victorian Cinema" (The British Film Institute). "As a magic lanternist, he understood the cutting techniques perfected with biunial and triunial (two-lensed and three-lensed) lanterns and brought this consciousness to his filmmaking."

Méliès (1861-1938) — considered the father of movie special effects — directed two silent holiday-themed films. In "The

"Santa Claus" (1898) has the earliest known film depiction of Santa.
© George Albert Smith Films

Christmas Dream" (1900) and "The Christmas Angel" (1904), there are superimpositions and deep-perspective painted sets, though whimsy and pathos, not FX, carry the day with both films.

Edison's company put out "The Night Before Christmas" (1905), which presents a vision of Santa's trek that utilizes independently moving silhouettes of Santa's reindeer and sled, traveling across a panoramic painted background of snowy mountains leading to a village. This must've wowed 'em way back in 1905.

So when the inevitable CGI-fest "A Transformers Christmas" finally opens, just stick with the 1898 "Santa Claus."

'The Christmas Dream' (1900) Georges Méliès crafted this ahead-of-its-time series of vignettes that move from dancing toys to angels on snowy rooftops to a bell-ringing to beggars outside of a holiday feast, all book-ended by dreaming children. © Star Film

'Scrooge; or Marley's Ghost' (1901) In the earliest known film adaptation of Dickens' tale, the Ghosts of Christmas Past, Present and Yet to Come have been sidelined, and Jacob Marley does all the salvation-ing. Directed by Walter R. Booth. © Paul's Animatograph Works

'The Night Before Christmas' (1905) The first film adaptation of the famous poem shows Santa slinging hay to his reindeer, tinkering in his shop, and marking his list with a quill pen before embarking on his trek. Directed by Edwin S. Porter. © Edison Manufacturing Co.

'A Little Girl Who Did Not Believe in Santa Claus' (1907) A rich boy in a Buster Brown-lookin' outfit forces Santa Claus at gunpoint (!) to bring presents and a tree to a poor girl. Directed by J. Searle Dawley and Edwin S. Porter. © Edison Manufacturing Co.

'Dreams of Toyland' (1908) A rich woman buys her spoiled son many toys, including a trolley car. In jittery but charming early stop-motion animation, the boy dreams that the car comes to life. Directed by Arthur Melbourne Cooper. © Alpha Trading Company

'The Star of Bethlehem' (1909) A surprisingly well-made telling of the Nativity. The angel Gabriel fades into view as he appears to Mary. There are many costumed extras as Mary and Joseph search for shelter. Directed by Edwin S. Porter. © Edison Manufacturing Co.

'A Trap For Santa Claus' (1909) After an unemployed drunk leaves his family, his wife inherits a fortune. Directed by D.W. Griffith. The film stars Henry B. Walthall, a player in Griffith's controversial epic of 1915, "The Birth of a Nation." © Biograph Company

'A Christmas Carol' (1910) With Marc McDermott (star of the first movie serial) as Scrooge, and Charles Ogle (the film world's first Frankenstein monster) as Cratchit. The three Christmas ghosts are combined. Directed by J. Searle Dawley. © Edison Manufacturing Co.

'March of the Wooden Soldiers' (1934)

THERE'S A WARNING FOR CHILDREN AT THE TOP of Gus Meins' and Charley Rogers' "March of the Wooden Soldiers," one that should be heeded. Alas, most kiddies won't have the wisdom to fathom its implications until it's too late.

We see Mother Goose (Virginia Karns) step out from within a giant storybook as a nearby live goose flaps its wings. She sings the song "Toyland" from the 1903 stage musical "Babes in Toyland," on which the film is based. Ostensibly, the song is about the fantasy world viewers are about to visit, populated by storybook figures such as Little Bo-Peep, Little Miss Muffet, and the Three Little Pigs. But really, the song is about the individual fantasy worlds that every child creates and inhabits — and, by degrees, departs as they begin to notice how the "real" world works.

Sings Mother Goose: *"Childhood joyland / mystic, merry Toyland / Once you pass its borders / you can ne'er return again."*

PRODUCER HAL ROACH — THE MAN WHO FIRST teamed Stan Laurel and Oliver Hardy — obtained Victor Herbert and Glen MacDonough's "Babes in Toyland," revamped it, and inserted his comedy stars as Stannie Dum (slight and trusting) and Ollie Dee (tubby and bossy). The ploy works beautifully.

The comedians do nothing to modify their act or adapt it to the Toyland motif. After all, their onscreen characters were always babes in adult bodies — innocent, none-too-bright, sometimes squabbling, but always loving one another. Thus, Laurel and Hardy fit in seamlessly among the costumed characters, fanciful architecture, and Toyland's carefully mapped municipal layout, with its Maypole, pond, winding walkways, decorative giant faces, and the churning center of the Toyland economy: its toy factory.

"March of the Wooden Soldiers" has the vital components of a

fairy tale: the chaste damsel, Bo-Peep (Charlotte Henry); the romantic hero, Tom-Tom (Felix Knight); and the villain, odorous miser Barnaby Silas (Henry Brandon).

As dawn breaks in Toyland, and we see its denizens go about their morning rituals. Jack Horner sticks his thumb in a pie and pulls out a plum. Miss Tuffet's meal of curds-and-whey is rudely interrupted by a spider. The cat with the fiddle chases a mouse. It's like Groundhog's Day around here.

We soon meet Mother Peep (Florence Roberts), "the old woman who lives in a shoe," as she sends her many children off to school. The eldest of the brood is our heroine Bo-Peep, who skampers off to — how did you know? — tend her sheep.

Santa Claus (Ferdinand Munier) visits the toy shop. Right: Tom-Tom (Felix Knight) romances Little Bo-Beep (Charlotte Henry). © Metro-Goldwyn-Mayer

Stan Laurel and Oliver Hardy in the film (originally titled "Babes in Toyland"). Below: Henry Brandon as Barnaby. © Metro-Goldwyn-Mayer

BO-PEEP'S ERRAND IS INTERRUPTED BY MEAN old Barnaby (played broadly, and appropriately so, by Brandon, then 22). With his top hat, gnarled cane and leering expression, Barnaby is, well, *skeevy*. There's no better adjective for a geezer who tells an innocent young lady, "I have ... gazed with wonder on your sweet, maidenly virtue." *Wha?*

Bo-Peep refuses the advances of Barnaby, who owns the mortgage on the shoe-house she lives in. Barnaby then tells cash-strapped Mother Peep he will forgive the mortgage in exchange for one small concession: Bo-Peep's hand. *Ew.*

Ollie, another boarder in the shoe-house, promises to borrow the payment from his boss, the toymaker (William Burress). But at the factory that morning, the toymaker is in a foul mood. The boys are late for work. They spill paint in his lap. A third offense is uncovered when Santa Claus himself (Ferdinand Munier) stops by the factory to see how his order is coming along.

Not so good, it turns out. Santa had asked for 600 wooden soldiers at 1-foot-high each. But when Stan took the order, he wrote "100 soldiers at 6-feet-high." After activating one of the life-sized soldiers, triggering a destructive ruckus, Stan and Ollie are fired by the toymaker. Santa, for his part, takes it all in stride, ho-ho-ho-ing as he is knocked butt-first into an outsized drum.

When Barnaby frames Bo-Peep's true love, Tom-Tom,

for the crime of "pignapping," Tom-Tom is banished to Bogeyland, a nightmarish zone populated by fanged monsters called the Bogeymen. Can Stan and Ollie save Bo-Peep and Tom-Tom from the clutches of Barnaby and the Bogeymen? I'll never tell.

SOME CAST MEMBERS WILL DELIGHT movie buffs, not least Laurel and Hardy, a legendary team that made 100-plus films between 1926 and '50.

Barnaby is the first of two all-time-great movie baddies played by Brandon. The other is Scar, the Comanche chief pursued by John Wayne in John Ford's classic western "The Searchers" (1956). Barnaby and Scar — the contrast is amazing.

Angelo Rossitto, standing at 2-feet-11, played Elmer, "pignapped" member of the Three Little Pigs. He was one of Tod Browning's "Freaks" (1932); a Munchkin in Oz; Bela Lugosi's sidekick in three films; the evildoer Master opposite Mel Gibson in "Mad Max: Beyond Thunderdome" (1985); and appeared on album covers alongside Bob Dylan and Tom Waits.

Decades later, "March of the Wooden Soldiers" was colorized for home video. The controversial process suits this film well.

A final thought about Mother Goose's warning at the top: You *can* go back to Toyland, sort of. The responsibilities and tragedies of life cannot be avoided, but sometimes, they can be set aside for a spell. Seeing "March of the Wooden Soldiers" is a way back to Toyland ... for 78 minutes, anyway.

111

Seymour Hicks is plenty miserly in the first sound feature film adaptation of Dickens' classic tale. © Julius Hagen Productions

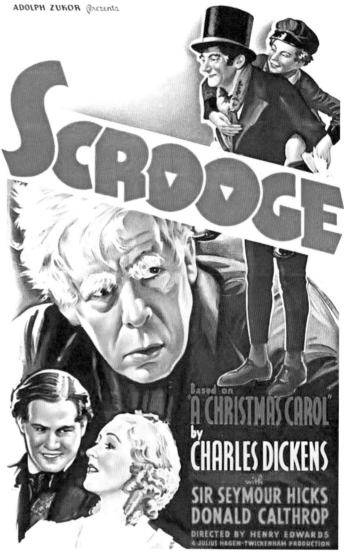

'Scrooge' (1935)

THE DOWNSIDES OF THE FIRST-EVER SOUND

feature film adaptation of Dickens' tale: It is stodgy and old-fashioned, and surviving prints are hardly pristine.

The upside: We are watching an actor give a performance informed by a lifetime spent playing the character. Only in this case, he is finally the approximate *age* of the character.

"Sir" Seymour Hicks — he was knighted the previous year — first played Ebenezer Scrooge when he was 30 in 1901, 64 years after the publication of Dickens' novella. Hicks was 42 when he played Scrooge in a 1913 silent adaptation of "A Christmas Carol." He was 64 when he filmed the 1935 version.

And the made-in-England '35 "Scrooge," directed by Henry Edwards, goes places that other adaptations don't.

Much of the film has a "spooky" feel. By design, it is darkly lit, which sometimes conjures the Expressionism that expatriate Germans were bringing to Hollywood. Some of the film's incidental music falls within the horror-comedy *milieu*.

There's an early sequence that can only be called Dickensian. We see ornate carriages arrive for the Christmas feast of the Lord Mayor of London. There is a hubbub of intense preparation in the massive, well-staffed kitchen. Wine is tested; cakes are decorated; fowl is basted. Then the chef throws scraps of meat through a grate to beggars outside, seen in shadow.

Another juxtaposition shows Scrooge — a man of means — at a dreary eatery as its sole customer, and a miserable one at that.

When the Lord Mayor toasts the Queen, he calls upon his opulently appointed guests to stand and sing "God Save the Queen." Outside, the cold, grimy beggars sing along.

Interestingly, of the four spirits in Dickens' story (counting Jacob Marley), we are only actually shown one: the Ghost of Christmas Present, in the stout form of Oscar Asche, lustily (and hilariously) eating while delivering his first lines. The other ghosts are obscured or outright invisible.

"Look well, Ebenezer Scrooge, for only *you* can see me," says Marley upon entering Scrooge's cheerless parlor. (Sure enough, *we* don't see Marley.) The Ghost of Christmas Past is a blurry sil-

houette, and the Ghost of Christmas Yet to Come is a shadow.

When the charwoman, laundress and undertaker sell off the "deceased" Scrooge's purloined possessions to the rag man, it is played as the blackest of black comedy. Mind you, the sequence was always morbid, but *this* is like something out of James Whale.

We aren't usually shown Tiny Tim's body after the child has passed away. The 1935 "Scrooge" presents a heartbreaking scene in which Bob Cratchit (Donald Calthrop) regards the body of his late son (Philip Frost) and kisses his forehead.

This "Scrooge" also employs a subtle storytelling device that could only result from the use of then-new sound technology.

In the present, we eavesdrop on the Cratchit family feast, which ends with Tiny Tim singing, in a reedy little voice, "Hark! The Herald Angels Sing." (This comes right after Scrooge asks the Ghost of Christmas Present if the boy will live.) Tim's voice gives way to a church-y choir, and the camera pulls back to a panoramic view of the rooftops of old London (albeit, in filmed miniatures).

Later, when the redeemed Scrooge attends the dinner party of his nephew Fred (Robert Cochran), Scrooge approaches a well-decorated tree. While gazing at the tree, he appears wistful and again "hears" Tiny Tim singing the first line from "Hark! The Herald Angels Sing" — an audio reminder that there are more promises to keep for the new, improved Ebenezer Scrooge.

'A Christmas Carol' (1938)

CASTING A BRITISH ACTOR AS SCROOGE HARDLY masks the fact that Edwin L. Marin's 1938 "A Christmas Carol" is a decidedly Hollywood production. Reginald Owen, wearing an iffy bald-head appliance, nonetheless makes a fine Scrooge. (Owen also played Sherlock Holmes and the admiral in "Mary Poppins.")

The first of several twists has Bob Cratchit (Gene Lockhart), after departing the office on Christmas Eve, throwing a snowball at Scrooge — he didn't realize it was his boss — and knocking off Scrooge's top hat, which is promptly flattened by a passing carriage. Scrooge fires Cratchit on the spot, Christmas Eve or no.

The Cratchits cast is a family affair. Mrs. Cratchit is played by Lockhart's wife, Kathleen, and one of the children by their daughter, June (later the mom in TV's "Lassie" and "Lost in Space").

Always a handy player for an oddball role, Leo G. Carroll ("Tarantula," "The Man From U.N.C.L.E.") is well cast as Marley.

Another twist has Scrooge, during Marley's visit, shouting out his window to town watchmen, "There's an intruder in my room!" The men investigate, find no intruder, and exit laughing.

The Ghost of Christmas Past is a willowy blonde (Ann Rutherford) with a spangly star atop her head. She and Owen play flying scenes akin to those of George Reeves in TV's "Superman."

The role of Scrooge's nephew, Fred (Barry MacKay), is built up almost to the level of a romantic lead. Fred is on hand when Scrooge brings armloads of food and cheer to the Cratchits. At first, Bob thinks Fred is there to remove his uncle, who has apparently taken leave of his senses. Why *else* would he restore Bob's job — with a raise, to boot — wishing one and all a merry Christmas?

GREATER THAN "DAVID COPPERFIELD"

Charles Dickens'
A CHRISTMAS CAROL

with REGINALD OWEN
GENE LOCKHART
KATHLEEN LOCKHART

The chain-bedecked ghost of Jacob Marley (Leo G. Carroll) appears before Ebenezer Scrooge (Reginald Owen). © Metro-Goldwyn-Mayer

'Holiday Inn' (1942)

SURE, "HOLIDAY INN" COVERS ALL THE HOLIDAYS, not just Christmas. The musical comedy — starring the dream team of Bing Crosby and Fred Astaire as on-again, off-again stage partners (and competitors in romance) — has production numbers built around Valentine's Day, Independence Day, Easter, etc.

But Christmas is clearly the movie's flagship.

Mark Sandrich's film — based on an idea by composer Irving Berlin, who wrote all the songs — opens on Christmas Eve, with Astaire dancing in the snow and ringing the bells of a street Santa, and closes two years later on New Year's Eve, with a resounding singalong of "Happy Holidays" while snow falls outside.

And Berlin's song "White Christmas," making its movie debut here (and heard twice at that), is the film's keynote.

In "Holiday Inn," Crosby is a crooner, Astaire is a hoofer — no surprises here — and singer-dancer Virginia Dale completes the trio. Crosby and Dale are engaged and, according to his plan, will retire from showbiz to the calm of Connecticut farm life.

But Crosby gets an unpleasant surprise: Astaire has stolen Dale's heart. (That's right, Astaire is playing a rat for once.)

Crosby takes the news surprisingly well, telling the guilty-looking couple, "I hope ... you dance yourselves into beautiful nervous breakdowns." He then proceeds with his dream to become a farmer, while Astaire and Dale carry on as a nightclub duo.

Problem is, Crosby makes one clumsy, and exhausted, farmer. After a year of getting up at 4 a.m. to pitch hay and milk cows, he concocts a new plan: to transform his farmhouse into a resort with live entertainment that will only be open to the public on holidays.

He will call it ... *Holiday Inn.*

Crosby meets an unknown, ambitious singer-dancer (Marjorie Reynolds), and hires her to perform at his resort. He is starting to fall for Reynolds when, during a packed New Year's Eve at Holiday Inn, a very drunk Astaire stumbles in. (Go figure, Dale has dumped him for a Texas millionaire.) Astaire does an impromptu, drunken dance with Reynolds — in real life, Astaire hoisted a few to properly convey inebriation — and brings down the house.

The next morning, a hungover Astaire — who needs a new partner for his act, remember — has no recollection of his drunken dance, but is told by his manager (Walter Abel) to *find that girl.*

Hmmm ... it seems Crosby has been through this before.

The musical numbers are memorable, such as a comical mashup of minuet and swing (for Washington's birthday) and Astaire tap-dancing while setting off firecrackers (for Independence Day). Crosby then sings a patriotic number amid footage of a munitions factory, fighter planes and FDR. The song was a hasty add-on; Pearl Harbor was bombed while "Holiday Inn" was in production.

ANOTHER NUMBER IS MEMORABLE FOR A NOT-so-good reason: Crosby and Dale wear blackface for a production number built around Irving's song "Abraham" (for Lincoln's birthday). Worse, the waitstaff and band also wear blackface in the sequence. *Worser,* it's a plot point; Crosby puts the makeup on Dale to keep Astaire from recognizing her. The regrettable number is sometimes chopped when the film airs on television.

In a way, "Holiday Inn" is an alternate-universe prequel to the 1954 musical "White Christmas," which also stars Crosby. The sprawling, distinctive farmhouse resort that gives "Holiday Inn" its title — with its sunken rooms, ornate staircases and cozy windows looking out on Hallmark-card-perfect exteriors — is the *exact same one* that Crosby and Danny Kaye rescue in "White Christmas," beam for beam.

And, yes, the Holiday Inn hotel chain, which was founded in 1952, was named after Sandrich's 1942 film.

Marjorie Reynolds, Bing Crosby and Fred Astaire.

A phony lifestyle columnist (Barbara Stanwyck) is serenaded by a war hero (Dennis Morgan) in "Christmas in Connecticut."

'Christmas in Connecticut' (1945)

IN THE GOOD OLD DAYS WHEN PATIENTS COULD still smoke in hospitals, two survivors of a torpedoed destroyer recuperate. Both men are hailed as heroes, though only one is fed well during their six-week stay at a Naval hospital on Staten Island.

"Sink" Sinkewicz (Frank Jenks) gets thick, juicy steak — he knows how to schmooze the nurses — while Jefferson Jones (Dennis Morgan) is served raw eggs in milk. *Ugh*.

Jefferson longingly reads the holiday menu published by the lifestyle columnist of *Smart Housekeeping* magazine: roast goose, walnut dressing, cranberry-orange relish, candied sweet potatoes, celery souffle, mince pie, and old-fashioned plum pudding.

A nurse (Joyce Compton), who is sweet on Jefferson, takes the liberty of writing to the columnist, Mrs. Elizabeth Lane (Barbara Stanwyck), on Jefferson's behalf, requesting he be invited to Christmas dinner at Elizabeth's famous, fabulous farmhouse in Connecticut — the one she writes about so vividly in her columns.

Problem #1: There *is* no farmhouse. Problem #2: Elizabeth has no husband. Problem #3: She can't cook.

The grim reality: She lives in a cramped Manhattan apartment and gets her recipes from a Hungarian restaurateur, Felix (S.K. Sakall), who always has her best interests at heart. (Case in point: Felix actively discourages suitors who are, in his eyes, unworthy.)

Smart Housekeeping's portly publisher Alexander Yardley (Sydney Greenstreet) — himself hoping to taste Elizabeth's holiday fare — gets wind of Jefferson's request and envisions the headline "American Hero Spends Christmas on Perfect Farm."

Elizabeth tries hard to wriggle out of the obligation, but Yardley is a man accustomed to getting his way.

This poses a threat to Elizabeth's livelihood. Yardley doesn't know she is a fraud. Such a reality would not be tolerated by the publisher. As Yardley tells the editor of her column: "I expect two things from my editors: Print the truth and obey my orders."

What to do? It so happens Elizabeth has a wealthy suitor (Reginald Gardiner) who has been pushing for marriage and — suspension-of-disbelief alert — owns a gorgeous farmhouse in Connecticut. Would he take part in a charade? Felix certainly would, as Elizabeth's "Uncle Felix" who will "help" her to cook.

WITH A TWIST-HAPPY SETUP LIKE THAT, IS IT ANY wonder that once Elizabeth and Jefferson lay eyes on each other, they are both smitten? Peter Godfrey's "Christmas in Connecticut" is a romantic comedy with subtle hints of bedroom farce.

It's also an interesting snapshot of the time when World War II was winding down. "Christmas in Connecticut" was released 95 days after V-E Day, and has references to "postwar planning."

Still, the film is a Christmas movie through-and-through. The trappings are everywhere: the Christmas dinner, a romantic sleigh ride, a Christmas dance, a flirty tree-trimming scene.

And Stanwyck, an Oscar winner, borrows an old Three Stooges bit. When Yardley insists that Elizabeth demonstrate the proper way to flip a flapjack — something she's never done in her life — it sticks to the ceiling. Move over, Moe Howard.

Mary (Donna Reed), George (James Stewart) and Zuzu Bailey (Karolyn Grimes) bask in a Christmas miracle. © Republic Entertainment

'It's a Wonderful Life' (1946)

GOING IN, WE MUST ACKNOWLEDGE THREE THINGS about "It's a Wonderful Life." No. 1, George Bailey is kind of a jerk. No. 2, Pottersville is a much cooler place than Bedford Falls. No. 3, Frank Capra's movie classic is basically a two-hour "Twilight Zone" episode.

"It's a Wonderful Life" centers on idealistic George (James Stewart) who, when contemplating suicide at his darkest hour, learns what the world would be like had he never been born, with the help of a dotty angel-in-training (Henry Travers). It's an exquisitely told story that spans American milestones from the Roaring '20s through the Great Depression and World War II, all swirling around a small, bucolic everytown.

As the film opens, folks are praying for George in voiceover while we view landmarks of snowy Bedford Falls. Meanwhile, up in Heaven, two celestial overseers decide to dispatch "that clockmaker," wanna-be angel Clarence, to redeem George. If successful, Clarence will finally earn his angel's wings. But first, Clarence must review George's life story, starting with the time George rescues his kid brother from drowning in a sledding accident. Quick-witted young George also prevents a distraught, drunk pharmacist from inadvertently poisoning a customer.

More flashbacks: George, now an adult, attends the Class of '28 senior dance and rocks the Charleston with a childhood friend, Mary Hatch (Donna Reed), who has grown into a looker ... they harmonize on "Buffalo Gals" during the soggy walk home ... George's sage-like father

LIBERTY FILMS INC. Presents Frank CAPRA'S "IT'S A WONDERFUL LIFE" starring James STEWART and Donna REED

LIONEL BARRYMORE · THOMAS MITCHELL · HENRY TRAVERS ·

(Samuel S. Hinds) dies of a stroke, leaving the future of his floundering firm, Bailey Savings & Loan, in question ... wealthy, wheelchair-bound curmudgeon "Old Man" Potter (Lionel Barrymore), Bedford Falls' own Scrooge, makes a play for the firm ... George, who'd planned to see the world, stays home to assume responsibility for his father's firm ... he marries Mary, but their honeymoon is effectively canceled as the firm narrowly side-steps, in Depression-era parlance, a run on the bank.

But George faces the test of his life when his absent-minded Uncle Billy (Thomas Mitchell) — who ties strings around his fingers as "reminders" —makes a mistake that throws Bailey Savings & Loan into dire legal jeopardy.

Uncle Billy is bursting with pride that his nephew, George's brother Harry (Todd Karns), won the Congressional Medal of Honor for valor in battle. Screams the front page of *The Bedford Falls Sentinel:* "President decorates Harry Bailey." As Uncle Billy brags to Potter, he unknowingly drops into Potter's lap an envelope containing the $8,000 he was about to deposit.

We now find out just how evil Potter is. Rather than return the eight grand, Potter pockets it, surreptitiously delighting in the pain it causes Bailey Savings & Loan. "You're worth more dead than alive," Potter purrs when George begs his elderly rival for a loan.

This brings George to the brink — and Clarence to the rescue.

OK, SO WHAT MAKES GEORGE A JERK? LET US count the ways. He constantly disparages Bedford Falls in front of fellow lifers, with refrains like "I'm shaking the dust of this town off my feet." When, during that impromptu first "date," Mary loses her robe and hides, nearly naked, in a large flower bush, George leaves her stranded. (Granted, he just learned his father had a stroke, but before rushing off, he should have seen to her safety. *She was nearly naked.*) He calls Uncle Billy a "stupid old fool," his daughter Zuzu's teacher "stupid" and "careless," and terrorizes his family, kicking furniture and yelling at another daughter to "stop playing that silly tune!" The prosecution rests.

And how is Pottersville — the alternate-universe town from a world where George was never born — so much hipper and less repressed than Bedford Falls? The chief entertainment in Bedford Falls is "The Bells of St. Mary's" at the Bijou. But Pottersville? Billiards ... bowling ... fights every Wednesday night ... dime a dance ... burlesque with "20 gorgeous girls" ... "Welcome, jitter-bugs" ... *this* is a town that knows how to party.

Supporting roles are cast with familiar faces: Ward Bond and Frank Faylen as the original Bert and Ernie, a cop and cabbie respectively; *noir* queen Gloria Grahame as town flirt Violet; tough-guy actor Sheldon Leonard as tough-guy bartender Nick; H.B. Warner (Jesus in Cecil B. DeMille's 1927 "The King of Kings") as troubled pharmacist Mr. Gower; and Alfalfa himself, Carl Switzer of Little Rascals fame, as a jealous prankster.

Barrymore was not in terrific health when he played Old Man Potter, and he masterfully used his infirmity in his performance. Just when you might feel sympathy for Potter, or fall for one of his honey-laced come-ons, you suddenly remember that this guy is part reptile. Unlike Scrooge, Potter never gets redeemed. (His final line in the film is "Happy New Year to you — in jail!") Studio movies at the time tended to redeem such characters, to put a nice, pretty bow on everything. Capra chose wisely to keep Potter as the unmitigated cad, the "scurvy little spider," that he is.

Potter is rich, but friendless. Clarence's inscription on a gift to George is the message of "It's a Wonderful Life." It reads: "No man is a failure who has friends."

Uncle Billy (Thomas Mitchell, right) gets the best of Old Man Potter (Lionel Barrymore, seated) ... for the moment, anyway.

George and his self-proclaimed guardian angel, Clarence (Henry Travers), are the odd men out at Nick's bar.

Bedford Fall-ites, including Bert the cop (Ward Bond, with accordion) and Harry Bailey (Todd Karns, in uniform), harmonize.

'Miracle on 34th Street' (1947)

A RISING ATTORNEY CONVINCES A NEW YORK court that an eccentric senior citizen is the "one and only Santa Claus" in George Seaton's "Miracle on 34th Street." But the *real* miracle is how the film nearly convinces the viewer of the same.

Movie Santa Clauses are generally a homogenous lot. They live at the North Pole. They wear the requisite fur-trimmed red costume and shiny black boots. And their efforts are meant to satisfy one overriding concern: to deliver joy every Christmas Eve.

In Seaton's film — which the director scripted based on a story by Valentine Davies — Santa is conceived in real-world terms. Kris Kringle (Edmund Gwenn) wears tweed civvies and resides in an old folks home in Great Neck. On those occasions when Kris dons the familiar costume, it's understood he is "playing" Santa, like any department-store, Salvation Army or parade surrogate.

By outward appearances, Kris is, as a little girl named Susan Walker (Natalie Wood) puts it, a "nice old man with whiskers." The fact that *he* believes he is Santa Claus is regarded as a charming idiosyncrasy by some — and a dangerous delusion by others.

We first see Kris as he strolls through Manhattan on Thanksgiving morning to, we assume, take in the Macy's parade, then in its 22nd year. While instructing the parade's faux Santa (Percy Helton) in the proper technique to crack a whip ("It's all in the wrist"), Kris discovers that the gentleman is stinking drunk. Outraged, Kris reports this to Doris Walker (Maureen O'Hara), the Macy's executive in charge of organizing the parade. Doris takes note of Kris' parade-ready physiognomy — white beard, a bit of girth, and twinkling eyes — and asks if he's had any experience playing Santa. Kris says with understatement, "Oh, a *little*."

So Kris fills in on a moment's notice, and proves to be the hit of the parade. An exhausted Doris makes a bee-line for her apartment building, where her daughter Susan is watching the parade with Fred Galley (John Payne), a neighbor who, we learn, is using

the girl as a means to meet her mother. Yeah, it's sneaky, but Doris looks so smart in those Charles LeMaire "power" outfits.

Susan is an adult in a 9-year-old's body, casually deflecting Fred's attempts to engage her in childish whimsy. Doris is raising Susan to not only disbelieve in fairy tales, but to actively avoid even *hearing* them. Make believe is for other people's children.

So later on, when Doris hires Kris as Macy's in-store Santa Claus and he meets Susan, he soon realizes he has his work cut out for him to transform this girl, *and* her mother, into believers.

Maureen O'Hara reacts to a crisis, above, and Natalie Wood starts to believe in Edmund Gwenn in "Miracle on 34th Street."

For a last-minute substitution, Gwenn makes a surprisingly good Santa in Macy's Thanksgiving parade. © 20th Century Fox Film Corp.

AS A DISPENSER OF GIFTS, KRIS LABORS WITHIN real-world limitations. Elves don't make the toys; Kris is well aware they are purchased by parents at stores (and he's not about to "push" overstocked items on customers). Likewise, elves didn't build the X-ray machine needed by a doctor at the Great Neck group home. And when Susan tells Kris what *she* wants for Christmas, he is taken aback: "It's a tall order, but I'll do my best."

The cast is yet another miracle in a film that tops many Best Christmas Movie Ever lists. Gene Lockhart plays Judge Harper, who finds himself in a tough spot. If he admits the possibility of Santa's existence, he'll be the laughing stock of the legal profession. If he doesn't, his grandchildren won't kiss him good night.

William Frawley plays Charlie, a cigar-chomping henchman, er, adviser who warns the judge that in denying Santa's existence, he'll draw the ire of the unions, department stores, Christmas card companies, candy manufacturers and the Salvation Army.

Jerome Cowan — Humphrey Bogart's doomed partner in "The Maltese Falcon" — is the district attorney. Alvin Greenman is the broom-pushing Brooklynite who is the first to believe in Kris.

Marlene Lyden, then 7, plays a skittish Dutch orphan girl, a stranger in a strange land, who speaks no English and convinces her adoptive American mother to bring her to Macys to meet who she recognizes as the real Santa. It's pure movie magic when Kris and the girl duet on "Sinterklaas, Kaapoentje." Clearly, Lyden's missing front teeth are not the handiwork of a Hollywood makeup artist.

O'Hara and Payne create good rom-com chemistry, but pint-sized Wood steals the movie with her killer smirk and deadpan.

Another character is New York City. Parade exteriors were shot on Thanksgiving 1946. O'Hara played scenes at 81st and Central Park West, a location that remains the parade's organizing base.

BY ORDER OF STUDIO BOSS DARRYL F. ZANUCK, "Miracle on 34th Street" was released in June. A rather tortured trailer disguised the fact that this was a Christmas movie. Not to worry; it proved so popular that it played through December.

It's a film that remains eminently quotable. "Christmas is not just a day, it's a frame of mind," says Kris at one point. Following Doris' conversion to Santa-believer, she tells Susan: "Faith is believing in something when common sense tells you not to."

There was even a memorable *off*-screen quote. When Gwenn accepted the Best Supporting Actor Oscar for his portrayal of Kris Kringle, he said in his speech: "Now I *know* there's a Santa Claus."

119

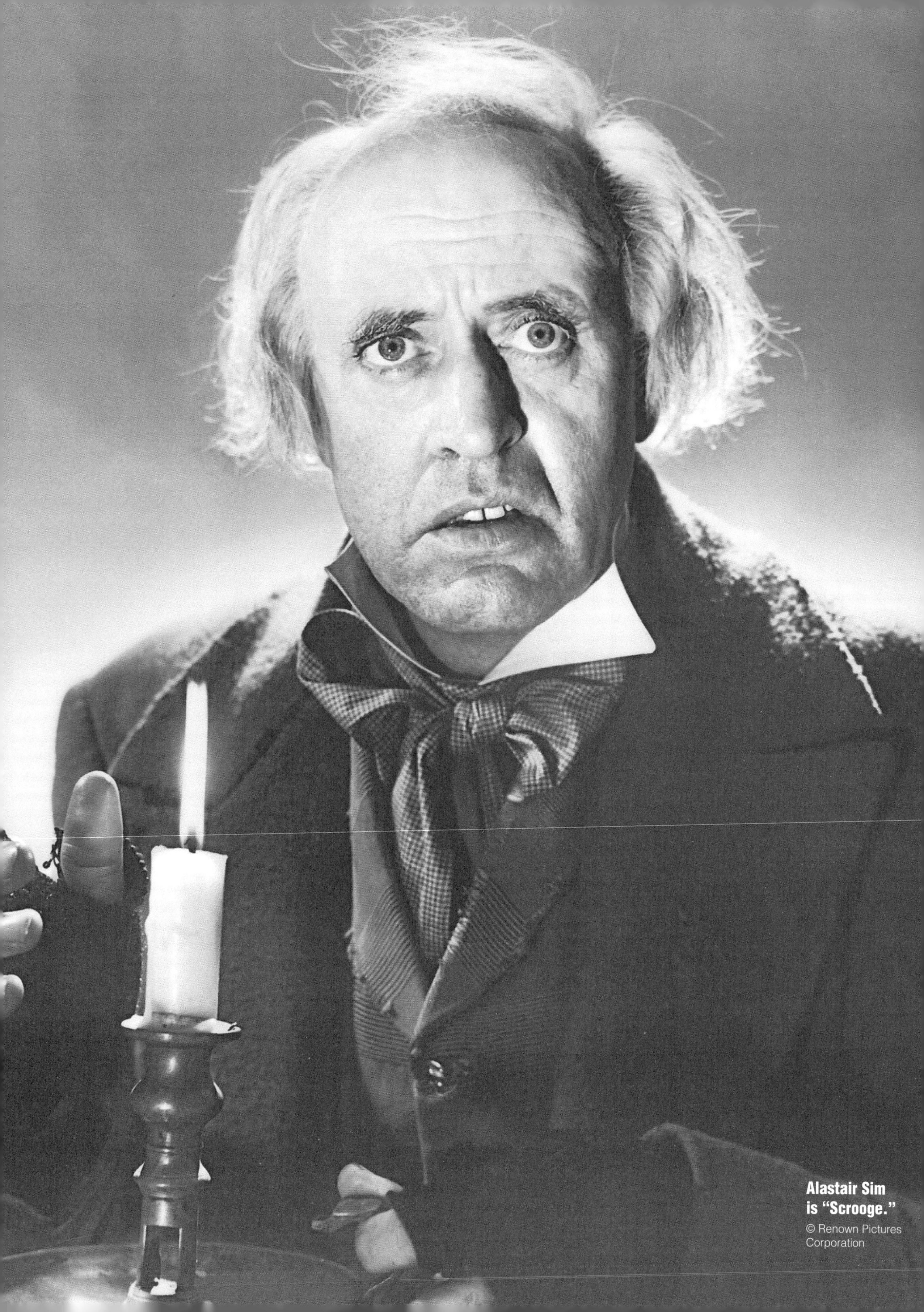

Alastair Sim is "Scrooge."

'Scrooge' (1951)

EVERY ACTOR WHO PLAYS EBENEZER SCROOGE
faces formidable challenges. He must make the audience hate him.
Then, he must make them root for him. Toughest of all, he must
make Scrooge's transformation from Christmas-hating curmudgeon to grinning, clear-eyed convert believable, a tall order. Has
any actor achieved this with such quintessence as Alastair Sim?

In Sim's hands, Charles Dickens' miserly moneylender is not
merely an unfeeling, friendless skinflint; he is, if you'll pardon
the vulgarity, a bastard to his core.

This is made clear out of the box in Brian Desmond Hurst's
1951 British film "Scrooge" (titled "A Christmas Carol" in the
United Kingdom). In an early sequence, one of two representa-
tives of a local charitable organization ill-advisedly requests a
donation from Scrooge on Christmas Eve.

"Some of us are endeavoring to create a fund to provide food
and comfort for those who are less well off," says the do-gooder.

"Why?" deadpans Sim's Scrooge, with what seems like a hint
of glee at how despicable he sounds.

This reply, from screenwriter Noel Langley's adaptation, is
not in Dickens' 1843 novella. No film version is, or can hope to
be, perfectly faithful. This will not be the last time Langley elab-
orates on (as opposed to differs from) Dickens' prose.

Still, much of the script is virtually word-for-word faithful.
Sim delivers Dickens' speech in which Scrooge, still addressing
the do-gooders, feigns concern over whether the prisons, union
workhouses, treadmill and Poor Law are still operating "in their
useful course," while knowing full well they are. It's no mere
case of an actor reciting dialogue from a century-old tome. You
feel Sim's Scrooge. You can see into his black heart.

Sim is the engine that runs Hurst's film — it's a tour de force
performance — but the actor has plenty of help.

THE BLACK-AND-WHITE "SCROOGE" HAS ASPECTS
of film *noir* and even tumbles into horror-movie territory, with
superb cinematography (by C.M. Pennington-Richards), sets and
costuming. The FX are certainly crude by today's standards, but
somehow, you wouldn't trade them for digital perfection.

The music — by Richard Addinsell — is particularly effective
and memorable. The bombastic Scrooge theme ... the wild, foreboding chorus as Marley rejoins his fellow phantoms ... and, of
course, the polka ... these perfectly complement the story.

Classics are interspersed, too. "Hark! The Herald Angels
Sing" is heard in the opening credits and later sung by carolers,
while "Silent Night" is played by a trio of street urchins. The
plaintive 17th-century Scottish ballad "Barbara Allen" is used as
the theme of Ebenezer's ill-fated sister, Fan, and is later sung
during the Christmas party of her son, Scrooge's nephew Fred.

But it is the cast that brings the story alive: Michael Horden
as Marley; Brian Worth as Fred; Mervyn Johns as Bob Cratchit;
Hermione Baddeley as Mrs. Cratchit; Glyn Dearman as Tiny
Tim; Carol Marsh as Fan; George Cole as young Ebenezer;
Patrick MacNee as young Marley; Rona Anderson as Alice,
Scrooge's fiance; Olga Edwardes as Fred's wife (a character
unnamed in the book and the film); Kathleen Harrison as house-
keeper Mrs. Dilber; and, as the spirits, Michael Dolan (Christmas
Past), Francis de Wolff (Christmas Present) and Polish dancer
Czeslaw Konarski (face obscured as Christmas Yet to Come).

**Michael Horden
as Jacob Marley**

**Kathleen Harrison
as Mrs. Dilber**

**Mervyn Johns
as Bob Cratchit**

**Glyn Dearman
as Tiny Tim**

**Carol Marsh as Fan,
Scrooge's sister**

**Brian Worth as Fred,
Scrooge's nephew**

SURPRISES AWAIT THOSE WHO ARE INTRODUCED
to "A Christmas Carol" via the 1951 film, and later backtrack to
the original book. For instance, the death of Fan — and Scrooge's
resentment of his nephew for surviving the birth which took her
life — is not expressly depicted by Dickens, but only hinted at in
dialogue spoken by the Ghost of Christmas Past.

This dialogue is repeated, virtually intact, in the 1951 film.
"Always a delicate creature, from whom a breath might have with-
ered ... she died a woman, and had, as I think, children," the spirit
says of Fan. Scrooge corrects him tersely: "One child."

But Langley dares to bring us to the scene where Dickens did
not: Fan is on her deathbed after giving birth.

"Not here," Scrooge implores the Ghost of Christmas Past.

"Yes, here," answers the spirit.

Present is a doctor; a younger man who is presumably Fan's
husband; and young Ebenezer, who, thinking Fan has already
died, storms out angrily at the sound of the baby's cry.

Young Ebenezer is out the door, but the old Scrooge remains in
the room to hear Fan's faint final words: "Ebenezer ... promise me
you'll take care of my boy ..."

"Forgive me, Fan! Forgive me!" old Scrooge says, sobbing into
his hands.

I can never watch this scene without bawling fat tears, and I
submit that no other adaptation of "A Christmas Carol" has presented so dramatic a moment.

Langley's script also fleshed out the character of Fezziwig —
young Ebenezer's stout, jovial onetime employer — in a way that
is faithful and appropriate. Dickens' Fezziwig is a boss who really
knows how to throw a Christmas party. But in the 1951 film, in a
scene that likewise does not appear in Dickens, Fezziwig (Roddy
Hughes) explains to cunning competitor Jorkin (Jack Warner) why
he initially declines an offer to sell off his business.

"It's not for money alone that one spends a lifetime building up
a business," Fezziwig says, in dialogue worthy of the master. "No,
I won't surrender to the new vested interests. I shall cling to the
old ways, and die out with them, if needs must."

But Fezziwig's young clerk, Ebenezer, is eventually lured away
by Jorkin. Fezziwig later watches from a coach, teary-eyed, as his
old sign is taken down, replaced by one that says "Scrooge &
Marley." It feels like betrayal, and adds layers of dramatic com-
plexity to the long-ago dynamic between Ebenezer and Fezziwig.

AS WITH THE 1935 "SCROOGE," HURST'S FILM
descends into pure black comedy during the sequence, set in the
"future" following Scrooge's death, in which the undertaker
(Ernest Thesiger), the charwoman (Louise Hampton) and the
housekeeper Mrs. Dilber sell Scrooge's pilfered belongings to Old
Joe the rag man (Miles Malleson). I can't resist pointing out that
the casting here is a horror-film buff's dream. Thesiger played Dr.
Pretorius, no less, in "The Bride of Frankenstein" (1935); he and
Harrison had roles in "The Ghoul" (1935); and Malleson played
the doddering undertaker in "Horror of Dracula" (1958).

Harrison later steals the movie out from under Sim for a few
minutes, when Mrs. Dilber becomes the first person to encounter
the converted Scrooge on Christmas morning. As a giddy Scrooge
attempts to stand on his head, Mrs. Dilber bolts from the room
shrieking, despite her apron covering her eyes.

Holiday-themed movies and TV specials always must end with
a "Christmas miracle" — *another* thing for which we have Dickens
to thank. The Alastair Sim "Scrooge" is, itself, a Christmas miracle, one we can relive year after year and be touched anew by
familiar moments, yet still delight in fresh discoveries.

William Frawley as one of 11 unsavory Santas in "The Lemon Drop Kid." Right: Bob Hope and Marilyn Maxwell introduce "Silver Bells."

'The Lemon Drop Kid' (1951)

BOB HOPE VENTURES SLIGHTLY — *SLIGHTLY* — outside of his wheelhouse in Sidney Lanfield's remake of "The Lemon Drop Kid." This is a Damon Runyon adaptation, albeit, a musical-comedy-ization. Some of the author's knack for colorful observations of New York denizens survives, but after all, it stars *Bob Hope*. As the title con artist, Hope more or less plays his usual character: quipping, hustling, up to his ski-nose in trouble.

Put it this way: In Runyon's short story, the Lemon Drop Kid never makes cracks about Milton Berle or Bing Crosby.

The Kid's specialty is as a racetrack "tout": He imparts advice to bettors, who, if they win big, are apt to demonstrate their gratitude with a tip. At a Florida track, he gives bad advice to an expensively dressed dame (Andrea King), not realizing she is the mistress of mob boss Moose (Fred Clark).

Moose reckons that the Kid's bad advice cost him 10 grand. Moose gives the Kid until Christmas Eve to raise the money, even allowing him to go to New York City to do it. If the Kid fails, he will have an appointment with Moose's murderous henchman Sam (Harry Bellaver), a.k.a. "the Surgeon."

In snowy New York, the Kid runs into sweet old Nellie Thursday (played by Ma Joad herself, Jane Darwell), a down-on-her-luck granny hawking newspapers to get by. Later, the Kid puts the bite on his perennial fiancee, a singer-dancer known as Brainey (Marilyn Maxwell), for 10 bucks. He only has $9,990 more to raise.

The Kid hits on a scheme that puts this film in a rarefied position among Christmas movies: It has 11 Santas, played by a rogue's gallery of familiar Hollywood faces. The scheme: Moose owns an idle casino on Long Island, which the Kid will convert into an old ladies' home — named after Nellie, yet — thus attaining a city license to collect donations as streetcorner Santas. The Kid presses all of his underworld buddies into service to don the suits and ring the bells.

Problem is, the Kid doesn't tell his buddies, Brainey or Nellie that "Nellie Thursday's Home for Old Dolls" won't get the moolah collected. To save the Kid's skin, it will go to Moose.

AMONG THE SANTAS ARE WILLIAM FRAWLEY (Fred Mertz himself), Sid Melton (Alf the carpenter in "Green Acres"), Jay C. Flippen (a ubiquitous movie tough guy), and — are you sitting? — Swedish wrestler Tor Johnson ("Plan 9 From Outer Space"). Hope has fun playing off of Johnson, even kissing the wrestler's bald dome.

So the quandary becomes: Will the Kid do the right thing by finally marrying Brainey, and coughing up the dough to the Old Dolls' Home?

The film introduced Jay Livingston and Ray Evans' song "Silver Bells," which is sung by Hope and Maxwell as they stroll a Christmas-y backlot that looks nothing like New York City. (Actually, Frawley growls a few lyrics first in his Santa suit, making him technically the first person to sing "Silver Bells" on screen.)

Jane Darwell as Nellie Thursday

Frawley is also in the 1934 film version of Runyon's story, which debuted that year in *Colliers*, and makes no mention of Christmas. Runyon died five years before the release of Hope's "The Lemon Drop Kid." Maybe that's a good thing?

Bob Wallace (Bing Crosby) sings "White Christmas" for the troops on Christmas Eve 1944 in "White Christmas."

'White Christmas' (1954)

WORLD WAR II NOSTALGIA — THAT'S WHAT "White Christmas" is all about. And since Michael Curtiz's glossy, color, VistaVision movie musical was released in 1954, it was not even 10 years out from the epic historic conflict.

"White Christmas" is a fantasy — not so much for those who kept the home fires burning, nor for later generations looking back on World War II, but for the boys, by then *men,* who once bid farewell to their families and sweethearts, and left home to face the dangers that come with defending America and the free world. It's a fantasy about getting together with your old war buddies and putting on your uniforms one more time.

The heart of "White Christmas" is tied into devotion to "the Old Man": General Waverly, masterfully underplayed with humor, authority and a well-placed silver toupee by Dean Jagger. Hasn't everyone had an authority figure who was tough but fair? Who made you a better person? Who you would drop everything for?

"White Christmas" opens with a Christmas Eve 1944 flashback depicting American troops in an overseas war zone watching makeshift entertainment — not a USO show, but a modest little by-soldiers-for-soldiers holiday revue — surrounded by rubble in the midst of ongoing bombing. It so happens one of the performers is Bob Wallace (Bing Crosby), a famous stage professional in civilian life who is just another soldier here — albeit, one who can coax a tear from his fellow GIs with his rendition of, meta alert,

"White Christmas," while his somewhat goofy buddy Phil Davis (Danny Kaye) accompanies him on a plinky windup music box.

The plot thickens when a Jeep arrives with General Waverly and his replacement, General Carlton (Gavin Gordon), a fresh-from-the-Pentagon wonk who aims to enforce the rules. (He's sort of an alternate-universe version of Captain Queeg.) First order of business: no entertainment in a war zone. But Waverly manages to temporarily divert Carlton, and the Christmas Eve show continues.

The boys have a big finish for the program, a number dedicated to General Waverly. Sample lyrics: *"We'll follow the Old Man / Wherever he wants to go … because we love him / we love him / especially when he keeps us on the ball ..."*

The show is interrupted by more bombing. Pandemonium hits as everyone scatters for cover. A collapsing wall almost takes out Bob, but for quick action by Phil, whose arm is injured in the act.

Phil, an aspiring entertainer, later plays on Bob's gratitude to coerce him into singing a duet with him, once the war is over and they're back in civvies. Bob and Phil eventually form a double act, headlining a radio show and a Broadway revue.

In that brisk 11-minute prologue, the seeds have been planted. For the time being, "White Christmas" settles into a backstage romantic comedy. To get workaholic Bob to take a breather — and get a little break himself — Phil plays Cupid, attempting to set up Bob with a lady friend. But Bob sees through Phil's ploy.

It's looking like a merry Christmas for, from left, Vera-Ellen, Danny Kaye, Crosby and Rosemary Clooney. © Paramount Pictures

BOB AND PHIL CATCH THE ACT OF THE SINGING
Haynes Sisters, Betty (Rosemary Clooney) and Judy (Vera-Ellen). There's a spark between Bob and Betty, which is just fine with Phil and Judy, who form an alliance, scheming behind their backs to nudge the flicker into a full-fledged fire. The girls have a booking at the Columbia Inn, a resort in Pine Tree, Vermont, and the boys tag along, all psyched to romp in the snow.

But when they arrive, there's nary a snow-flake to be found. Freak warm weather has left Pine Tree bereft of snow — and the Columbia Inn bereft of customers. The boys are ready to leave when in walks General Waverly, wearing civvies and toting an armload of firewood.

On instinct, Bob and Phil snap to attention.

"General Waverly, a janitor!" exclaims Phil.

"As a matter of fact, it's worse than that," Waverly replies. "I *own* this hotel."

And so the conflicts are all in place. Can the boys help rescue General Waverly's struggling inn? And will Bob and Betty ever fall in love?

It took some years to get "White Christmas" off the ground. The 1952 death of Crosby's wife, Dixie Lee, caused the crooner to take a hiatus. Fred Astaire was set to reteam with Crosby, but for another commitment. Donald O'Connor was then cast, but fell ill. Kaye finally landed the gig.

Vera-Ellen, she of the freakishly long legs, gave "White Christmas" some of the dancing oomph Astaire would have brought. Kaye dances remarkably well with her in two numbers,

Dean Jagger as the Old Man.

but when Vera-Ellen needs a *real* ringer as a dancing partner, they bring in John Brascia, who plays a variety-show choreographer.

(Years later, in pointing out that Vera-Ellen's vocals were dubbed, Clooney joked: "If they could have dubbed my dancing, we would have had a perfect picture.")

An Our Gang cast member makes a cameo of sorts. Carl "Alfalfa" Switzer is seen in a photograph as an old Army buddy of Bob and Phil's.

Crosby and Kaye play a song in drag — well, *partial* drag, anyway. In a gag bit, the boys lip-synch to a recording of the Haynes sisters while wearing spangly headpieces and light makeup. When a goofup on one of the takes caused Crosby and Kaye to crack up, it played so well that this was the take used, mistake be damned.

The movie has a raft of Irving Berlin tunes. "Snow" makes you want to revel in the white stuff. "Counting Your Blessings" is a charming Crosby-Clooney duet. "Choreography" is a clever, biting sendup of then-current dance trends, with the movie-stopping scene of Vera-Ellen's legs, sheathed in cotton-candy pink hose, dropping into the screen and tapping with inhuman precision. "Love, You Didn't Do Right by Me" is a torch song by Clooney with a recognizable George Chakiris (seven years before "West Side Story") as a dancer. The war-themed rousers "The Old Man," "What Can You Do With a General" and "Gee, I Wish I Was Back in the Army" offer more proof of wherein lies the heart of "White Christmas."

'Santa Claus' (1959)

IT'S NOT A CLASSIC IN THE "MIRACLE on 34th Street"/"It's a Wonderful Life"/"White Christmas" sense. But the 1959 "Santa Claus" — a Mexican movie made by horror specialists — is indeed counted as a classic by a certain strain of movie buff: those who prefer, let's say, "Plan 9 From Outer Space" to "Citizen Kane."

The Mexican "Santa Claus" raked in American dollars on the weekend matinee circuit by masquerading as Disney-quality fare. Its deceptive advertising campaign ("An Enchanting World of Make-Believe!") made American moms feel safe to drop off their kids at mall theaters while they got in a couple of offspring-free shopping hours.

What children got in the bargain was brain-twisting, sometimes downright creepy entertainment.

A bit of history: "Santa Claus" was one of many films imported and dubbed into English by producer/huckster K. Gordon Murray of Coral Gables, Florida. (I mention the town because it appears prominently in the credits of just about every Murray import.) Murray carved a niche repackaging foreign horror, wrestling and kiddie films, chiefly from Mexico, for the U.S. market. That's his exuberant voice you hear narrating "Santa Claus," billed as Ken Smith.

DIRECTOR RENÉ CARDONA HONED A niche making horror and wrestling movies — the kind that turned up on American television beginning in the '60s. Typical of Cardona's *oeuvre* were "Doctor of Doom" (Mexican title: *"Las luchadoras contra el médico asesino"*) and "Wrestling Women vs. the Aztec Mummy" (Mexican title: *"Las Luchadoras contra la Momia"*).

Even Santa had a checkered past. Horror fans remember José Elías Moreno, who stars as Santa, as the mad surgeon who transplants a gorilla's heart into his son's body in the gory "Night of the Bloody Apes" (Mexican title: *"La horripilante bestia humana"*), also by Cardona. That infamous film ruled the midnight movie circuit, thanks to the questionable rumor that it has footage of actual open-heart surgery.

Despite its horror-ific pedigree, "Santa Claus" generally keeps things funny and family-friendly. But owing to lost-in-translation weirdnesses, there are some eerie moments. Among these are the tribunal of hooded devils — they look like the KKK, but in red robes instead of white — convening in a fire-and-brimstone vision of Hell. There's also "little Lupita" (played by Lupita Quezadas, who appears to be about 4), looking worried and confused while surrounded by dancing dolls who taunt her. Santa matches wits with Pitch (José Luis Aguirre), a red devil who wears dime-store horns and ears, and dances with a flourish that outpaces his actual talent.

The Mexicans invented some novel customs for Santa. He lives on a cloud, not the North Pole. His palace is staffed by children from all over the world, not elves. His reindeer are windup robots that snort steam. He carries a flower that makes him invisible, and

An Enchanting World Of Make~Believe!

Bursting upon our BIG SCREEN in all the colors of the rainbow... a prize-winning blue ribbon treat for old and young alike! Here's something for the whole family to see together! The Management.

K. Gordon Murray presents

SANTA CLAUS

See FULL LENGTH! FULL COLOR!

SAN FRANCISCO BEST FAMILY FILMS AWARD FILM FESTIVAL

in EASTMAN COLORSCOPE

ALL THE WEIRD AND WONDERFUL CHARACTERS OF MAKE-BELIEVE.

THE FABULOUS REALM OF THE CANDY-STICK PALACES.

Advertisements for the Mexican "Santa Claus" promised "An Enchanting World of Make-Believe!" But this was no Walt Disney movie. © Azteca Films

"dreaming" powder to keep children unconscious during Christmas Eve deliveries. His "main food" is "pastry and ice cream made of soft clouds." And he fusses over a large, ornate Nativity display while singing "Silent Night" — thus fudging the unwritten Santa-movie rule to avoid mixing church and state.

Also, there is no sight, nor mention, of a *Mrs.* Santa. The only other adult occupants of Santa's palace are a robed wizard and a muscular, shirtless, hairy-chested, bearded blacksmith.

Does *this* Santa prefer the company of men?

The plot can be summarized in 21 words: A devil tries to coerce children into committing crimes; poor girl Lupita wants a dolly for Christmas; Santa to the rescue!

From top left: José Elías Moreno as Santa Claus; singing children; Lupita and mama; snowy Toyland. Below: A devil! © Azteca Films

WE FIRST SEE SANTA CLAUS IN HIS PALACE "IN the heavens," which an interior decorator might describe as oil-rich-country-crown-prince *chic*. Santa plays an organ with a video screen that shows a "We Are the World" of children amid giant candy canes and falling snow. Represented are Africa, China, England, Japan, "the Orient," Italy, the Caribbeans, South America, Central America, the United States and Mexico. "Even Russia has a delegation," says the narrator. (*Even* Russia?)

Of course, the children are styled as stereotypes. The Africans have bones in their hair and wear leopard skins; the Russians wear cossack hats; the French are dressed as painters; the Americans are dressed as cowboys. Even the Mexican children wear sombreros and serapes.

Meanwhile, in Hell, Lucifer (who is heard but not seen) presides over dancing devils and mysterious hooded figures. He commands a devil known as Pitch to get the children of Earth to "do evil." If he fails, Pitch will face the ultimate punishment: eating chocolate ice cream. (Get it? Devils hate good stuff.)

On Earth, families are gawking at toys in a store window. Among the spectators is little Lupita, looking glum because her unemployed father and clinically depressed mother haven't given

her much hope of snagging a doll on Christmas morning.

Pitch convinces three delinquents to throw rocks at the store window. Later, Pitch — knowing that Lupita's greatest wish is for a doll all her own — tries to get the girl to steal one. Lupita resists the temptation, but dreams of bizarro dancing dolls in a jaw-dropping sequence that should be on every schlock movie aficionado's clip reel.

Back at the palace, Merlin the wizard is making like Q in a James Bond movie, outfitting Santa with the latest magic devices for his Christmas Eve trek.

Lately, children have been mailing wishlists to Santa. When the kids ask for siblings, Santa laughs knowingly and puts those letters in a box marked with a stork image and the word "Paris." (Huh?)

Will Santa visit Lupita's hovel? Lupita has her doubts. She tells her *madre:* "I don't think he likes me. He has never brought me any dolly." And this Christmas, Pitch is stalking Santa's sled in the hopes of sabotaging the Jolly One's joy-dispensing mission.

The Mexican "Santa Claus" is not a case of "So bad, it's good." It's more like "So weird, it commands attention." This cinematic oddity is the perfect thing to watch when you've had too much eggnog and cookies, and your glucose levels are kablooey.

'Santa Claus Conquers the Martians' (1964)

THERE'S SCIENCE FICTION, AND THEN again, there's *science fiction*.

The title alone — "Santa Claus Conquers the Martians" — should clue you in that this is not a film to be counted alongside "Metropolis" or "2001: A Space Odyssey." But that's OK. To criticize Nicholas Webster's low-budget quickie "Santa Claus Conquers the Martians" for its inane plot, cheezy FX and ridiculous Martian costumes is to miss the point.

The made-on-Long-Island movie is intended as lightweight children's entertainment. Yet, there are knowing winks that keep it kind of hip — a gift for adults who find themselves trapped in the crowded TV room of a relative's home over the holidays.

The film kicks off with an up-to-the-minute 1964 pop song over the opening titles. The peppy "Hooray for Santy Claus," composed by Milton DeLugg and Roy Alfred, sounds like something out of a Frankie Avalon-Annette Funicello "Beach Party" movie, except sung by a chorus of children. Sample lyric: *"He's fat and round but jumpin' Jiminy / He can climb down any chim-i-ney ..."*

As the action begins, a newscaster visits the North Pole toy shop of Santa Claus (John Call), who injects the first bit of hip-ish humor when he mistakenly refers to one of his reindeer as "Nixon." Santa shows off a prototype Martian doll, musing, "I wonder if there really *are* people on Mars?"

THERE *ARE*, WE LEARN, AND THEIR costumes are identical to the one on the doll: helmets with antennae and vacuum cleaner hoses; onesies that terminate in hot pants; leotards; gloves; and "Batman"-style utility belts. All are dyed or painted in puke green, as are the actors' faces. It makes "The Far Out Space Nuts" look like "Things to Come."

Martian children Bomar (Chris Month) and Girmar (Pia Zadora ... that's right, Pia Zadora) are obsessed with Earth TV, especially programs about Santa Claus, even as they're mystified by the topics discussed. "What is a doll?" asks Girmar. "I don't know. What is tender loving care?" replies Bomar.

Their concerned father is Kimar, leader of Mars (played by Leonard Hicks who, but for a cruel twist of fate, could have been in a John Ford war movie). Goofy Martian gofer Dropo (Bill McCutcheon, doing his best Ray Bolger) tells Kimar and his wife, Lady Momar (Leila Martin), that the kids seem depressed and have lost their appetites. (A running joke: Martians eat pills, not food, in flavors like hamburger, buttered asparagus, mashed potatoes and chocolate cake.)

Bomar and Girmar aren't the only kids affected. "Something is happening to the children of Mars," says Kimar, who meets with the one entity who may have a solution: Chochem, "the Ancient One" (Carl Don). Styled in a long white wig and beard, Don appears to be seeking favor with the Oscars nominating committee as he pleads in a weary croak, "The children must be allowed to be children again ... We need a Santa Claus on Mars."

SANTA BRINGS CHRISTMAS FUN TO MARS!

Blast off for Mars... with Santa and a pair of Earth Kids! Science-Fun-Fiction at its height!

JOSEPH E. LEVINE presents

SANTA CLAUS CONQUERS THE MARTIANS

IN SPACE-BLAZING COLOR

SAT.-SUN. MATINEE SPECIAL

♪ Hear: "HOORAY FOR SANTA CLAUS" On Four Corners Records

SEE: The Martians Kidnap Santa!
Santa's North Pole Workshop!
The Fantastic Martian Toy Factory!
Earth Kids Meeting With Martian Kids!
Space-ship Journey from Earth to Mars!
Santa Turn Mars-Robot Into a Mechanical Toy!

Written by GLENVILLE MARETH · Produced by PAUL L. JACOBSON · Directed by NICHOLAS WEBSTER · A Jalor Production · An Embassy Pictures Release

It's easy to call "Santa Claus Conquers the Martians" a stinker. Though a low-budget quickie, it is a clever movie with a hip sensibility. © Embassy Pictures

Kimar takes a spaceship and crew to Earth in search of Santa, to the consternation of Voldar (Vincent Beck), his sneering second-in-command. Wearing a shaggy porn 'stache and those tight Martian duds, Voldar looks like the lost Village Person.

Flying over New York City, the Martians spot a streetcorner Santa, thinking he is "the" Santa. Then they see Santas on other blocks. Confused, they land in a wooded area, where they encounter two siblings, Billy (Victor Stiles) and Betty (Donna Conforti) Foster. The squeaky-clean children inform the Martians that the "real" Santa lives at the North Pole. At the urging of that rat Voldar, the children are abducted as the Martians head north.

From top left: Santa and Earth kids; Martian family; spaceship cockpit; Mrs. Claus, media darling. Below: The robot! © Embassy Pictures

THE MARTIANS BRING ALONG A ROBOT, TORG,
who makes the one in "The Robot vs. the Aztec Mummy" seem like the one in "Forbidden Planet." You look at it and wonder if the silver spray paint is dry yet.

Dispatched to Santa's shop, the lumbering Torg breaks down the door and freaks out the elves, but inspires curiosity in Santa. "You're the biggest toy I've ever seen," he says, "and very well-made, too."

The Martians enter and fire freeze-ray guns at the elves and Mrs. Santa (Doris Rich), turning them into statues. Santa sadly regards his frozen wife and says, "You know, my dear, I can't recall a time when you were so silent."

(A digression: Toy buffs will recognize the freeze-ray guns as undisguised pump-and-shoot Air Blasters from Wham-O, a hot seller at the time.)

Billy, Betty and Santa are taken to Mars, where they are set up with a toy factory quite different from Santa's North Pole enterprise. He laments: "Look at me — Santa Claus, the great toymaker, pushing buttons. That's automation for you. Technology!"

Bobby and Betty befriend Dropo, Bomar and Girmar. (Stockholm syndrome?) But they rightly conclude that Voldar is evil. (It must be the mustache.)

Voldar infiltrates the factory and sabotages its wiring. The next day, when Santa cranks up the toymaking machinery with the help of Bomar and Girmar, the toys come out wrong, giving Zadora her most dramatic line: "The doll has a teddy bear head, and the teddy bear has a doll head!" Sputters Santa, "This never happened when we made toys by hand."

Will Voldar get his comeuppance? Will Billy, Betty and Santa get back to Earth? Will Mars get its own Santa Claus? Do you seriously not know the answers to these questions?

Zadora starred in "The Lonely Lady" (1983) and was nominated for a Grammy in 1984. McCutcheon played Uncle Wally on "Sesame Street." Beck was all over '60s-'70s TV ("Mr. Ed," "Gilligan's Island"), as was director Webster ("Mannix," "Bracken's World"). DeLugg was a onetime musical director for NBC. And — *Merrrry* Christmas — there was a "Santa Claus Conquers the Martians" album (Golden Records) and comic book (Dell Publishing).

129

Albert Finney (in Santa suit) leads the dance in the musical "Scrooge." Below: Alec Guinness' creepy Marley.

'Scrooge' (1970)

THE FIRST COLOR MOVIE ADAPTATION OF "A CHRISTMAS Carol," and the first big-screen musical version of Dickens' tale, was Ronald Neame's "Scrooge" starring Albert Finney, which alternates between bleak and bouncy, and has an eerie, captivating performance by Alec Guinness as Marley.

At 33, Finney was younger and more conventionally handsome than his movie predecessors in the role. Finney's hair is a rusty gray rather than the traditional white. Wearing little discernible "old age" makeup, Finney scrunches up his face, scowling and sneering his way through the film. Thus, he avoids one fate of his older forebears as Scrooge: the indignity of wearing a dark wig atop a fallen face in flashback scenes. (We're looking at *you,* Seymour Hicks.)

This "Scrooge" is unafraid to take several considerable liberties with Dickens. Here, Scrooge walks around town collecting payments from street vendors — a clothing concession, a soup seller, a "Punch and Judy" show puppeteer. When the vendors beg for more time, Scrooge ups the interest and helps himself to some of their goods (a scarf, a stein of soup). It's a power trip akin to Don Fanucci preying on old New York in "The Godfather Part II."

In flashback, young Scrooge's sweetheart, Eva (Suzanne Neve), is the daughter of Mr. and Mrs. Fezziwig. Dating the boss's daughter — *that* can get you in hot water (and it's a twist found nowhere in Dickens).

In a big production number, one of Scrooge's debtors dances atop Scrooge's coffin as it winds through the cobblestone streets of Victorian London to the cheers of townfolk. Referring to Scrooge's act of dying, they sing, with ironic sprightliness, "That's the nicest thing that anyone's ever done for me."

A daring liberty comes courtesy of the Ghost of Christmas Yet to Come (who looks like something out of "Dr. Phibes"). After being shown his gravestone, Scrooge descends into Hell — with *Marley* returning as his guide! Says he: "I heard you were coming down today, so I thought I'd come to greet you."

Scrooge-palooza

THAT SKINFLINT EBENEZER SCROOGE has many on-screen faces. On TV, there was Fredric March (with a false nose) opposite Basil Rathbone as Marley in 1954; Rathbone (no false nose needed) as Scrooge in 1959; and TV movies starring George C. Scott (1984) and Patrick Stewart (1999).

"Alternate universe" movie Scrooges include Bill Murray's jerk of a TV executive in "Scrooged" (1988) and Taryn Manning's peroxided trailer-park party girl in "All American Christmas Carol" (2013).

Among kid-friendly adaptations are Brian Henson's "The Muppets Christmas Carol" (1992). Michael Caine as Ebenezer Scrooge? Dream casting. Caine pulling off the role while performing alongside zany puppets? Nothing short of an acting feat.

Familiar Muppets "play" Dickens' characters, such as Kermit the Frog and Miss Piggy as Mr. and Mrs. Bob Cratchit, and Fozzie the Bear as "Fozzi-wig." (If you wonder what happens when a male frog mates with a female pig, this film has the answer: Boys come out as frogs, girls come out as pigs.)

But Caine grounds the film. "I'm going to play this movie like I'm working with the Royal Shakespeare Company," said the actor (as quoted by Henson). "I will never wink, I will never do anything Muppety."

See also Robert Zemeckis' motion-capture version of 2009, with scenes of flight that pose a motion-sickness hazard, and a Scrooge (Jim Carrey) who resembles Uncle Creepy as a lifelong crack user.

In Bharat Nalluri's "The Man Who Invented Christmas" (2017), Christopher Plummer is, at 86, the embodiment of Scrooge, wearing a top hat and a lined face. But with a twist. Plummer's Scrooge is a figment of Charles Dickens' (Dan Stevens) imagination — a ghost, you might say, haunting Dickens' thoughts as the author collects ideas, quotations and other fragments for his next book following three flops.

A sickly nephew (Pearce Kearney) who gets around with a crutch is the inspiration for Tiny Tim. A wealthy snob (Bill Paterson) extols the necessity of workhouses and decreasing the surplus population. An Irish maid (Anna Murphy) repeats a legend her grandmother used to tell: "On Christmas Eve, the veils between this world and the next thin out, and that's when the spirits cross over and walk among us."

Up against a tight deadline, soaring debt and a returning ne'er-do-well father (Jonathan Pryce), Dickens is constantly visited by the characters of "A Christmas Carol," especially Scrooge, who acts as a taunting conscience — and muse.

From top: Basil Rathbone (1959), George C. Scott (1984), Michael Caine and friends (1992), Bill Murray (1988), Patrick Stewart (1999), Jim Carrey (2009) and Christopher Plummer (2017).

Ralphie (Peter Billingsley) takes aim with his official Red Ryder 200-shot air rifle in "A Christmas Story." Below: The leg lamp.

'A Christmas Story' (1983)

WE THINK "A CHRISTMAS STORY" IS ABOUT the BB gun. But really, it's about the dad.

Young Ralphie (Peter Billingsley) pins all of his hopes and dreams on finding a shiny, new, official Red Ryder carbine-action 200-shot-range model air rifle — the "holy grail of Christmas presents" — under the tree on the big morning. It won't just be a cool Christmas gift. It will redefine him.

The kid is a loner. He's not the smartest boy in class. He is bullied. And he feels like a disappointment to his father (Darren McGavin). But bespectacled Ralphie has honed the ability to daydream his way out of his often joyless existence. In his fantasies, that Red Ryder BB gun transforms him into a heroic figure in a 10-gallon hat.

But, as he does with everything else in his life, Ralphie is gearing up for a letdown. His mom (Melinda Dillon) has already uttered the "classic mother BB gun block," which is — all together, now — "You'll shoot your eye out."

So when Christmas morning comes, and it seems like every last gift has been torn open by Ralphie and his goofy little brother, Randy (Ian Petrella), an all-too-familiar feeling of resignation comes over Ralphie like a heavy cloak.

Another Christmas, another fail.

That's when Ralphie's father points out one more unnoticed gift in a corner. Ralphie's father — who tussles with blown fuses, faulty furnaces, flat tires, Christmas tree salesmen and rowdy neighborhood dogs, and never seems to hear a word

Ralphie says — has a knowing look in his eye.

The wrapped box appears to be the perfect shape and size to hold a Red Ryder BB gun.

Bob Clark's "A Christmas Story" is set in the 1940s. The exact year is unspecified, but there are war toys at Higbee's Department Store, and Bing Crosby songs from 1943 are heard. The action takes place in cold, icy Indiana in the days before Christmas.

The script was co-written by Jean Shepherd, derived from his radio monologues. (Many fans of the film assume the adventures of Ralphie are based on Shepherd's real-life experiences, but this is not strictly the case.) Shepherd also narrates the film as the "adult" Ralphie.

Ralphie's father is, himself, something of a sad sack, one who has grown accustomed to life's little indignities. It's there in Ralphie's observations of his father, such as: "The Old Man could replace fuses quicker than a jackrabbit on a date" ... "(He is) one of the most feared furnace fighters in northern Indiana" ... "In the heat of battle, my father wove a tapestry of obscenity that, as far as we know, is still hanging in space over Lake Michigan" ... "Some men are Baptists, others Catholics. My father was an Oldsmobile man" ...

So how does a movie make a lamp shaped like a woman's leg — complete with fishnet stocking, heel and tassled skirt — into holiday iconography? "A Christmas Story" is a one-of-a-kind, a perfect illustration of the truism, "The more specific something is, the more universal."

PEOPLE BINGE-WATCH THE FILM BECAUSE IT
tells truths. We've all known a bully like Scut Farkas (Zack Ward), of whom adult Ralphie narrates: "He had yellow eyes! So help me God, yellow eyes!" We've all had a distant, older relation who tended to send us duds as Christmas gifts, though Aunt Clara's bunny onesie takes the fluffy, pink cake. (Says adult Ralphie: "Aunt Clara had, for years, labored under the delusion that I was not only perpetually 4 years old, but also a girl.")

We're reminded of our own pasts when we see timeless kid stuff like Randy being (over)dressed for the snow ... Ralphie letting slip the "queen mother of dirty words" ... the Bumpus' motley dogs ... and Flick (Scott Schwartz) ill-advisedly taking a triple-dog-dare by placing his tongue on a pole in December.

Even the timely 1940s stuff rings a bell, such as "The Little Orphan Annie Show" sponsored by "rich, chocolate-y Ovaltine," which yields the anticlimactic Little Orphan Annie Secret Society Decoder Pin.

The leg lamp is a reflection of the Old Man's frustrations. He learns that a "major award" will be coming his way. (We assume it's some sort of a sweepstakes prize.) Victories are few and far between for this man, and in his wild anticipation, he has built the thing out of proportion.

It arrives unceremoniously in a crate marked with the Italian word *fragilé* — or maybe it's just the English word "fragile." He is rendered speechless by its beauty. His wife is aghast. His boys are confused. On some subconscious impulse, Ralphie reaches up the "skirt."

Where to display so exquisite a work of art? Nothing less than the front parlor window will do. "It could be seen up and down Cleveland Street, a symbol of the Old Man's victory," says adult Ralphie.

But the Old Man is crestfallen, near tears, when his precious leg lamp is broken under mysterious circumstances. (Narrator: "With as much dignity as he could muster, the Old Man gathered up the sad remains of his shattered major award.")

"A Christmas Story" wraps with one more truism: having Christmas dinner at the Chop Suey Palace. In a sense, haven't we all been there? Even if it was eating a Swanson's Frozen Turkey Dinner on Thanksgiving, or a McDonald's Big Breakfast on Easter morning.

Flick (Scott Schwartz) painfully accepts a triple-dog-dare.

Town bully Scut Farkas (Zack Ward) enjoys his work.

Ralphie's "pink nightmare"

Ralphie is dispatched by a store elf (Drew Hocevar) as Santa Claus (Jeff Gillen) waves goodbye. *"A Christmas Story"* © Metro-Goldwyn-Mayer

133

From top left: The holy grail of Christmas trees; Clark (Chevy Chase) enjoys the attention of a lingerie salesperson (Nicolette Scorsese); Cousin Eddie (Randy Quaid) tidies up; Clark finds a trove of home movies; Clark's fantasy; the Griswolds rejoice.

"National Lampoon's Christmas Vacation" © Warner Bros. Pictures

134

'National Lampoon's Christmas Vacation' (1989)

EVEN THE MOST RABID FAN OF "NATIONAL LAMP-
oon's Christmas Vacation" couldn't say the film has a finely crafted script. It's mostly a series of holiday tropes jazzed up with
broad, incongruous slapstick. And let's face it: The Scrooge surrogate's climactic salvation is cynically written and hard to swallow.

But the film itself has yielded some indelible holiday tropes.

The most garishly overdecorated home on a given block is
often called a "Clark Griswold house." Cousin Eddie, with his
dilapidated trailer and chemical toilet, symbolizes every unwel-
come, ne'er-do-well relative who darkens one's doorstep over the
holidays. And who can hear "Mele Kalikimaka" — Bing Crosby's
Hawaiian-themed Christmas song of 1950 — without picturing
Nicolette Scorsese peeling off her red bathing suit on the diving
board of Clark's fantasy swimming pool?

All that, and the occasional touching moment, makes
"Christmas Vacation" a cut above forgettable '80s-'90s holiday
drivel like "Santa Claus: The Movie" and "Jingle All the Way."

"Christmas Vacation" — written by John Hughes, directed by
Jeremiah S. Chechik — repeats the formula from its predecessor,
1983's "National Lampoon's Vacation." Clark (Chevy Chase) is
optimistic to the point of manic, and dead-set on having family
fun, *no matter what*. Aiming to keep the peace is Clark's wife,
Ellen (Beverly D'Angelo), as their two sullen teenagers (Juliette
Lewis and Johnny Galecki) roll their eyes at Clark's polly-
anna-ish outlook in the face of disaster.

"An old-fashioned family Christmas" is what
Clark professes to want. But as with most
inept father figures in the movies, what
Clark wants for his family is *really* what
he wants for himself.

The Scrooge of the film is Frank
Shirley (Brian Doyle-Murray), the
Napoleonic CEO of the company
Clark works for. There, Clark's
big-gun project is the Crunch
Enhancer, a "non-nutritive cereal
varnish." Explains Clark to a
colleague: "It's semi-permeable
... it coats and seals the flake,
prevents the milk from penetrat-
ing it."

Shirley has taken notice of
the innovation, if not
Clark's name. Clark is certain this recognition will
translate into a big, fat
holiday bonus — which
will pay for the swimming
pool he's already put a down
payment on as a sur-
prise Christmas gift

for his family. (Hmmm, are you sensing a setup here?)

Then come the tropes — and the gratuitous slapstick. When
the Griswolds drive to a Christmas tree farm, Clark gets in a road
rage contest and careens precariously beneath a gigantic tractor
trailer. A sledding expedition goes haywire when an experimental
lubricant is applied to Clark's sled. As he puts up his exterior
house lights, Clark staples his sleeve to his gutter. Stuff like that.

But there's a bit more going on here. It dawns on us that Clark
is something of an outsider in his own home. When both sets of
grandparents stay over for the holiday, Clark skips a family breakfast. While trapped in a cold attic as the rest of his family goes on
a shopping outing, he gets teary-eyed watching old home movies.

THE FILM REALLY COMES ALIVE WHEN COUSIN
Eddie (Randy Quaid in the role of a lifetime) shows up with his
motley brood in tow, including a large dog named Snots. Scato-
logical humor alert: Somehow, it's become a heartwarming holiday tradition to watch Eddie in front of Clark's home in his bath-
robe, Meister Brau in hand, emptying his trailer's toilet into the
sewer, and volunteering to Clark's yuppie neighbors: "Merry
Christmas! S***er was full!" It wouldn't be Christmas without it.

But it's hard to summon that "Christmas miracle" feeling when
the miracle is a fat corporate bonus meant to pay for a swimming
pool. (Not exactly Dickensian, is it? But, hey, this *was*
the '80s, when "Greed is good" was a mantra.)

"Christmas Vacation" boasts several references to old classics. Frank Capra's "It's a
Wonderful Life" is watched on TV. When
Clark — in manic phase — chainsaws a
post on his staircase, it's akin to Jimmy
Stewart's exasperation at a loose post
in Capra's film. During a meltdown,
Clark exclaims: "We're going to have
the hap-hap-happiest Christmas since
Bing Crosby tap-danced with Danny
(expletive) Kaye!"

And *speaking* of old classics,
"Christmas Vacation" gave a sweet,
career-capping moment to Mae Questel,
then 80, as doddering Aunt Bethany. In
the '30s, Questel was the voice of Betty
Boop and Olive Oyl. You can still hear it,
plain as day, when she sings "The Star-
Spangled Banner," as Clark's flaming
decorations become airborne, following an explosion triggered by
Eddie's, um, discards. Questel
then exclaims "Play
ball!" — her final
words in her
final film.

Clark cracks up.
© Warner Bros. Pictures

Short & sweet

The first question for modern audiences: What was a "short"?

In the olden days — that is, prior to the proliferation of TV — when you went to the movies, you were provided with a full evening of entertainment. The main feature was preceded by these things alternately called "film shorts," "short films" or just "shorts." These could be comedies, histories, how-to films, travelogues, newsreels (the forerunner of television news) or cartoons.

Top animators of the period made holiday shorts: Walt Disney, Max and Dave Fleischer, Jack Hannah, Wilfred Jackson, Rudolph Ising, Burt Gillett, Seymour Kneitel, Ub Iwerks, Bill Tytla and Izzy Sparber.

But Hollywood wasn't the only purveyor of Christmas-y shorts. Some were imported from Czechoslovakia ("A Christmas Dream"), England ("Christmas is Coming"), and Russia ("The Christmas Visitor").

IF ONE SHORT CAN BE SAID

to encapsulate the holiday *and* the period, it is Dave Fleischer's color gem "Christmas Comes But Once a Year" (1936), 8-minutes-and-change about an old, bearded professor who rescues Christmas for a poverty-stricken orphanage.

Legacy-wise, Fleischer Studios was overshadowed, to put it mildly, by their onetime competitor Walt Disney. But where Disney's output emphasizes family friendliness, the Fleischer brothers' stuff can be downright *weird*. "Koko the Clown" shorts are acid trips; "Popeye" shorts celebrate violence; "Betty Boop" shorts idle at fetishy. Kraków-born Max Fleischer's rotoscoping

---

Prof. Grampy is the MacGyver of Santas in "Christmas Comes But Once a Year" (1936).

process, whereby character movement became smoother and more realistic, changed forever the art of animation.

The Fleischers' penchant for innovation is on full display in the 1936 Christmas short. Prof. Grampy sets about creating toys out of kitchen doo-dads and household clutter. A washboard, wooden hangers and crowbars become a sled. A coffee percolator, teapot, serving forks and plateware become a choo-choo train. A sewing machine, funnel, portable stove and a box of unpopped corn become an automatic popcorn stringer. When Grampy — truly the MacGyver of the Santa set — lights up a rotating "tree" (made of umbrellas) for the orphans, rotoscoping is employed to charming effect.

LIVE-ACTION SHORTS ALSO RANG IN the season. Members of the Three Stooges donned Santa costumes in five of their comedy shorts (though two of these used recycled footage). "Star in the Night" (1945) is a thinly disguised update of the First Noël, with three gift-bearing cowpokes as stand-ins for the Wise Men, and the grumpy proprietor of a cafe in the middle of a dark desert (J. Carrol Naish) refusing shelter to a Mexican woman who is about to have a baby. "Silent Night: The Story of the Christmas Carol" (1953) is a history and travelogue in fuzzy color that brings viewers to quaint, storied Oberndorf, Austria, to learn how the hymn "Silent Night" came into existence. Theaters also screened interactive singalong shorts from Fleischer Studios and Paramount, in which patrons were invited to sing hymns and carols by following a "bouncing ball" atop printed lyrics. A movie theater full of neighborhood folks united in song? This *was* a less jaded time.

'Midnight in a Toy Shop'

(1930) Director: Wilfred Jackson

In this peyote nightmare of a kiddie film, a blizzard rages outside of Ye Toy Shoppe. Seeking shelter, a spider slips through a keyhole and learns that a toy shop after dark is a creepy place. As the spider dances on a piano, dormant toys come to life: elephants, soldiers, Jack-in-the-boxes, rocking horses, monkey puppets, a teddy bear band, and a stereotypical black doll that says "Mammy." (Apparently, racism was inescapable back then.) A box of ignited firecrackers puts an end to the mayhem. Jackson later directed "Cinderella," "Peter Pan" and "Lady and the Tramp."

'Mickey's Orphans'

(1931) Director: Burt Gillett

At Christmastime, a woman in a raggedy shawl leaves a basket of kittens at the doorstep of Mickey Mouse. After he, Minnie Mouse and Pluto take in the diaper-clad kittens, we learn *why* they're unwanted. The little monsters destroy Mickey's house by sawing, axing and hammering the piano, furniture and lamps; and breaking the windows and china. Even after Mickey dresses as Santa and gives presents to the kittens, they drop hot embers from the fireplace down his pants! Gillett directed 90 shorts between 1920 and '40, including the Oscar-winning "Three Little Pigs."

'Toy Time'

(1932) Directors: John Foster, Harry Bailey

In a plot reminiscent of "Midnight in a Toy Shop," a mouse couple has a romantic evening in a toy store after hours. They dance on a xylophone, drums, and a clarinet. But their dalliance is interrupted when they are pursued by a mean, mangy cat. They confuse the cat using a windup mouse, soldiers, a toy cannon, and a blowup cat, which explodes and vanquishes the antagonist. The boy mouse then serenades his girlfriend at the piano. *Awww.* The short was part of the "Aesop's Fables" series from Van Beuren Studios, a predecessor and competitor of Walt Disney.

'Santa's Workshop'

(1932) Director: Wilfred Jackson

At Santa's headquarters, elves cheerily paint the sleigh and groom the reindeer as their boss sorts through the mail. Santa's cranky secretary brings children's wish lists into the factory, which is a whirlwind of activity. Santa apparently adopted Henry Ford's assembly-line model. Rocking horses, for instance, are shown being constructed in five stages. Doll faces and checkerboards are painted, dresses are sewn and ironed. It's charming, inventive, and funny. But political incorrectness again rears its ugly head with toys based on old black, Asian and Jewish stereotypes.

'The Night Before Christmas'

(1933) Director: Wilfred Jackson

On Christmas Eve, eight children sleep in a single bed (with a ninth child hidden under a conspicuous patch in the blanket). Santa and his reindeer make a slippery landing on their snowy roof. He slides down the chimney, shakes off soot and endures a butt burn. When Santa opens his bag, a parade of toys marches out to decorate the tree. (There's even a Mickey Mouse toy.) Christmas balls are shot onto the branches with toy canons; a circling airplane wraps holly around the tree; a dirigible places the star on top. This was Jackon's sequel to "Santa's Workshop."

© Walt Disney Productions

'Parade of the Wooden Soldiers'

(1933) Director: Dave Fleischer

A Betty Boop doll, complete with negligee, garter and heels, arrives at a toy shop. She utters her first words — "Boop-oop-a-doop," naturally — and spins her head like Linda Blair in "The Exorcist." This animates the wooden soldiers, who play a fanfare on tiny trumpets, awakening the other toys. Their revelry annoys a large gorilla toy who makes like King Kong, wreaking destruction and snatching Betty. (This was one year after the release of the movie "King Kong.") The title song is performed by Russian violinist David Rubinoff, who appears "live" in the film.

© Famous Studios

'The Shanty Where Santy Claus Lives'

(1933) Directors: Hugh Harmon, Rudolph Ising

An urchin who resembles a Dead End Kids refugee enters a hovel to escape the cold. Turns out, Santy Claus lives there! The boy hops on Santy's sleigh and they fly to his shop, where the toys come to life. A Kate Smith figure sings a snippet of "Shine on Harvest Moon." Bagpipes extinguish a Christmas tree fire. But — here we go again — there are three instances of offensive stereotypes: the "Sambo jazz band," dancing "pickaninnies," and a doll that tumbles into a coal shuttle, emerges covered in soot, and exclaims (as if you haven't guessed) "Mammy!"

© Warner Bros. Pictures

'Christmas Night'

(1933) Director: James Tyer

The fat, bearded Little King — traveling on Christmas Eve via a "litter" manned by ice-skating minions — joins two unkempt hobos ogling toys through a store window. The King brings the bums home, where they all disrobe, share a bathtub and a bed. (Um, these things happened in the olden days.) Santa arrives, drills a hole in the tile floor, and plants instant Christmas-tree seeds. The Little King was the star of a syndicated comic strip by Otto Soglow, which ran for 45 years beginning in 1930. Van Beuren made 13 Little King shorts between 1933 and '36.

© Van Beuren Studios

'Jack Frost'

(1936) Director: Ub Iwerks

Elf-like Jack Frost arrives in the forest with a palette and brush, painting green leaves into fall colors. "Summer's gone, play no more, for winter's knocking at your door," he warns the animals. A bear family hibernates, but the little boy bear sneaks out. He encounters autumnal creatures such as dancing Jack o'lanterns and a scat-singing scarecrow, before the forest is enveloped in snow. Old Man Winter — fearsome in blue with a long, snow-white beard — imprisons the bear in a log. Can Jack Frost save him? Iwerks co-created Mickey Mouse with Walt Disney.

© Celebrity Productions Inc.

'Christmas Comes But Once a Year'

(1936) Director: Dave Fleischer

At a dilapidated orphanage, toddlers awake to one *sad* Christmas. A dry, dead Christmas tree sags. Tattered stockings hang over an unlit fireplace. Someone left toys for the children, but they are faulty. A tricycle falls apart on its maiden journey, a teddy bear disintegrates. Soon, the children are all bawling. "What's the matter here, I wonder?" says Prof. Grampy before entering. Christmas magic ensues. Jack Mercer (Popeye) and Mae Questel (Olive Oyl) provided voice talent. The theme was composed by longtime pros Sammy Timberg (music) and Bob Rothberg (lyrics).

© Famous Studios

'A Christmas Dream'

(1945) Director: Karel Zeman

In this charming Czechoslovakian film that mixes live action with stop-motion animation, a girl forsakes her worn rag doll for the new toys under the Christmas tree. As she sleeps, a ghost-like vision of Santa Claus appears and gives her a dream in which the rag doll comes to life and says, "I'm still a lot of fun even though you have new Christmas toys!" He dances on a piano and "skates" on the piano's polished lid. The Santa footage was added to the American version. Austria-Hungary native Karel Zeman directed seven "Voyage of Sinbad" shorts in the 1970s.

© Castle Films

'The Night Before Christmas'

(1946) Director: Uncredited

The famous poem is enacted in this cute — but *weird* — old-fashioned short that mixes live action with animation. As three children sleep in their bed, cartoon sugar plums dance over their heads. Scenes of Santa Claus and his "eight tiny reindeer" flying through the night sky are done in cartoon form, while close-ups of Santa calling the reindeer's names show an actor in costume. Inside the children's home, Santa smokes a pipe and laughs maniacally, in a movie moment that would be right at home in "Reefer Madness" or Ed Wood's "Glen or Glenda."

© Castle Films

'Santa's Surprise'

(1947) Director: Seymour Kneitel

Unbeknownst to Santa, when he returns to the North Pole after satisfying his Christmas Eve duties, he has seven little stowaways: a Latin American girl, a Russian boy, a Chinese boy, an island girl, a Dutch boy, a black boy and the star of the short, Little Audrey. Yes, the black child is drawn as an offensive stereotype —what *else* is new? Still, "Santa's Surprise" is a sweet story in which the kids conspire to clean Santa's house while he sleeps, as a Christmas present. Kneitel spearheaded "Popeye" shorts from the Fleischer brothers' glory days to the not-so-hot TV days.

© Famous Studios

'Hector's Hectic Life'

(1948) Director: Bill Tytla

Poor Hector. He's a dog who is apparently hated by the stout lady of the house. She threatens to throw Hector out in the snow — on Christmas, yet — if he isn't a good boy. There's a knock at the door, and Hector finds a basket containing three puppies with identical markings to his. (So, guess who the *father* is?) Hector brings them in, and the pups wreak havoc, upsetting a fishbowl, tearing open a cushion and destroying the Christmas tree. Will Hector be blamed? For Disney, Tytla earlier played a major role in animating the seven dwarfs and Dumbo.

© Famous Studios

'Rudolph the Red-Nosed Reindeer'

(1948) Director: Max Fleischer

The song "Rudolph the Red-Nosed Reindeer" is *not* heard on the original short, which was released the year before the ditty debuted. The opening credits say "Christmas Greetings from Montgomery Ward," the department store chain that commissioned the Rudolph character. A realistically drawn Santa Claus is seen delivering toys only to animals (deer, bunnies), not human children. Santa awards Rudolph a medal for guiding his sleigh, "the No. 1 job on the No. 1 day." The short was re-released in 1951 with the song added and the Montgomery Ward credit removed.

© Jam Handy Organization

'Toy Tinkers'

(1949) Director: Jack Hannah

Chip 'n' Dale's cozy winter snooze is rudely interrupted by Donald Duck chopping down a tree. The furry little guys follow DD to his abode, where he decorates the tree for Christmas. But what Chip 'n' Dale *really* notice is the abundance of nuts throughout Donald's quarters. Before long, duck and chipmunks are at war, using Christmas toys (presumably earmarked for unseen Huey, Dewey and Louie) as weapons. The short was nominated for an Oscar, and comic-book-icized by Dell. We have Hannah to thank for much of Donald Duck's irascible disposition.

© Walt Disney Productions

'Toys Will Be Toys'

(1949) Director: Seymour Kneitel

We're back in a toy shop after dark. A cuckoo clock sentry announces, "All is well. Day is done. Come on, toys. Have your fun!" This short has celebrity "cameos": A Carmen Miranda-esque doll; a Harpo-Marx-in-the-box; a "ski slide" in the image of Bob Hope; even Popeye. There's a "mammy" doll (ugh, will it *never* end?) and boxing kangaroos (a Rock 'Em Sock 'Em Robots precursor). It all ends in a sing-along to "Oh, You Beautiful Doll." The same year, the George Jessel-produced musical "Oh, You Beautiful Doll" was released, based on the song composed in 1911.

© Famous Studios

'Christmas is Coming'

(1951) Director: Lotte Reiniger

In fascinating silhouette-style animation, angels prepare for Christmas by trimming a tree and prepping Santa Claus' boots. But cranky Santa declares: "I'm on strike!" The angels appeal to St. Peter, who says all will be well if people mail their parcels by Dec. 19 and cards by Dec. 20. "Christmas is Coming" is a brief (one-minute) public service announcement from England encouraging folks to mail their Christmas-related items on time. The silhouette technique was executed by Reiniger, a revered animator who fled Germany during the rise of the Nazi party.

© BFI National Archive

'The Three Little Dwarfs'

(1951) Director: Uncredited

In captivating stop-motion animation, Santa is joined on his Christmas Eve trek by "three little men only two feet high, singing to Santa way up in the sky." The action is narrated via a holiday ditty sung by an a capella chorus. The elves are Hardrock, the driver; Coco, the navigator; and the candy cane-wielding Joe, whose talents are unspecified. (From the song: "Though old Santa really has no need for Joe, he takes him 'cause he loves him so.") This TV short became a Christmas Eve tradition on certain local television stations, notably WGN in Chicago.

© Centaur Productions

'True Boo'

(1952) Director: Izzy Sparber

On Christmas Eve at Casper's creepy homestead, the young ghost writes to Santa asking for a friend. He then heads downtown to *find* one. Casper plays Santa for a poor child, making like Prof. Grampy from "Christmas Comes But Once a Year" and improvising toys on the fly. He fashions a bow-and-arrow with a toilet plunger; a rocking horse from an ottoman, broom and rocking-chair legs; and, stealing directly from Grampy, an airplane from a curtain rod and spoon; and a percolating coffee-pot choo-choo. This is the 16th "Casper" short in a series that began in 1945.

© Harvey Films, Inc.

'The Story of the Tin Soldier'

(1956) Director: Uncredited

Hans Christian Andersen's "The Steadfast Tin Soldier" is loosely adapted in an episode of TV's "Mr. Piper." A spoiled boy receives a tin soldier for Christmas, but is disappointed: "Why, it doesn't move!" His sister is likewise unhappy with her ballerina. "This silly soldier can guard my doll," she says, and the siblings relegate the toys to a shelf. When the soldier and ballerina fall in love, a Jack-in-the box plots to thwart their budding romance. "Mr. Piper" host Alan Crofoot, who sings in a booming tenor, played Mr. Bumble in "Oliver" on Broadway in 1965.

© Productions Unlimited

'The Star of Bethlehem'

(1956) Directors: Lotte Reiniger, Vivian Milroy

Another silhouette-style animated short from German film-maker Reiniger, "The Star of Bethlehem" introduces a shepherd boy who plays a wooden flute for his animal friends. When Jesus is born in Bethlehem, the boy is among those who present a gift to the child — his flute. The animation (in which characters are seen in black shapes against color backgrounds) is, by design, not "smooth," but fascinating to watch. The short was produced by Rev. James K. Friedrich for Cathedral Films, which released 170 films on biblical topics from 1939 to '68.

© Cathedral Films

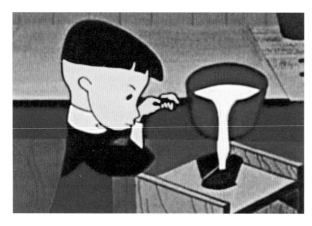

'The Candlemaker'

(1957) Directors: John Halas, Joy Batchelor

Every Saturday, young Tom's father the candlemaker delivers a pair of tall, perfect, white candles to the church for Sunday service. In the days before Christmas, the candlemaker must leave home to deliver Christmas candles to far-flung customers. He entrusts Tom with a sacred mission: to make the second of the two church candles, and deliver them on time. The simple, exquisite animation is by Hungarian Halas and his wife, British Batchelor, who co-directed "Animal Farm" (1954), an adaptation of the George Orwell novel and England's first animated feature.

© Cathedral Films

'The First Christmas'

(1959) Director: Uncredited

The story of the First Noël is told using puppets. But *these* puppets are not animated via stop-motion; these are true puppets, with fluid movement furnished by unseen human hands. The vibe is very religious, but the beautifully sculpted puppets — they look like a Nativity set come to life — will hold children's interest. The black-and-white lighting is moody and effective. The Mary and Joseph puppets are given large, circular halos that appear almost sci-fi-ish. "The First Christmas" was the final of 24 Christmas-themed shorts from Castle Films (1924-77).

© Castle Films

'The Christmas Visit'

(1959) Director: Pyotr Nosov

A boy in Moscow trims his Christmas tree with lion, whale and penguin decorations. (Hint: It's *foreshadowing*.) His father, a weatherman, is away in Antarctica. "If only there was some way Daddy could have a Christmas tree," the boy laments. He encounters Santa, who flies around in a plane made of stars, sort of like Wonder Woman. Santa lends the boy his plane, and makes the rest of his deliveries in a cab (!). The boy then encounters ... a lion, a whale and a penguin. This enchanting Russian short is beautifully drawn, with just a bit of lost-in-translation weirdness.

© Soyuzmultfilm

'The Christmas Visitor'

(1959) Director: John Halas

With its very '50s, very modern look, this British short offers twists on both "The Night Before Christmas" and "The Steadfast Tin Soldier." Santa is delivering toys when he spies a bit of repast left for him by children: cookies, wine and a cigar. (The kids must've had input from their parents.) While Santa digs in, the toys come to life. A sailor in a boat and a girl on a music box are threatened by a Jack-in-the-box that bounces around on its spring. The villain ties the girl to toy train tracks, a la "Perils of Pauline." Halas' wife, Joy Batchelor, co-wrote the script with Halas.

© Halas and Batchelor Cartoon Films

'Spinach Greetings'

(1960) Director: Seymour Knietel

"Everyone's happy at this time of the year, and it's all Santa Claus' fault," says the wicked Sea Hag who — like her fellow green-skinned Christmas-hater, the Grinch — wants to stop the holiday. When she dispatches her purple vulture to kidnap Santa, the Jolly One's reindeer-design plane crashlands at Popeye's house. The episode gets a bit morbid when Popeye shows up at the Sea Hag's ramshackle abode with the vulture killed, plucked and roasted on a platter, saying, "Does you likes yours with or without stuffins?" Popeye veteran Knietel also wrote the script.

© King Features Syndicate

'When the Littlest Camel Knelt'

(1963) Director: Al Joyce

A revisiting of the Nativity, this time through the eyes of the Littlest Camel, who is "wooly in spots and curious all over." Upon hearing older camels Cappy and Mogo brag about carrying gifts to a king, the Littlest Camel dearly wants to do the same. As the three Wise Men organize their expedition, the older camels are too tired to make the trek, so the Littlest Camel is pressed into service. When the party stops at a modest stable instead of a marble palace, the Littlest Camel is confused. There is no actual animation in the short; illustrations are panned-and-scanned.

© Cathedral Films

Not exactly Christmas movies

YOU'RE WATCHING FRANCIS FORD COPPOLA'S "The Godfather" (1972). Somewhere between "I'm gonna make him an offer he can't refuse" and "Leave the gun, take the cannoli," suddenly it becomes a *Christmas* movie. Mike and Kay go shopping in Manhattan! Tommy Hagen buys a sled for the kiddies!

It's a special sub-category of film, and a fun thing to spot for movie buffs: Non-Christmas Movies That Have Christmas in Them. "The Man Who Came to Dinner" (1942) is set during the holiday, but it just *feels* more like a drawing-room comedy. "Christmas Eve" (1947) has Christmas in the *title*, but at heart, it's a lightweight comedy with George Raft. "Double Dynamite" (1951) isn't on many must-watch-at-Christmas lists, but much of it is set during the holiday. Other movies have brief sequences set at Christmastime, such as Jack Lemmon's drunken encounter with Santa in "The Apartment" (1960); Mia Farrow's ill-fated meetup in "Rosemary's Baby" (1968); and Divine's meltdown over not getting cha-cha heels for Christmas in "Female Trouble" (1974).

Harry Earles and Lon Chaney Sr. (wearing drag) bamboozle Matthew Betz in "The Unholy Three" (1925). © Metro-Goldwyn-Mayer

Stan Laurel and Oliver Hardy play bumbling Christmas tree salesmen in "Big Business" (1929). © Metro-Goldwyn-Mayer

Myrna Loy and William Powell as Nora and Nick Charles toast the season in "The Thin Man" (1934). © Metro-Goldwyn Mayer

Arthur Hohl as a miniaturized man scurries beneath a Christmas tree in "The Devil-Doll" (1936). © Metro-Goldwyn-Mayer

Barbara Stanwyck, left, Fred MacMurray, center, and fellow cast members in "Remember the Night" (1940). © Paramount Pictures

Know-it-all World War I soldier James Cagney drops in on Christmas Eve Mass in "The Fighting 69th" (1940). © Warner Bros.

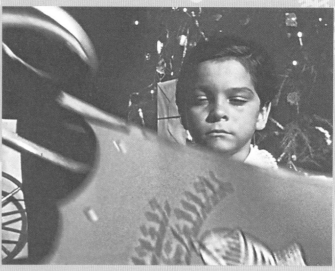

Young Charles Foster Kane (Buddy Swann) regards a Christmas present in Orson Welles' "Citizen Kane" (1941). © RKO Radio Pictures

Bette Davis in the film adaptation of the Broadway comedy "The Man Who Came to Dinner" (1942). © Warner Bros.

Judy Garland sings "Have Yourself a Merry Little Christmas" to Margaret O'Brien in "Meet Me in St. Louis" (1944). © Metro-Goldwyn-Mayer

Ann Carter has an overactive imagination — or does she? — in "The Curse of the Cat People" (1944). © RKO Radio Pictures

Bing Crosby reprises Father O'Malley opposite Ingrid Bergman as a nun in "The Bells of St. Mary's" (1945). © RKO Radio Pictures

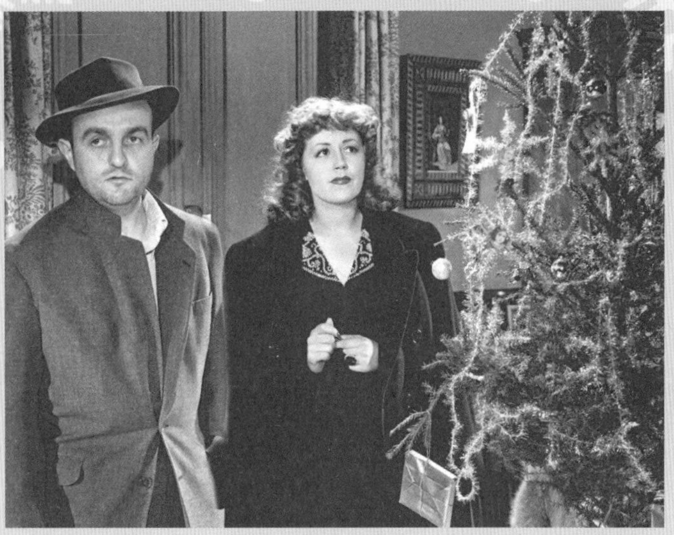

Bernard Blier, Suzy Delair and tree in Henri-Georges Clouzot's French drama "Quai Des Orfèvres" (1947). © Coronis

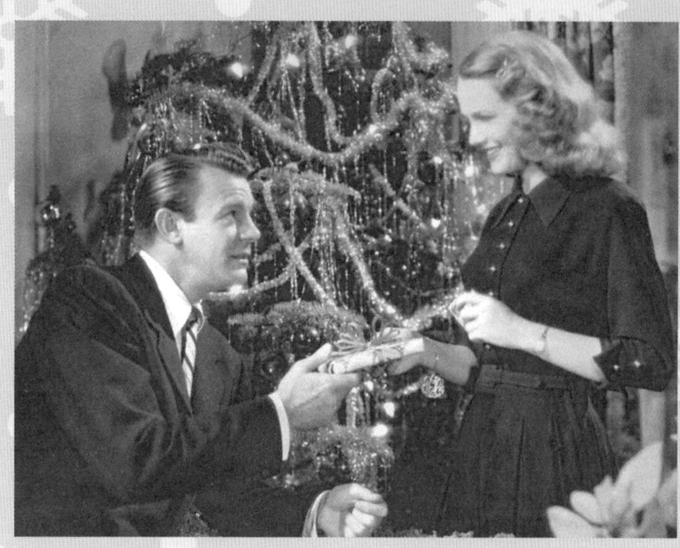

Dennis O'Keefe and Barbara Britton take a breather from a murder investigation in "Cover Up" (1949). © Strand Productions

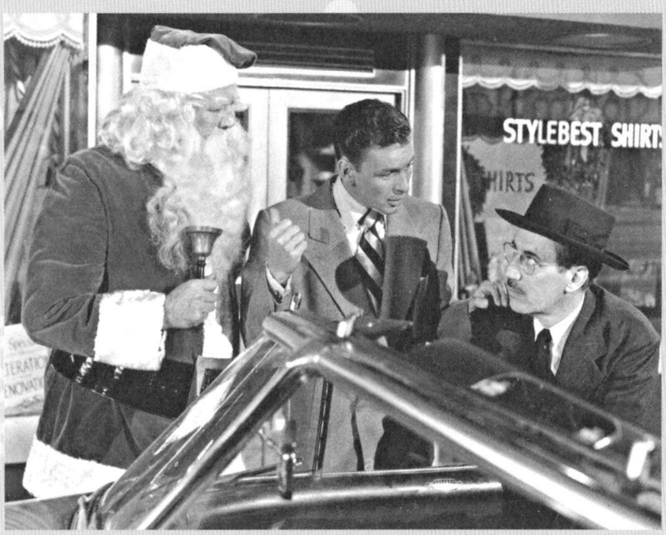
STYLEBEST SHIRTS

Ring-a-ding-ding! Frank Sinatra, Groucho Marx and a street Santa confer in "Double Dynamite" (1951). © RKO Radio Pictures

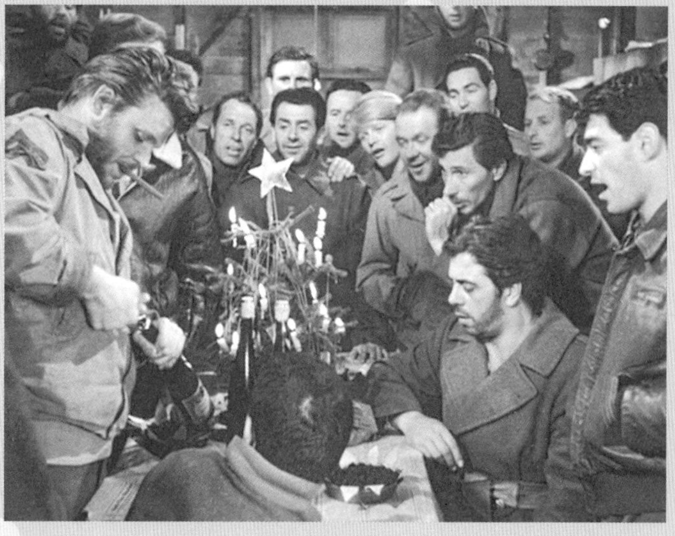

Neville Brand, left, Robert Strauss, seated, and fellow cast members mark the holiday in "Stalag 17" (1953). © Paramount Pictures

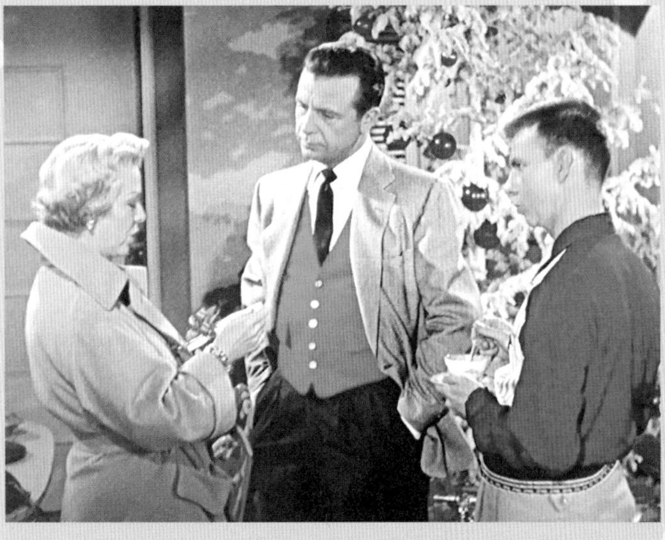

Glenda Farrell, Dick Powell and Alvy Moore confab by the Christmas tree in "Susan Slept Here" (1954). © RKO Radio Pictures

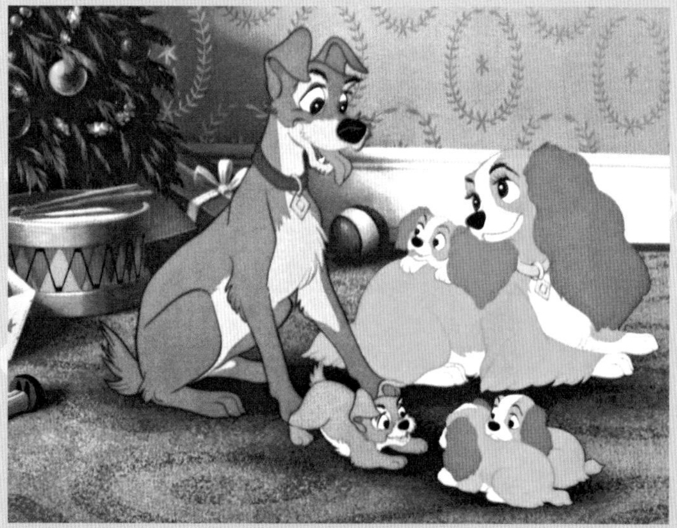

Tramp and Lady enjoy their growing family in the animated feature "Lady and the Tramp" (1955). © Walt Disney Productions

Escaped prisoners Humphrey Bogart and Aldo Ray decorate for a holiday party in "We're No Angels" (1955). © Paramount Pictures

Katharine Hepburn (in red), Joan Blondell and co-workers have an office Christmas party in "Desk Set" (1957). © 20th Century Fox

Dour Jack Lemmon gives the stink-eye to jolly Hal Smith in Billy Wilder's "The Apartment" (1960). © United Artists

Mike Mazurki portrays one of the Wise Men at a Christmas pageant in John Ford's "Donovan's Reef" (1963). © Paramount Pictures

Rosemary (Mia Farrow) awaits a friend she'll never see again in Roman Polanski's "Rosemary's Baby" (1968). © Paramount Pictures

Diane Keaton and Al Pacino get in a little holiday fun before receiving bad news in "The Godfather" (1972). © Paramount Pictures

Dawn Davenport (Divine, right) gets a big Christmas-morning letdown in John Waters' "Female Trouble" (1974). © Dreamland

Oliver Reed, Barry Winch and Ann-Margret have an uneasy Christmas morning in "Tommy" (1975). © Robert Stigwood Organisation L.T.D.

Christopher Plummer plays a gun-brandishing Santa in the Canadian thriller "The Silent Partner" (1978). © Carolco Pictures

Brian Backer and Robert Romanus talk about (what else?) girls in "Fast Times at Ridgemont High" (1982). © Universal Studios

Batman (Michael Keaton) basks in the splendor that is Gotham City at Christmastime in "Batman Returns" (1992). © Warner Bros.

Down-and-out Charlie (Michael Townsend Wright) is given a gift in "The Life and Times of Charlie Putz" (1994). © Radmks

Christmas with the Stooges

"Some people think that Ebenezer Scrooge is / Well he's not, but guess who is? / All Three Stooges," sings Adam Sandler in "The Chanukah Song," his correction to the dearth of Chanukah music in pop culture, and a comical shout-out to Jewish celebrities.

Of course, there were actually *six* Stooges at different points in the long career of the slapstick movie trio, and every lineup participated in some form of Christmas buffoonery.

Bossy Moe Howard, middleman Larry Fine and childlike Jerry "Curly" Howard wear Santa suits in "Wee Wee Monsieur" (1938). Moe and Curly's big brother, Shemp Howard — the original "third Stooge" — dons the white beard and fur-trimmed suit in "Malice in the Palace" (1949) and "He Cooked His Goose" (1952). In the latter short, Moe electrocutes himself while trimming a Christmas tree. Joe Besser, the third "third Stooge," makes like Santa in "Triple Crossed" (1959), a cannibalization of "He Cooked His Goose." And Curly-Joe DeRita, the fourth and final "third Stooge," sang on Christmas recordings with the trio.

Moe Howard, Larry Fine and Jerry "Curly" Howard pose for a publicity photo wearing Santa suits (1938). © Columbia Pictures

Curly, Larry and Moe are delighted to encounter a group of harem girls in "Wee Wee Monsieur" (1938). © Columbia Pictures

Shemp Howard in, yep, a Santa Claus suit examines a pricey bauble in "Malice in the Palace" (1949). © Columbia Pictures

What could go wrong? Moe puts the finishing touch on a Christmas tree in "He Cooked His Goose" (1952). © Columbia Pictures

Joe Besser, Shemp's replacement, takes aim with a fireplace bellow in "Triple Crossed" (1959). © Columbia Pictures

Cathode ray yule

Holiday episodes of beloved TV series give us valuable information about the respective universes (universae?) these shows are set in.

How do they celebrate Christmas in Mayberry? With a skinny Santa and Aunt Bee's turkey.

How do they celebrate Christmas in the Twilight Zone? With a drunken Santa and a magic bag o' gifts.

How do they celebrate Christmas in Bensonhurst? With an orange-juice squeezer in the shape of Napoleon. (The juice comes out of his ears.)

Holiday episodes, which date back to the medium's inception, are like Christmas specials unto themselves, and are often rerun during the season, sometimes as stand-alones or in marathons.

Two tropes that are universal throughout Christmas Culture are prevalent in such episodes, one being the "Christmas miracle." *You* know, the "fifth Santa Claus" in the Ricardos' kitchen … that bag o' gifts found in a trash-strewn alley by Art Carney … Carol Brady regaining her singing voice in time for the Christmas church service … the scruffy patrons of a "greasy spoon" pooling their change to pay for Kelsey Grammer's Christmas platter …

The second universal trope is the redemption of a surrogate Scrooge. That would be low-down old Ben Weaver on "The Andy Griffith Show" … skeptical orphan Billy Mumy on "Bewitched"… skeptical advertising client Charles Lane, also on "Bewitched" … spoiled rich brat Butch Patrick on "The Monkees" …

Season sampler: Series with Christmas episodes

Comedy: "The Honeymooners," "I Love Lucy," "Our Miss Brooks," "Amos 'n Andy," "Burns and Allen," "Topper," "Make Room For Daddy," "Father Knows Best," "Ozzie and Harriet," "Dobie Gillis," "The Donna Reed Show," "Dennis the Menace," "McHale's Navy," "Lassie," "The Andy Griffith Show," "Hazel," "The Lucy Show," "The Beverly Hillbillies," "The Dick Van Dyke Show," "Bewitched," "The Patty Duke Show," "The Addams Family," "Petticoat Junction," "Gilligan's Island," "Family Affair," "The Monkees," "Green Acres," "The Flying Nun," "The Odd Couple," "That Girl," "Julia," "The Brady Bunch," "The Partridge Family," "The Mary Tyler Moore Show," "All in the Family," "The Jeffersons," "Maude," "M*A*S*H," "Happy Days," "Welcome Back, Kotter," "Good Times," "The Simpsons." **Drama:** "Racket Squad," "Highway Patrol," "Dr. Kildare," "Alfred Hitchcock Presents," "The Twilight Zone," "The Man From U.N.C.L.E.," "Adam 12." **Western:** "Annie Oakley," "The Lone Ranger," "Gunsmoke," "Wagon Train," "Bonanza," "Daniel Boone." **Kids' stuff:** "Howdy Doody," "The Flintstones," "Davey and Goliath" … and on and on.

IN TV'S EARLY DAYS, ANTHOLOGY DRAMAS WERE
a staple. Some of these yielded Christmas episodes that remain watchable and relevant, despite old-fashioned production values.

In 1955, "The 20th Century Fox Hour" presented a thoughtfully condensed adaptation of the 1947 film "Miracle on 34th Street" for television. It starred Thomas Mitchell — Uncle Billy from "It's a Wonderful Life" — as Kris Kringle. Teresa Wright played the Maureen O'Hara role; Sandy Descher played the Natalie Wood role; and Macdonald Carey played the John Payne role.

More anthology series that presented Christmas episodes were "Actors Studio," "The Alcoa Hour," "Cavalcade of America," "Fireside Theatre," "General Electric Theater," "Gruen Guild Playhouse," "Hallmark Hall of Fame," "Kraft Television Theatre," "The Loretta Young Show," "Lux Video Theatre," "Schlitz Playhouse of Stars," "Studio 57," and "Westinghouse Studio One."

THERE WAS THE RECURRING TENDENCY FOR A
gritty (or gritty-*ish*) dramatic series which didn't usually go in for sappiness to put that policy aside for the holiday. We're thinking of shows like "Dragnet," "Racket Squad," "Highway Patrol," "City Detective," "Naked City," "Deadline," "The Untouchables," "The FBI," "Dragnet 1967" (a color reboot), "Adam 12," "The Mod Squad," "Kojak," and "S.W.A.T."

In the holiday episode of "Racket Squad" (1952), an elderly neighborhood man (Lloyd Corrigan) seeks to earn money to buy Christmas gifts for underprivileged local kids. He is "hired" by grifters to collect money for "charity" as a street Santa. Says Captain Haddock (Reed Bradley) in his intro: "It put me on a spot I never want to be put on again. I had to arrest Santa Claus."

In the holiday episode of "Highway Patrol" (1956), gravel-voiced Chief Matthews (Broderick Crawford) investigates the disappearance of a 6-year-old girl (Michelle Ducasse) whose parents are estranged. Carrying a wounded puppy, the girl approaches a street Santa in front of a soup kitchen. She tells him, "Santa? I know just what I want for Christmas: mommy and daddy together."

CHRISTMAS EPISODES PROVIDE AN OPPORTUNITY
for the cast of a given TV series to put their extracurricular talents on display. On "The Andy Griffith Show," Griffith and his TV girlfriend (Elinor Donahue) harmonize on "Away in a Manger." On "The Brady Bunch," Florence Henderson belts out "O Come All Ye Faithful." On "The Dick Van Dyke Show," the cast sings, dances, plays instruments — everything short of juggling.

Few episodes illustrate this better than one from "Car 54, Where Are You?," a police comedy set, and filmed, in the Bronx. In the episode titled "Christmas at the 53rd" (1961), the precinct puts on a holiday variety show for its families. Captain Block (Paul Reed) sings about his leadership prowess; a patrolman (Mickey Deemes) demonstrates the properly worn uniform in a parody of fashion models; Officer Toody (Joe E. Ross) croons "You're Nobody 'Til Somebody Loves You"; Officer Muldoon (Fred Gwynne) sings a ditty about declining respect for the law; Toody's brother-in-law (Carl Ballantine) performs feats of magic; and Muldoon's kind-of girlfriend (Alice Ghostley) sings a torch song. What's affecting is that the episode ends without some big, happy, Christmas-y climax. Following the cops' little variety show, the camera lingers as they cheerlessly return to their duties.

Alice (Audrey Meadows) opens a gift from Mrs. Stevens (Anne Seymour) as Ralph (Jackie Gleason) and Ed (Art Carney) look on.

'The Honeymooners' (Dec. 24, 1955)

MORE THAN ANY OTHER TV SHOW — OR MOVIE, for that matter — "The Honeymooners" Christmas episode, which is mostly set on Christmas Eve, makes the viewer feel like it actually *is* Christmas Eve. Those who watched the original performance live (on stage in New York City and in living rooms across America) were literally seeing it on Dec. 24th.

It has something to do with the intimacy of the live audience ... it is a living, breathing, laughing, coughing organism ... the laughter is the opposite of "canned" ... some gags hang on the precarious thread of audience recognition ... but the audience melds with the players as another cast member ... it's almost mystical ...

And so, oh future generations, whenever you watch this historic episode, this one-of-a-kind, this Christmas miracle unto itself, make sure it's on Christmas Eve.

"The Honeymooners" — starring Jackie Gleason as everyschlub Ralph Kramden, a Brooklyn bus driver with big ideas and a waistline to match — began in 1951 as a recurring skit on the Gleason-hosted "Cavalcade of Stars." The show is best remembered for its so-called "Classic 39" episodes (1955-56), which co-starred Audrey Meadows as Ralph's long-suffering wife Alice, Art Carney as dimwitted sewer worker Ed Norton, and Joyce Randolph as Trixie, Ed's wife and Alice's sounding board.

Ralph and Alice live in a tiny Bensonhurst flat amid worn furniture and ancient facilities. There is love in this household, but the couple squabbles, often about money. During these arguments, Alice — lovely and petite to Ralph's big and blustery — stands her ground, eyes flashing and hands on her apron-clad hips.

The Classic 39 are noted for their play-like feel and realistic quality. "The Honeymooners" is undoubtedly a show that solidified the situation comedy form. Many critics and fans point to it as the greatest sitcom in the medium of television.

In the Christmas episode, the four-person company is joined by only two guest actors. Together, they enact the simple tale of a gift-exchanging fiasco involving deception, near misses, a bit of slapstick, self-reflection, regret and, ultimately, forgiveness. There's an O Henry-esque twist, a stirring soliloquy by Ralph on the spirit of Christmas, and an unprecedented (for the series) breaking of character. All in under 30 minutes.

THESE ELEMENTS ARE SET IN MOTION WHEN TRIXIE drops in on Alice to borrow an orange. Ed, you see, can't wait to demonstrate his Christmas gift to Trixie: an orange juice squeezer in the shape of Napoleon. The juice squirts out of Napoleon's ears.

Later, Ralph shows Ed his gift for Alice, which is no better: a box for hairpins made of 2,000 matchsticks with a secret compartment for bobby pins. But this is no ordinary box. According to the salesman, it was once owned by the emperor of Japan.

When Alice's friend Mrs. Stevens (Anne Seymour) brings Alice a gift, it is — oh, the irony — a box for hairpins made of 2,000 matchsticks with a secret compartment for bobby pins. Mrs. Stevens bought it at a novelty store, and she is a bit embarrassed, as the kitchen thermometer Alice got her is so much nicer.

Realizing he was duped, Ralph makes a full confession to Ed: He had saved $22 for Alice's gift, but instead bought a bowling ball. "I had to be selfish and think of myself," laments Ralph, facing the reality that he is flat broke without a gift. What now?

The festivities end with Ralph's little speech about the power of Christmas. He talks about how people who might bump into each other on a busy street are less likely to react with anger: *"Especially when it gets real close to Christmas night. Everybody's walkin' home. You can hardly hear a sound. ... And, boy, what a pleasure it is to think that you got some place to go to, and the place that you're goin' to has somebody in it that you really love. Someone you're nuts about."*

Gleason then does something that happened just this once in the Classic 39. Breaking the fourth wall, he and Meadows are joined by Carney and Randolph to take a bow — not as Ralph, Alice, Ed and Trixie, but as themselves.

THERE IS A TANGIBLE REASON WHY THE EPISODE seems fraught with tension, and therefore, so naturalistic. That the show was performed before an audience was not unique among TV series in the 1950s. But the tension was elevated due to Gleason's preferred working style, as one cast member explained.

"Jackie would only work live," Randolph told me in 2002.

"He said, 'Comedy is not funny if it's on film and rehearsed many times.' So we did not rehearse much. You saw him only the day of the show, which was Saturday. We had very little rehearsal with Jackie. But it worked. Somehow, it worked."

Not that the cast ever got comfortable with the situation.

"Oh! Everybody was scared," Randolph said with a laugh.

"I've seen actors who didn't know that this was the routine, and thought they were going to have days of rehearsal — I've seen them vomit in the wings, they were so scared."

According to Randolph, the show was performed at what was then CBS-TV Studio 50, later known as the Ed Sullivan Theater.

"It's at Broadway and 53rd, but it's the same old vaudeville house — just a regular proscenium stage," she recalled.

"We always had a live audience. And we had no teleprompters. We just did it as if it were a play. You'd see that little red light go on and know that millions were watching you, and you've only gone through this once with Jackie. Even if things went wrong, he said, 'Just ad-lib in character.' That helped to keep it very real.

"I think, yes, he was some sort of comedic genius. He knew what was right and wrong with comedy. He ran the whole show. He was really the producer, the director, he was everything."

Ralph mulls over his options in the gift debacle as Ed trims the Kramdens' Christmas tree.

Alice and Ralph trade presents on Christmas morning.

Ed Norton's tinsel-tossing technique

Select tinsel strands

Wind up from behind back

Toss along a forward arc

Watch strands land perfectly

Lucille Ball and A. Cameron Grant in the 1956 Christmas episode of "I Love Lucy" (colorized version). © Desilu Productions

'I Love Lucy' (Dec. 24, 1956)

THE "I LOVE LUCY" TEAM FASHIONED A WARM,
casual Christmas episode that doubles as a "best of" clip show.

It's Christmas Eve at the Manhattan apartment of the Ricardos: zany Lucy (Lucille Ball) and her Cuban bandleader husband, Ricky (Desi Arnaz). Their son, Little Ricky (Keith Thibodeaux), wants to keep an all-night vigil by the fireplace for Santa's arrival, and his parents take turns explaining why he must go to bed.

Once Little Ricky is safely tucked in, the tree is snuck in by the Ricardos' landlords, the Mertzes: Lucy's frequent co-conspirator Ethel (Vivian Vance) and grouchy skinflint Fred (William Frawley).

Some gently played holiday-related comedy follows: the untangling and checking of the Christmas lights; a little mistletoe smooching; Lucy's off-key singing during "Jingle Bells"; and the trimming of the tree. One of the bits has entered the lexicon: when Lucy keeps asking Fred to saw a little off of a branch to "even out" the tree. The next thing you know, all that's left is a sad-looking trunk with some scraggly leftover branches.

Once the troupe begins to engage in "remember when" chit-chat, we're in Flashback City, with clips centered around Ricardo family milestones such as Little Ricky's arrival.

Meanwhile, back in the present, it's Christmas morning at the Ricardos. Ricky — who is a percussionist as well as a bandleader, after all — buys a shiny new drum kit for Little Ricky. The tyke hops on the stool and gives a recital like a miniature Buddy Rich.

The four principles, who all have dressed in Santa suits, convene in the kitchen. If you watch closely, you'll notice that a fifth Santa (A. Cameron Grant) slyly materializes. Surprised by this costumed interloper, the Ricardos and the Mertzes tug at each others' beards until the real Santa goes "ouch" — because, of course, *his* whiskers aren't phony. The routine is a little bit corny, a little

Desi Arnaz, Ball, William Frawley, Vivian Vance and tree.

bit childish, but these pros pull it off — no pun intended.

Thibodeaux did not take drumming lessons especially for the Christmas episode. "I was a professional drummer at the age of 3 doing one-night-stands across the nation," he told me in 2003.

"I auditioned for the part of Little Ricky. The first day on the set, Lucy was there. She looked at my dad and she said, 'Well, he's cute, but what does he do?' My dad said, 'Well, he plays the drums.' She couldn't believe it.

"They happened to have a set of drums on the stage there. I walked over to the set and played it. All the stagehands started gathering around. Sheldon Leonard, the big producer, came around. And then finally, Desi himself came over and started jamming with me on the drums. He stood up and laughed and he said, 'Well, I guess we found Little Ricky.'"

154

'The Howdy Doody Show' (Nov. 1951)

It's Christmas Eve at the weird homestead of Buffalo Bob Smith, his puppet sidekick Howdy Doody, and their live-in clown with a cow's name, Clarabell (Bob Keeshan). Bob trims the tree; Howdy hangs the stockings; and Clarabell chews on the popcorn-and-cranberry strings. When Santa doesn't show up immediately at midnight, the trio flies to the North Pole in a rocket that appears to be lifted from some underfunded sci-fi serial. Poor Santa has been tied to a chair by Ugly Sam, who pegs him as the "bearded bandit" in the news. Team Howdy straightens out the mess, and a generation of young viewers have their brains twisted anew.

"The Howdy Doody Show" © National Broadcasting Co.

'The Amos 'n Andy Show' (Dec. 15, 1952)

Not to be confused with the offensive "blackvoice" radio series, the TV "Amos 'n Andy" was groundbreaking as the medium's first black-cast series. In this episode, Andy (Spencer Williams) is the godfather of little Arbadella (Patti Marie Ellis), daughter of Amos (Alvin Childress). While window-shopping, Andy learns her dearest Christmas wish: a talking doll. But, Arbadella tells him, her father said "Santa Claus couldn't afford it this year." Broke as usual, Andy takes a job as a department-store Santa in order to buy that doll. The show ends with an eye-misting bedside sequence in which Amos explains the Lord's Prayer to Arbadella.

"The Amos 'n Andy Show" © CBS Television Network

'Alfred Hitchcock Presents' (Dec. 18, 1955)

Diminutive, Dublin-born Barry Fitzgerald — he of the scrunched up face and bog-thick brogue — basically played the same character in films like "Going My Way" (1944) and "The Quiet Man" (1952). Fitzgerald was Fitzgerald, a wary man with an impish humor who says what he thinks, albeit in a flowery language all his own. Here, he plays Stretch, a paroled burglar hired as a store Santa. Says Stretch of Santa's duties: "Sure, sure, I've shilled before," and "Kids? On me lap?" Regarding a mob of children, he thinks in voiceover: "Look at the little monsters. The joint's *crawlin'* with 'em!" But Stretch makes a better Santa than he reckons.

"Alfred Hitchcock Presents" © CBS Television Network

'Dobie Gillis' (Dec. 20, 1960)

High-schoolers Dobie (Dwayne Hickman), Zelda (Sheila James) and Chatsworth (Steve Franken) perform "A Christmas Carol" in class, leading Mr. Pomfritt (William Schallert) to look skyward and say, "Sorry, Charlie." When Maynard (Bob Denver) says that he feels like a social outcast, Mr. Pomfritt suggests he host a Christmas Eve party. Meanwhile, Zelda convinces Dobie that his financial future depends on attending Chatsworth's high-society function the same night, even *if* Maynard is Dobie's best buddy. After having a Dickensian dream in which Maynard is a spirit, Dobie keeps seeing Maynard in spirit form at Chatsworth's party.

"Dobie Gillis" © 20th Century Fox Television

Ben (Will Wright, center) scowls as Aunt Bee (Frances Bavier) and Andy (Andy Griffith) serve a turkey in jail.

'The Andy Griffith Show' (Dec. 19, 1960)

A COMICAL ENSEMBLE POPULATED MAYBERRY'S business district on "The Andy Griffith Show": Floyd the barber, Goober the pump jockey, Emmett the repairman. One of the most memorable was store owner Ben Weaver (Will Wright), the uncontested Scrooge of Mayberry. Wright perfected the role of the cantankerous old-timer in supporting bits in movies and on TV. He fixed his imposing scowl on the motorcycle gang of Marlon Brando, no less, in "The Wild One" (1953) — not that they were much fazed.

Set in the improbably bucolic town of Mayberry, "The Andy Griffith Show" (1960-68) starred Griffith as fair-minded authority figure Sheriff Andy Taylor, Ron Howard as his mostly obedient son Opie, and Frances Bavier as his self-sacrificing Aunt Bee. For the first five seasons, Don Knotts played Andy's jittery sidekick, Deputy Barney Fife.

In this Bob Sweeney-directed episode, Barney tells Andy he can't play Santa at the Christmas party that night, because he has to watch the five prisoners at the jailhouse. Andy's solution: Set the prisoners free for the holiday on the honor system. (Ah, the good old days, when criminals were trustworthy.)

In walks a scowling (of course) Ben with townie Sam Edwards (Sam Muggins) in tow. Ben caught Sam red-handed operating a still. Andy sniffs the jug of moonshine, winces and says, "It ain't exactly sarsaparilla."

Miffed that the sale of moonshine cuts into his store's profits, Ben demands that Sam be locked up, Christmas or no. "If that ain't the meanest, orneriest, low-downest man," Andy declares.

Later, Andy jails Sam's wife and kids, so the Edwards clan can spend Christmas together with all the fixings, including Aunt Bee's turkey. This only makes Ben madder — at first. But then Ben, who has no apparent family, starts to wish *he* could take part in the celebration.

One of the most touching moments in any TV series follows as Andy and his gal Ellie (Elinor Donahue) sing a duet of "Away in a Manger" in the jailhouse, as the assembled party (including Barney wearing a Santa suit) looks on. In one fluid shot, the camera pans from the singers to their admiring audience, into the darkened jail cell, and up to the barred back window. From outside, an unnoticed Ben clings to the bars and sings along. (The director of photography was Sidney Hickox.)

Can the meanest, orneriest, low-downest man in Mayberry turn into Santa Claus?

Let's just hope those five prisoners at the top of the episode kept up *their* end of the bargain, and returned to the jailhouse on Dec. 26th.

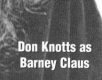

Don Knotts as Barney Claus

156

It suddenly dawns on an alcoholic vagrant (Art Carney) that he might really be Santa in "The Twilight Zone." © Cayuga Productions

'The Twilight Zone' (Dec. 23, 1960)

IN AN ALTERNATE CINEMATIC UNIVERSE, "Miracle on 34th Street" might have followed the exploits of that drunken, slurring, flask-wielding Santa at the beginning of the film, rather than the perfect Santa who castigates him.

Rod Serling — creator, host, and main writer of the fantasy anthology series "The Twilight Zone" (1959-64) — went there, kind of. Serling's thoughtful Christmas episode, "The Night of the Meek," is often dark, occasionally funny, and explores themes of alcoholic despair and Dickensian poverty.

Art Carney — then known as a comedic actor for his role of Ed Norton on "The Honeymooners" — was afforded a dramatic stretch as Henry Corwin, the world's least likely department-store Santa Claus. And Carney *ran* with it.

From the look of Henry, it's a wonder he ever got hired. His beard and costume are filthy. And this unlaundered, unshowered, unloved man probably stinks somethin' awful.

We first see Henry, in costume, downing shots at a sleazy dive. When neighborhood kids peer into the window, Henry laments, "Why isn't there a real Santa, for kids like that?"

Replies the burly bartender (Val Avery): "You know what your trouble is, Corwin? You let that dopey red suit go to your head."

Henry arrives at the store late to a crowd of antsy shoppers, and promptly falls on his face. "Look, Mom, Santa Claus is loaded!" a boy exclaims. Henry is fired by his boss, Mr. Dundee (John Fiedler), but doesn't leave without imparting a farewell speech.

Nearly in tears, Henry says of the boy's mother: "Someone should remind her that Christmas is more than barging up and down department-store aisles, pushing people out of the way." He speaks of poor souls for whom "the only thing that comes down the chimney on Christmas Eve is more poverty."

Series host Rod Serling sermonizes on a snowy street.

Then comes the "Twilight Zone" twist. As Henry stumbles down a snowy street, an alley cat upsets a bag of cans that land in a clatter. When Henry looks into the bag, he sees ... presents.

"The Night of the Meek," directed by Jack Smight, is one of six episodes in the second season to be shot on videotape (rather than film) as a cost-cutting measure. Each sequence is staged "live," like a soap opera, to great effect. The sets and vibe are *noir*-ish. In this world, it's always dark, it's always snowing, and Carney/Henry is always wearing that soiled Santa suit.

Sounds like Christmas Eve in ... "The Twilight Zone."

157

From left: Donna Douglas, Max Baer, Irene Ryan, Buddy Ebsen, Paul Winchell and Bea Benaderet harmonize on "Jingle Bells."

'The Beverly Hillbillies' (Dec. 19, 1962)

WHEN YOU'RE HILL FOLK, IT'S A PLUMB FACT you're gonna spend Christmas in the hills — and we don't mean *Beverly* Hills. "It's December everywhere else but here, dad-blamed Californy," says irascible Granny (Irene Ryan).

So, for the first Christmas episode of the 1962-71 corn-pone comedy "The Beverly Hillbillies" — about a backwoods family that relocates to the land of swimming pools and movie stars after striking oil — the Clampetts load up their truck and move *out* of Beverly. Granny is joined on the holiday trek by sage Uncle Jed (Buddy Ebsen), stunning tomboy Elly May (Donna Douglas) and her doofus cousin, Jethro (Max Baer).

"Six days' hard drivin'" is the ETA for the trip, so Granny makes sure to pack a wood stove, an *entire* wood stove, since the hard-living Clampetts aren't about to squander their money on fancy restaurants like city folks do.

Showing up in the nick of time is bank president Milburn Drysdale (Raymond Bailey), riding shotgun as usual in the spiffy convertible of his fastidious secretary, Jane Hathaway (Nancy Kulp).

Drysdale, that money-grubber, wants to make certain that the Clampetts aren't leaving permanently, lest Jed withdraw his $25 million from the Commerce Bank of Beverly Hills.

Drysdale talks the Clampetts into letting *him* make the arrangements: a luxurious private plane on TWA (talk about product placement), in-flight movie, mink coats for the ladies, the works.

Meanwhile, back in the hills, Cousin Pearl (Bea Benaderet) and her daughter Jethreen (Baer in hilarious drag) are planning a surprise Christmas trip … to Beverly Hills.

It all ends with a rousing rendition of "Jingle Bells" in Pearl's parlor.

This was a two-parter. The following week's episode brings us to Christmas morning, when Granny unveils her holiday menu: red cabbage, green turnip tops "swimming with sorghum," and what Granny calls "heavenly hash": grits, chitlins, possum belly, hog jowls and cabbage, "all minced together and simmered in gopher gravy," and topped with poached hawk eggs.

Because Christmas dinner is when you serve your very best.

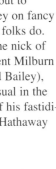

Elly May and friend on Christmas morning.

158

'The Dick Van Dyke Show' (Dec. 18, 1963)

The conceit of this show-within-a-show: It's a special Christmas episode of "The Alan Brady Show" put on by the staff. Santa-suited Alan (Carl Reiner) watches as a choir sings his praises. Man-hungry Sally (Rose Marie) sings "Santa, Send a Fella." Buddy (Morey Amsterdam) plays a plaintive "Jingle Bells" on cello until Sally goofs it up with peppy piano. Rob (Dick Van Dyke) and Laura (Mary Tyler Moore) dance in Santa suits. Little Richie (Larry Matthews) sings "The Little Drummer Boy" in a quavering falsetto. The finale has the entire cast as musical toy soldiers. It's all a showcase for one of TV's most talented troupes.

"The Dick Van Dyke Show" © Calvada Productions

'The Patty Duke Show' (Dec. 25, 1963)

The sitcom about that most rare of human anomalies — identical twin cousins — has Patty Duke in dual roles as Patty, a rock 'n' roll-loving Brooklyn Heights girl, and Cathy, her worldly cousin who adores minuets and crêpes Suzette. Patty's dad, Martin (William Schallert), is a newspaper editor whose twin brother, Kenneth, is a foreign correspondent. When Kenneth is arrested in Kurdistan on phony espionage charges, it looks like he won't make it home for Christmas. Still, his daughter Cathy's faith is unshaken. Another pickle: Kenneth's boss (John McGiver), that Scrooge, wants him fired the moment he sets foot on U.S. soil.

"The Patty Duke Show" © United Artists Television

'Bewitched' (Dec. 24, 1964)

"Santa Claus is a kid's father stuffed with pillows," says Michael (Billy Mumy), the orphanage troublemaker. The Stevenses — Samantha the witch (Elizabeth Montgomery) and Darrin the "mortal" (Dick York) — collect Michael from the orphanage to bring him home for Christmas. Samantha makes it her mission to convince Michael there really *is* a Santa Claus. Even though she is a practitioner of witchcraft, Samantha is buddies with Santa (perfectly cast Cecil Kellaway). She flies the boy to the North Pole, where Santa tells him, "Remember, Michael, the real happiness of Christmas isn't found in what we get, but what we give."

"Bewitched" © Screen Gems Television

'The Flintstones' (Dec. 25, 1964)

Hanna-Barbera's prime-time 'toon commented on advancing technology and burgeoning suburbia, and stole more than a little from "The Honeymooners." Blustery caveman Fred (voiced by Alan Reed) applies for a job at Macyrock's department store. After failing as a gift-wrapper, stock boy and toy salesman, Fred replaces the store's ailing Santa Claus. Fred wears the suit well, singing "Christmas is My Favorite Time of Year" and fooling his wife Wilma (Jean Vander Pyl) and pet Dino. When the *real* Santa also falls ill, he dispatches elves to bring Fred to the North Pole for a special Christmas Eve mission. Any guesses what that might be?

"The Flintstones" © Hanna-Barbera Productions

'The Addams Family' (Dec. 24, 1965)

Gomez (John Astin) and Morticia (Carolyn Jones) are miffed when a neighbor tells their kids, Pugsley (Ken Weatherwax) and Wednesday (Lisa Loring), that Santa Claus isn't real. Uncle Fester (Jackie Coogan) is elected to don a Santa suit, and give Pugsley a bow-and-arrow set and Wednesday a Marie Antoinette doll. When rotund Fester gets stuck in the chimney, Gomez strolls into town and rents the costume off of a streetcorner Santa ... for $25,000. Meanwhile, Grandmama (Blossom Rock), Cousin Itt (Felix Silla), Lurch (Ted Cassidy) and Morticia also don the beard and red suit, thus giving the kids too many gifts. But where is the *real* Santa?

"The Addams Family" © Filmways Television

'Green Acres' (Dec. 21, 1966)

Manhattan lawyer Oliver Douglas (Eddie Albert) and his high-maintenance Hungarian wife Lisa (Eva Gabor) go Christmas tree-shopping on Park Avenue, but find that all of the trees are flocked in blue, pink or white. "These trees are a travesty on Christmas," Oliver says, vowing that some day, he will own a farm and chop down his own natural tree. When that day comes, in the topsy-turvy town of Hooterville, Oliver finds that the neighboring farmers go in for artificial trees (with "spruce juice" and "sap oozers"), plastic candy canes, and pre-strung wax popcorn. Worse yet, an "old-fashioned" Christmas tree in Hooterville is made of ... aluminum.

"Green Acres" © Filmways Television

'Dragnet 1967' (Dec. 21, 1967)

Someone has stolen the Baby Jesus statue from the Nativity set at the San Fernando Mission Church. "We could get a new one, but it wouldn't be the same," says Father Rojas (Harry Bartell) to Sgt. Joe Friday (Jack Webb) and Officer Bill Gannon (Harry Morgan). The cops will try their best to find the culprit and retrieve the statue in time for morning Mass on Christmas. Their Scrooge of a boss (Byron Morrow) wants them on another case, but he punts when Friday and Gannon tell *him* to explain it to Father Rojas. Greg Brady, er, Barry Williams plays an altar boy. The twist ending is steeped in hokey religiosity, but that's not a bad thing.

"Dragnet 1967" © Universal Television

'The Monkees' (Dec. 25, 1967)

The Monkees *think* wealthy Mrs. Vandersnoot (Jeanne Sorel) hired them to play a party. Really, she's off on a Christmas cruise, and wants the boys to babysit her bespectacled son, Melvin (Eddie Munster, er, Butch Patrick), who says, "I've always felt that if one stripped away all the tinsel of Christmas, underneath you'd find nothing but more tinsel." The Monkees face an uphill battle converting this pint-sized Scrooge. But the group's *true* Christmas present to the world is their a capella performance of the Spanish carol "Ríu Chíu." The solemn rendition — no funny business — was arranged in part by Monkees producer Chip Douglas.

"The Monkees" © Raybert Prod. Inc. ™ Screen Gems, Inc.

Cindy Brady (Susan Olsen) asks Santa Claus (Hal Smith) for nothing short of a miracle on "The Brady Bunch." © Paramount Television

'The Brady Bunch' (Dec. 19, 1969)

TV'S FIRST BLENDED FAMILY, "THE BRADY BUNCH" (1969-74), didn't spend much time exploring the resentments and conflicts that may arise when three boys and three girls become instant siblings. Greg never said, "You're not my real mother!" Marcia never said, "You treat your sons better than you treat us!"

But the first season's Christmas episode at least *hints* at the elephant on the shag carpet. More than once, the impending holiday is referred to as "our first Christmas together as a family."

The central conflict has mom Carol (Florence Henderson) contracting laryngitis prior to her vocal solo in the Christmas church service. Nothing is helping her malady — not even an old family remedy recreated by the Bradys' housekeeper, Alice (Ann B. Davis): oil of camphor, tar, pepper, mustard powder and vinegar.

When dad Mike (Robert Reed) brings little Cindy (Susan Olsen) to see a department-store Santa Claus (Hal Smith), she doesn't ask for a toy. Rather, she asks Santa to cure her mother's "larry-gitis." And Santa, in a weak moment, says yes.

In a locker room, Mike confronts the repentant Santa, who admits he was powerless against "those big baby blues."

After bedtime on Christmas Eve, some of the kids gather downstairs: Greg (Barry Williams), Marcia (Maureen McCormick), Peter (Christopher Knight) and Jan (Eve Plumb). In discussing their mother's illness, they consider postponing Christmas.

They are overheard by Alice, who uses reverse-psychology to convince them that postponing Christmas would crush their parents. (You really feel sorry for those kids, who can't un-see Alice's bedtime look: robe, slippers, hairnet, pink sponge rollers.)

The service goes on as planned. But who sings the solo?

Though "The Brady Bunch" was canceled in 1974, it kept coming back to life in other forms, like George Romero zombies.

"The Brady Bunch Variety Hour" (1976-77) and "The Brady Brides" (1981) paved the way for the TV movie "A Very Brady Christmas" (1988), which proved an unexpected ratings bonanza.

In some ways, "A Very Brady Christmas" is a sequel to the 1969 Christmas episode of "The Brady Bunch." Both have Christmas miracles predicated on Carol singing "O Come All Ye Faithful." In the 1988 TV movie, she sings at the edge of a construction site collapse in which Mike is trapped. Cindy is played by Jennifer Runyon, but a clip from the 1969 episode of Olsen as Cindy asking Santa to cure her mother's "larry-gitis" is used as a flashback — a little Christmas gift for fans of the original series.

The reunited Bradys hope for another holiday miracle in the TV movie "A Very Brady Christmas" (1988). © Paramount Television

Vintage variety

TV's extinct, lamented variety format — a descendant of vaudeville and radio — was a made-to-order vehicle for holiday cheer.

And this entertainment genre of yore can still conjure cozy memories of old-guard stars in their career twilights making, as Bob Cratchit once put it, "rather merry" in schmaltzy TV specials.

"Happy Holidays With Bing and Frank" (1952) — do I *really* have to tell you Bing Who and Frank Who? — is a Frank Sinatra-directed stand-alone filmed in color. In the setup, Bing Crosby and Sinatra get together to drink, decorate, sing, plug their latest records, time-trip to Victorian England, and drink.

The backstory has it that Crosby wanted to film late in the day to maximize his golfing time, while Sinatra wanted to film earlier to maximize his carousing time. Sinatra deferred to the elder crooner.

That same year, as Bud Abbott and Lou Costello were nearing the end of their long career as a comedy team, they co-hosted a Christmas episode of "The Colgate Comedy Hour." The boys played a skit in which Abbott is thrown through two shop windows decorated for Christmas. The dancing Nicholas Brothers gave a wowzer of a performance. Costello then sang "White Christmas" straight — no goofing around — with OK-ish results. But the huge chandelier above his head was a prop for the pandemonium that erupted when he attempted to conduct an orchestra.

THESE TV EVENTS – THE BING-AND-FRANK AND Bud-and-Lou specials — illustrate the two types of Christmas variety program from the era: one-shots and holiday episodes of a variety series. More stars who got in on the hosting honors over the years were Bob Hope, Julie Andrews, Dean Martin, Jackie Gleason, Perry Como, Red Skelton, George Burns, Johnny Cash, Andy Williams, Dolly Parton, the Carpenters, John Denver, the Osmonds, the Captain and Tennille, and Luther Vandross.

Crosby's "White Christmas" co-star, Danny Kaye, often presided over holiday-themed episodes of his variety series. On Kaye's

Dorothy Collins hosts "Your Hit Parade" (1955); Nat King Cole sings "The Christmas Song" (1961); Judy Garland frolics (1963).

1963 show, Nat King Cole sang his hit "The Christmas Song," and sat with Kaye to kibitz and harmonize. In his 1965 show, when Kaye read the Cratchit family dinner scene from "A Christmas Carol," he had a trick up his sleeve. Kaye first pretended to read from a book, but before long, he looked straight into the camera and recited Dickens with warmth and sincerity.

The family affair "Christmas With the Martins and the Sinatras" (1967) alternated between swingin' and corny. Fellow Rat-Packer Sammy Davis Jr. made a guest appearance wearing a Santa hat. (Davis did a line that was trendy at the time, but has no lasting resonance: "Do the name Ruby Begonia ring a bell?")

Nancy Sinatra, dancing with four Santas, sang a rewrite of her 1966 #1 hit "These Boots Were Made for Walkin'" retitled (*ugh*) "These Boots Were Made for Santa." Frank Jr. and Dean Jr. played a scene with a toy car track by a Christmas tree. (Dean Jr. was then a member of the hitmaking trio Dino, Desi & Billy.) The boys commiserated about having such high-profile papas, and sang a dopey song titled "How Do You Talk to Your Dad?"

MEANWHILE, CROSBY BREEZED THROUGH SOLO

Christmas specials with understated humor and grace. And he could get a line off — gently sniping at on- and offscreen pals Bob Hope and Sinatra, or with self-deprecating age jokes referencing his long-ago days as one of Paul Whiteman's Rhythm Boys.

The crooner trotted out his well-trained family — gorgeous second wife Kathryn and their kids Harry, Mary and Nathaniel — for "Bing Crosby and the Sound of Christmas" (1971). They were joined by Robert Goulet, whose eyebrows and mustache were freshly darkened, and whose baritone was set on Extra Hammy.

"Bing Crosby's Merrie Olde Christmas" (1977) had Der Bingle and brood travel to England to stay at the mansion of Sir Percival Crosby, a British relation. A rendition of "Jingle Bell Rock" by Twiggy and Crosby's sons was cringe-worthy, but impressionist Stanley Baxter did a dead-on Hope to Crosby's apparent delight.

Those bits are forgettable, but one song in the special has attained a permanent place in the Christmas pantheon. In a skit, "neighbor" David Bowie stops by, explaining, "Sir Percival lets

Sammy Claus and Dino (1967); Nancy Sinatra repurposes "Boots" (1967); Bob Hope and Raquel Welch salute the troops (1968).

Diahann Carroll on Santa's lap (1969); Perry Como croons (1969); Chewbacca in the reviled "Star Wars Holiday Special" (1978).

me use his piano when he's not around." Crosby, 73, and Bowie, 30, then exchange cute jokes centered on their age difference before singing a heartwarming duet. (What was next, we wondered, Carol Channing meets Wendy O. Williams?)

Some backstage drama yielded magical results. When Bowie initially balked at singing "Little Drummer Boy," an original song, "Peace on Earth," was whipped up by Ian Fraser, Larry Grossman, and Buz Kohan, and interpolated into the "Little Drummer Boy" arrangement. With about an hour's rehearsal, Crosby and Bowie nailed the tricky blended song, and thus, generations were bridged.

On the special, Bowie — then promoting his album "Heroes" — also lip-synced the title track (#24 in the U.K.), which he co-wrote with Brian Eno and which featured guitarist Robert Fripp.

The Crosby-Bowie collaboration happened not a moment too soon. The segment was taped on Sept. 11, 1977. The following Oct. 14, Crosby died in Madrid after completing 18 holes — a fitting end for the avowed golf nut. The TV special aired posthumously on Nov. 30 with a tacked-on introduction by Kathryn Crosby acknowledging her husband's passing.

Which brings us to "The Star Wars Holiday Special" (1978), a humiliation for all involved. It aired once, and disappeared for decades. Worse, it was barely holiday-related. Surprisingly, all of the "Star Wars" principles participated: Mark Hamill, Carrie Fisher, Harrison Ford, Anthony Daniels, Peter Mayhew, even the voice of James Earl Jones. Hamill wore some *crazy* eye-liner.

(In a 2006 interview on "Late Night With Conan O'Brien," Ford jokingly claimed not to recall appearing in the special, then denied its existence, and then pretended to strangle O'Brien when the TV host said he would play a clip.)

The "plot" centered around Chewbacca's family life — including his dad, wife and son Lumpy — as they celebrate "Life Day." Celebs conned into appearing include Bea Arthur as the gruff proprietor of the "Star Wars" cantina, Harvey Korman as a robotic pitchman, and Art Carney as an outer space trading post proprietor. (The phrase "incongruous casting" springs to mind.)

As a preamble to singing "This Minute Now," Diahann Carroll did some kind of weird, seductive, "video phone sex" thing, looking directly into the camera and wearing wild duds you might see at Studio 54. The sequence was meant to be sexy, and it *would* have been sexy, if not for Wookiee moaning in the background.

The special also presented the Jefferson Starship (!) in "holographic" form performing "Light the Sky on Fire." That's right — Grace Slick, Paul Kantner and Marty Balin survived both Altamont *and* "The Star Wars Holiday Special."

Santa, Lou and Bud on "The Colgate Comedy Hour" (1952). Danny Kaye with dancing Santas on "The Danny Kaye Show" (1966).

Andy Williams enlisted multi-generational relations for Christmas episodes of his variety show. "The Andy Williams Show" © National Broadcasting Co.

How 'Mr. Christmas' got his name

A SPOTLESS ENTERTAINER WITH A READY SMILE,
Andy Williams is remembered for his signature hit "Moon River";
for his breezy 1962-71 variety show; and for being a stand-up guy
who supported his ex-wife during her manslaughter trial.

But Williams also attained a special moniker: "Mr. Christmas."
It grew from the Christmas episodes of his show, not to mention his
swinging hit of 1963, "The Most Wonderful Time of the Year."

In real life, Williams (1927-2012) believed the sentiment in
that song's title from the time he was a boy.

"We lived in a small town — Wall Lake, Iowa — of 700
people," Williams told me in 2005.

"Christmas was a big family affair. And I mean *big,* in that
everybody's doors were open at Christmas. It was like a big
movie set. We would walk from one house to another. We
knew everybody. We'd go in and have a Coke and bring presents around and get in a sleigh ride and drive through the little
town and wish everybody a merry Christmas. Everybody knew
everybody. So it was a great, big family affair."

As for how Williams became associated with the holiday: "It
just happened naturally, because Christmas came as one of the
weeks in the weekly show. So when Christmas came around, we
did the Christmas show. It was still 'The Andy Williams Show.'

"I would bring my children on; my mother and father; my brothers and my sister; grandchildren; everybody. It became a big family
thing. Every year, people liked to see it again, to see how the children had grown up and how my mother and father were doing. My
brothers and I sang together, which we hadn't done for a long time."

How did Williams' family adapt to the world of television?

"Well, my brothers and I had been singing together since we
were little kids on radio and in movies and things," Williams said,
"so that was not a big thing. My mother and father had been around
it enough, so that it wasn't difficult for them. With children, it's no
problem, anyway. Because they just do whatever they want to
do. Whatever's natural. So everything seemed right.

"It was a great, great thing for me and for my family and
for the audience. Warren Beatty said to me one day, 'That
Christmas thing that you do is so great, because it's so
nice to see a family that gets along and enjoys
Christmas and loves each other. Oh my God, I love
that show.' So, everybody seemed to like it."

**"It became
a big family
thing," said
Williams of
his annual
TV specials.**

© Moon River Enterprises

Special treatment

From top: Walt Disney's "From All of Us to All of You" (1958); Bell Telephone's "The Spirit of Christmas" (1950); "Nestor the Long-Eared Donkey" (1977).

ANIMATED CHRISTMAS TV SPECIALS HAD precedents in theatrical cartoon shorts. But when did animated specials created specifically for television begin to appear? There were two important harbingers.

One was "The Spirit of Christmas" (1950), a charming "Bell Telephone Hour" episode that re-enacted "Twas the Night Before Christmas" *and* the Nativity (even depicting "wily" Herod) via the Mabel Beaton Marionettes.

Then there was Walt Disney's "From All of Us to All of You" (1958), a collection of filmclips from previous Disney releases "hosted" by Jiminy Cricket and Mickey Mouse. "Uncle Walt" himself appears in miniature on a fireplace mantle, telling viewers: "Jiminy Cricket and Mickey Mouse are putting on this Christmas program. They insist that I appear 'cricket size' because, as they put it, Christmas is bigger than all of us."

Christmas card graphics introduce each clip. Presented are two shorts — "Santa's Workshop" (1932) and "Toy Tinkers" (1949) — and songs or sequences from "Peter Pan," "Bambi," "Pinocchio," "Lady and the Tramp," "Cinderella," and "Snow White and the Seven Dwarfs."

"From All of Us to All of You" was a ratings bonanza, even in rebroadcasts, which *had* to get TV execs thinking.

FOUR YEARS LATER CAME THE FIRST animated Christmas special made expressly for TV: "Mr. Magoo's Christmas Carol" (1962). The 1960s proved a golden age for such specials, with three of the most memorable following in consecutive years: "Rudolph the Red-Nosed Reindeer" (1964), "A Charlie Brown Christmas" (1965), and "How the Grinch Stole Christmas!" (1966).

"Rudolph" was the first of many Christmas specials created by Rankin/Bass Productions, the company founded in 1960 (as Videocraft International) by producers Arthur Rankin Jr. and Jules Bass. Rankin/Bass was also responsible for "The Little Drummer Boy" (1968), "Frosty the Snowman" (1969), "Santa Claus is Comin' to Town" (1970), "The Year Without a Santa Claus" (1974), "The First Christmas: The Story of the First Christmas Snow" (1975), "Frosty's Winter Wonderland" (1976), "Rudolph's Shiny New Year" (1976), "The Little Drummer Boy, Book II" (1976), "Nestor the Long-Eared Donkey" (1977), and "Rudolph and Frosty's Christmas in July" (1979). *Phew!*

Animated Christmas specials kept on coming, like fruitcakes in the mail: "Raggedy Ann and Andy in The Great Santa Claus Caper" (1978), "A Garfield Christmas" (1987), "It's Christmastime Again, Charlie Brown" (1992), "Olive, the Other Reindeer" (1999), "Grandma Got Run Over by a Reindeer" (2000), "My Little Pony: A Very Minty Christmas" (2005), "The Smurfs: A Christmas Carol" (2011), "It's a SpongeBob Christmas!" (2012), "Scooby-Doo! Haunted Holidays" (2012), and on and on.

Mr. Magoo "as" Scrooge slams his door on pesky carolers. Below: Gerald McBoing-Boing "as" Tiny Tim.

'Mr. Magoo's Christmas Carol' (1962)

TOP-RATE VOICE TALENT, MODERN GRAPHIC design, a Broadway-worthy score — they pulled out all the stops for the first-ever animated special produced specifically for TV.

The novel conceit of Abe Levitow's "Mr. Magoo's Christmas Carol" is that it's a play within a play. Magoo, the vision-challenged senior voiced with gusto by Jim Backus, is not merely a Scrooge surrogate, nor is he Scrooge. Magoo is Magoo, *playing* Scrooge in a stage musical — a Broadway production, no less.

There's a good reason "Mr. Magoo's Christmas Carol" has what sounds like a bona fide Broadway score: The music was created by bona fide Broadway guys: lyricist Bob Merrill ("Funny Girl"), and composers Jule Styne ("Gypsy") and Walter Scharf (a 10-time Oscar nominee).

We first see Magoo in his 1910s roadster, careening through New York City en route to a theater with a marquee that reads, "Quincy Magoo Starring in A Christmas Carol." (Now we know Magoo's first name.)

As an actor, Magoo is a bit hammy, but he has his lines down pat. Gerald McBoing-Boing — like Magoo, a character in the UPA (United Productions of America) family — "plays" Tiny Tim.

The piece is fairly true to Dickens, though the opening credits warn it was "freely" adapted. Magoo as Scrooge goes through the paces of Dickens' story: rejecting the charity volunteers; threatening Bob Cratchit's livelihood; being visited by the ghost of Jacob Marley and the three Christmas spirits; and his redemption.

One major liberty was taken: The spirits appear out of order. For a reason never made clear, the Ghost of Christmas Present precedes the Ghost of Christmas Past.

It's little surprise that much of the morbidity of Dickens' story seems even *more* morbid in kiddie cartoon form.

Of course, it wouldn't be Mr. Magoo without — political incorrectness alert — blindness jokes. There are one or two. At one point, the Ghost of Christmas Present says, "You're the one who's too tight with a penny to buy himself a pair of spectacles."

For voice talent, the special reached beyond the usual suspects. Morey Amsterdam, Jack Cassidy, Jane Kean, Les Tremayne and Royal Dano all had roles. Mind you, the special was made during a time before "serious" actors flocked to animation.

Kean, a Broadway and film veteran, voiced Belle, young Scrooge's fiancee who relieves him of his obligation. Kean told me in 1999: "I loved doing that, because I was the leading lady, and I sang that beautiful song that Jule Styne wrote, 'Winter Was Warm.' It was fun. Jim Backus, the original Magoo, happens to have been married to my sister (Betty Kean) at one time — not during that period. So Mr. Magoo was my brother-in-law at one point," Kean added with a laugh.

The actress verified that, while working with Backus as Magoo, there was improvisation in the recording studio.

"He was quite creative," Kean said. "He had that character down pat, as you know. On 'Gilligan's Island,' if you recall, he has a similar character voice. He was very good at that."

167

'Rudolph the Red-Nosed Reindeer' (1964)

WHAT IS "RUDOLPH" ABOUT, REALLY?

Is it about one foggy Christmas Eve, when Santa asks a reindeer with a nose so bright to "guide my sleigh tonight?"

The true answer is as plain as the (red) nose on Rudolph's face. Rankin/Bass' 1964 TV special "Rudolph the Red-Nosed Reindeer" is about outcasts — the ostracized, the isolated, the bullied, the ridiculed, and even the self-loathing.

But the puppet-animation special calls them a word that is a bit more child-friendly: "misfits." (This was an early instance of "owning" a pejorative in order to weaken its effect.)

As for the misfits in the TV special: There's Rudolph, whose "non-conformity" gets him kicked out of reindeer games, forbidden to see his girlfriend, and banished from Santa's sleigh team. There's Hermey, an elf who would rather be a dentist than a toymaker, and is told by his boss, "You'll never fit in." And then there's an entire island of misfits. It's called, a-*hem,* the Island of Misfit Toys.

In a masterstroke, "Rudolph the Red-Nosed Reindeer" places Santa Claus — the jolliest, most toy-givingest guy on the planet — on the wrong side of history. Santa is (gasp!) one of the haters.

So if you were a child who didn't quite fit in, "Rudolph" had your back.

It opens with dapper Sam the Snowman (voiced by Burl Ives) in frosty Christmastown, recounting the familiar story. In a cozy cave, baby Rudolph's parents, the Donners, are welcoming their new arrival, when Santa drops by ... and spots Rudolph's red nose.

"He'll grow out of it," a nervous Donner promises his bearded boss.

"Let's hope so, if he wants to make the sleigh team some day," warns Santa. (Like I said: wrong side of history.)

Later, Rudolph is attending reindeer practice wearing a false black nose ... his takeoff acquires some extra oomph when a long-lashed doe, Clarice, tells him he's cute … his fake nose falls off, and he's kicked off the squad … Clarice likes him anyway, but her dad declares, "No doe of mine is going to be seen with a red-nosed reindeer" … Rudolph leaves home and befriends Hermey, an elf and would-be dentist … they meet blustery prospector Yukon Cornelius, and form a happy trio … while fleeing the Abominable Snowmonster, they wash up on the Island of Misfit Toys.

WHY ARE THESE "MISFIT" TOYS, EXACTLY?

We can understand what might be peculiar about a bird that swims, a water pistol that shoots jelly, or a choo-choo with square wheels. But what's wrong with a Dolly Named Sue? Or a Scooter for Jimmy? And the Spotted Elephant is actually pretty cool.

The island's ruler, a winged lion called King Moonracer, asks Rudolph to prevail upon Santa to find a home for the misfit toys, because after all, "A toy is never truly happy until it is loved by a child."

Back in Christmastown, the Donners and Clarice leave in search of Rudolph. And, considering the dire weather predicted for Christmas Eve, Santa is getting awfully nervous.

"Rudolph" was directed by Larry Roemer; produced by Arthur Rankin Jr. and Jules Bass; co-written by Romeo Muller (a onetime writer for Jack Benny) and Robert May (the character's originator); with animation supervised by Tadahito Mochinaga.

Sam the snowman.
© The Rudolph Company, L.C.

"Rudolph" characters, from opposite page left: the Bumble, Hermey, a lady elf, Santa, the Spotted Elephant, Charlie-in-the-Box, a Scooter for Jimmy, a Dolly for Sue, and Yukon Cornelius. Below: Clarice bats her lashes at Rudolph. © The Rudolph Company, L.C.

Designer gave form to iconic 'Rudolph' characters

AN UNDERSUNG HERO OF "RUDOLPH THE RED-Nosed Reindeer," Antony Peters created the charming, enduring character designs for the 1964 TV special — though you might not know that from the vague credit, "continuity design."

Peters, who died in 2009, worked for Rankin/Bass beginning when the company was called Videocraft International. After parting ways with Rankin/Bass, Peters was summoned back for this, his final, and most significant, collaboration with the company.

When I interviewed Peters in 2004, he seemed ambivalent — happy his work is remembered, but stressing he had "moved on."

"I designed the characters and did the storyboards," Peters said unambiguously when asked his role on the special. "I had worked for Rankin/Bass, actually, from *before* they were Rankin/Bass, doing TV stuff. I wrote and designed a number of their animated shows. I had struck out on my own, and then we decided to do this.

"I don't really remember now whether they lost the person who was going to do it, or they decided I was cheaper than anybody else," Peters added with a laugh. "But they asked me to do the design of the characters and background for the puppets and the sets and the storyboards. That was pretty much it."

Peters said this so matter-of-factly. And yet, the artist was told, these characters are indelibly etched in our consciousness. "Oh, dear," he said, "I'm sorry about that. I've moved on since then."

Still, Peters said he didn't mind talking about his work on the special — for instance, how his design of Sam the Snowman resembles Burl Ives, which was presumably Peters' intention.

"Yes, it was," he confirmed. "I happened to have been — and still *am,* actually — a great fan of Burl Ives as a folksinger going way, way back before he got to be quite so commercial. He was

thinner then, too," Peters said, laughing again. "So I was aware of Burl Ives and purposefully designed it to look like him."

The artist employed a set designer's trick — "forced perspective" — to make viewers feel as if they can see deeply into the elves' bustling North Pole workshop.

"These were all dimensional stop-motion puppets," Peters said. "These sets were built in Japan; actually, it was animated in Japan also. Basically, I just designed these sets and they built them. I designed them in perspective. Clearly, it's a 'forced perspective' — since they really didn't need all that room — with stuff getting smaller as it goes into the distance.

"I made pencil sketches, drawings, of all these sets. Really, it's a lot simpler than it seems at the end — *my* part, anyhow. Easy to design. But building these things, and then moving them in 'stop-motion' (puppet animation), is really tedious."

BUT PETERS DID NOT PERSONALLY MONITOR THE animation as it came back from Japan. "Actually, the stuff that they did in Japan — they were really very autonomous about the whole thing," the artist said. "I would send the material. At that point, the Japanese were the lowest-priced animators in the world.

"In animation, you do the soundtrack first. Because you need to have the voices in order to lip-sync the mouths. The voices were all done in Canada by a very talented group of people, but probably not the music and effects. The music for the songs comes in, of course, at that point, but not the musical background, which is usually matched to the animation. So they would do these things, and we would get the finished film back. The music and effects were then scored to the finished film, also in Canada."

Antony Peters' "forced perspective" view of the elves' workshop.

PETERS RECALLED HE "ABSOLUTELY" WATCHED the special when it premiered on NBC on Dec. 6, 1964.

"After I was done with that, I was finished with Rankin/Bass and out on my own," he said. "I did that and I moved on."

(In an offhand comment, Peters seemed to wonder aloud over whether his "Rudolph" credit was sacrosanct: "I haven't seen the show in years and years, you know. Although, I do have a credit on it — at least, I *did*. From what I know, it's still on there.")

Did Peters have any theories on "Rudolph's" enduring appeal?

"Absolutely none," he said. "Things just become very popular, and then they gather momentum. I believe it's probably that."

We then touched upon an apparent, and understandable, sore spot. Many "Rudoph"-related toys and figures have been marketed. Was there pain involved for Peters in seeing so much money change hands over his character designs?

"That's the reason I moved on, as a matter of fact." he said.

"I went into business for myself, where *I* made the money. Basically, I left Rankin/Bass and formed Instant Miracles, which started out producing animation and went into educational films, industrial films, and museum exhibits, the graphics for them."

As our conversation concluded, I thanked Peters for the innocent, naive, childlike character designs he created way back when.

"That's me — innocent, naive and childlike," the artist said.

"I'm still that way, for whatever it's worth. I'm a very, very immature person. People who do my kind of work tend to be that way, as it turns out. It's a big help.

"But I'm always delighted that people remember it. Every artist likes to hear people say they enjoy the stuff they did. There are two reasons for this, as my son the lawyer says: a real reason and a good reason, OK? The good reason is, you know, reinforcement. And the real reason is: It's nice to hear people say that."

'Rudolph's' musical journey

It's only fitting that the best-known iteration of the iconic holiday character Rudolph the Red-Nosed Reindeer is a musical — namely, Rankin/Bass' 1964 TV special. After all, the character was largely popularized in song.

Rudolph began life as a commercial mascot, in a 1939 poem written by Robert May (1905-1976), then a copy writer for the Montgomery Ward department store chain. May's brother-in-law happened to be an accomplished composer, Johnny Marks (1909-1985). Marks wrote the song based on May's poem, which was recorded by movie cowboy Gene Autry and went to #1 (albeit, briefly) in 1949. Many have since recorded "Rudolph," including Bing Crosby, Spike Jones and His City Slickers, the Cadillacs, the Supremes, the Temptations and the Jackson 5.

When producers Arthur Rankin Jr. and Jules Bass wanted new songs for their planned "Rudolph" animated TV special, they turned to the man who composed the original song — not that Marks was interested.

"At first, Johnny Marks didn't want to do the special," Rankin told Rick Goldschmidt, author of "The Enchanted World of Rankin/Bass" (1997, Miser Bros. Press).

"He was very protective of the song. The song provided a very large income to Marks, and he was afraid that overexposure of the hit song might interfere with its success as a popular song. He was a neighbor of mine at the time and I eventually persuaded him to do the show, and he wrote some very memorable songs in addition to 'Rudolph.'"

From top left: The gang skates; Charlie Brown and Linus commiserate; Lucy the psychiatrist; Snoopy goes commercial.

'A Charlie Brown Christmas' (1965)

"I think there must be something wrong with me, Linus. Christmas is coming, but I'm not happy. I don't feel the way I'm supposed to feel."

So says Charlie Brown to Linus, in the first words spoken in "A Charlie Brown Christmas" — a sign, right off the bat, that this Christmas TV special was going to challenge some norms.

Did any prior Christmas special explore the theme of holiday depression? For that matter, did any Christmas special before, or since, name-drop hypengyophobia, ailurophasia, climacophobia, thalassophobia, gephyrobia and pantophobia?

Not that the producer, director, sponsor and writer-artist behind the first special based on the comic strip "Peanuts" were patting themselves on the back once the special was completed. Quite the opposite. The men were convinced they had a bomb on their hands.

The rest of the world would think differently.

Charles M. Schulz's comic strip "Peanuts" — about a group of children navigating a world in which adults are never seen — debuted from United Feature Syndicate in 1950. By the '60s, "Peanuts" was carried in more than 2,600 papers.

Producer Lee Mendelson and director Bill Melendez collaborated on an unsold documentary about the "Peanuts" phenom, with music by jazz pianist Vince Guaraldi and some brief animation. "Peanuts" characters also showed up in a TV commercial for Ford.

Mendelson's campaign to sell a TV special bore no fruit until — following an April 1965 *Time* cover story about "Peanuts" — he received an out-of-the-blue call from Coca-Cola's ad agency inquiring about the possibility of a Christmas special. Over one busy weekend, he, Melendez and Schulz whipped up an outline.

From top left: A spirited rehearsal; Charlie Brown plays director; Linus recites from St. Luke; the gang loves the tree after all.

"Peanuts" © United Feature Syndicate, Inc.

THE PLOT HAS CHARLIE BROWN — MELANCHOLY figurehead of "Peanuts" — feeling anxious about Christmas. "I know nobody likes me," he tells his precocious friend, Linus. "Why do we have to have a holiday season to emphasize it?"

Meanwhile, others in the "Peanuts" gang — crabby Lucy, piano prodigy Schroeder, messy Pigpen and Charlie Brown's little sister, Sally — take part in winter festivities such as ice-skating and snowflake-tasting, accompanied (and sometimes sabotaged) by Snoopy, Charlie Brown's wisenheimer dog.

Lucy — who runs what resembles a lemonade stand, from which she peddles psychiatry — decrees that Charlie Brown is in need of "involvement," and prescribes that he direct the school's holiday play. In choosing a Christmas tree for the play, Charlie Brown — who feels unloved, remember — selects the scrawniest, least-desirable tree in the lot, to the scoffs and scolds of the gang.

Besides exploring the darker side of the holiday, "A Charlie Brown Christmas" also broke ground by hiring children to voice the characters. (In those days, adult actors usually voiced kiddies.) Another innovation was Guaraldi's score of original music and jazz-ified classics. The special explored the commercialization of Christmas (represented by Snoopy's gaudily decorated doghouse, the pooch's entry in a "Lights and Display Contest"), and introduced a note of religiosity when Linus reads a passage from Luke.

The special was produced on a tight schedule and a low budget. Some of the animation is less than smooth. The slapstick sequences don't seem necessarily representative of Schulz's thoughtful comic strip. The Coca-Cola folks complained that the show was slow-moving and the jazz score wasn't a good fit. Mendelson believed the special might never have aired, but for the fact that the scheduled broadcast date was fast approaching.

These "problems" contributed to the special's unique charm.

"A Charlie Brown Christmas" premiered on Dec. 9, 1965, and won an Emmy the following May. Said Schulz from the Emmys stage: "Charlie Brown is not used to winning, so we thank you."

173

From newsprint to TV

Cartoonist recalled making of a holiday classic

YOU COULD CALL "PEANUTS" A HAPPY-SAD comic strip. The syndicated feature's protagonist — nerdy, round-headed social misfit Charlie Brown — can never win, even at something as simple as flying a kite or kicking a football.

Much of the classic comic strip's melancholy vibe has to do with the sensibilities of it's creator, writer and artist: Minneapolis native Charles M. Schulz (1922-2000).

So when Schulz set about plotting the first-ever "Peanuts" TV special, "A Charlie Brown Christmas" (1965), it's no wonder that ambivalence regarding the holiday season became the central theme of the program.

"I know what it's like to be lonely at the holidays," the cartoonist told me in 1998, during a telephone interview from his studio in Santa Rosa, California.

"I know what it's like to spend all day on Christmas completely alone, and being downtown in St. Paul (Minnesota) eating by yourself in a cafeteria. I know what that's like."

Schulz acknowledged that such conflicted emotions are particularly acute during the holidays.

"I suppose it has something to do with our inability to rise to the occasion," Schulz, then 76, said.

"We see TV shows and movies and magazine articles and wonderful photographs of people having a great time, and it simply isn't true. Most of the time, our lives don't live up to those expectations. There are a lot of lonely people.

"So I am very well aware of how lonely holidays can be."

One example of this loneliness in the TV special has come to be known as the "Charlie Brown Christmas tree," a tree so scrawny and pathetic, no shopper would choose it from a pack of prettier, healthier — or, in some cases, more garish — trees. A tree that, as Linus puts it, "just needs a little love."

In the ensuing decades, the Charlie Brown Christmas tree has won a permanent place in holiday lore. Sometimes, people use it as criterion for selecting their Christmas tree. Reproductions are manufactured and marketed. And the term, which has long since entered the lexicon, is even repeated in non-holiday contexts.

"It's very gratifying to think that things like the Charlie Brown Christmas tree, which I have thought of, have become part of our language," Schulz said.

"And the security blanket and Charlie Brown having the football pulled away from him and losing the ball games and the kite-eating tree and all of those things. That's very gratifying.

"We had no idea that the Charlie Brown Christmas tree would become a cult thing when we first did it."

Charles M. Schulz said he was surprised when the "Charlie Brown Christmas tree" entered the lexicon.

"I know what it's like to be lonely at the holidays," said "Peanuts" creator Schulz, shown at his drawing board in 1956.

Roger Higgins/Library of Congress

"A CHARLIE BROWN CHRISTMAS" ALSO EXPLORES the commercialization of Christmas, though surprisingly, Schulz did not have a strong position on the phenomenon.

"I must admit that the commercialism of Christmas doesn't really bother me. It never *did* bother me as much as the show seems to indicate," the cartoonist said. "Because I doubt very much that Christmas was ever a religious holiday in the first place. I sometimes think we should try to abandon these feelings of guilt and just enjoy it for what it is. Enjoy the giving and the getting together, and stop feeling so guilty about it."

Another memorable aspect of the TV special is its jazz score by pianist Vince Guaraldi, a Grammy winner for 1962's "Cast Your Fate to the Wind." Guaraldi's participation led many fans to assume that Schulz was, himself, an aficionado of jazz music.

"I had nothing to do with it," Schulz said with a chuckle.

"(Producer) Lee Mendelson lives near San Francisco in what we call the Bay Area. He had heard Vince Guaraldi performing at one of the clubs in town. He just thought, 'Why not try something different?' and called Vince.

"Well, Vince had never written for any film before. He didn't even really know how to do it. He never saw the scenes that I believe a composer should when he or she is composing music for a film. So he just wrote out some music, and of course (the song) 'Linus and Lucy' has become a minor classic. So it was wonderful, but I never had anything to do with the selection of the music."

Schulz could not quibble with character designs in the special, which were wholly faithful to his comic strip illustrations. But he was initially irked by some inconsistencies in the animation, which resulted from the tight schedule in completing the special.

Said the cartoonist: "Obviously, everybody has noticed that the Charlie Brown Christmas tree changes in its appearance in a couple of scenes. In fact, I remember the first time I saw it. We looked at it and we thought, 'Oh, no, what have we done?' Even the animator agreed.

"You see, the show was done in only four months, which is much too short a time than is necessary. This is because different people drew it. The animation is usually farmed out to animators who have their own studios or work at home."

THE CRUX OF THE SPECIAL COMES WHEN LINUS — in response to the question "What is the meaning of Christmas?" — steps onto a stage and recites the oft-repeated excerpt from Luke about the birth of Christ.

Including this scene was not without risk, considering network skittishness over the possibility of alienating non-Christian viewers. But, as Schulz and his collaborators had hoped, the sequence comes off as heartfelt and innocent rather than sanctimonious.

"I think that's the revolutionary part of the show," Schulz said.

"I remember sitting in the living room with Bill Melendez, the animator, and Lee Mendelson, the producer, trying to put together a show. We had the story going the way it was. But I remember sitting there and finally saying to them, 'You know, I don't think there's any way we can get around it. If we're going to do this show right, we have to use the famous passage from St. Luke.'

"And of course, the scene where Linus comes out onto the stage and says, 'Lights, please,' and then recites that famous passage from St. Luke was quite revolutionary in an animated cartoon."

175

'How the Grinch Stole Christmas!' (1966)

CHUCK JONES KEPT ASKING THEODOR GEISEL TO let him make a TV special out of Geisel's 1957 book "How the Grinch Stole Christmas!" Geisel, a.k.a. Dr. Seuss, kept saying no.

It's not like Geisel wasn't aware of Jones' many accomplishments in the field of animation. Jones (1912-2002) was a driving force behind Warner Bros.' "Merry Melodies" and "Looney Tunes" animated shorts featuring Bugs Bunny and cohorts.

It also wasn't like Geisel hadn't already known Jones as a collaborator. During the years of World War II, the two men partnered on 11 out of 26 "Private Snafu" cartoon training films made between 1943 and 1955, with Jones as director and Geisel as writer. (Sharp-eyed Seuss-o-philes cite some decidedly Seuss-ical character design in the 1944 short titled "Rumors.")

But Jones finally wore Geisel down, and we are the richer for it.

The 1966 animated special "How the Grinch Stole Christmas!" — written by Geisel, directed by Jones — accomplished two seemingly disparate things at once. It was wholly true to Geisel's 1957 book. And it was a marked departure from same.

First on Jones' itinerary was to flesh out the book to accommodate the special's running time. "It was a good story. We felt we could add business to it," he said in a 1994 short film about the special. Jones called upon Geisel to make additions to the book's "script" in the form of extra verses, names for the Whos' toys, and lyrics for three songs.

It then fell to Jones to create animation-friendly character designs and — the most significant liberty of all — add color to Geisel's intrinsically black-and-white world. Jones' Who-ville is practically psychedelic.

Recalled Jones in the 1994 film: "I finished the drawings on the Grinch. Why, Dr. Seuss — Ted — takes a look at them. He said, 'It looks like *you.*' And I said, 'Well, it happens, you know.'"

Casting horror star Boris Karloff as the narrator and the Grinch was an inspiration. The Grinch is unrepentantly evil; he's a bigot (he hates Whos for being Whos); treats his dog Max more like a slave than a pet; and steals candy from babies. Karloff played some diabolical characters in his career, but the Grinch can stand alongside Hjalmar Poelzig, Mord the executioner and the Wurdulak.

Karloff switches between his two roles on a dime, reading the Grinch with maximum mean-

Max's little snow mishap gives the Grinch an idea. Below: The Grinch, too, uses a chimney. © Dr. Seuss Enterprises, L.P.

ness, while maintaining a genteel, grandfatherly tone in delivering Geisel's text. (A filter is added to Karloff's voice when in Grinch mode.)

Truth be told, you kind of see why the Grinch finds the Whos so annoying. The Whos are the happiest, singingest, nicest group of beings anywhere. They have tails, webbed feet and weird hairstyles. Women wear pink mohawks, men wear Brooklyn-hipster beards.

Cindy-Lou looks like an insect in the 1957 book; in the 1966 special, the blond-haired, blue-eyed Cindy-Lou is more humanoid, antennae notwithstanding.

Two indelible sequences in the special are a little bit creepy. One is ... "The Smile." What is The Smile in "The Grinch"? It's the moment when he sees Max covered in snow, and gets the Grinchy idea to dress as Santa and burglarize Who-ville. The resulting smile, which seems endless, is totally creepozoid.

But the sickest, most brain-twisting scene comes when the Mean One extracts candy canes from five sleeping Who children. The Grinch's shadow crossing their bed is like something out of "Nosferatu." He removes the candy almost lovingly. Even the Wurdulak might have sensed a kindred spirit.

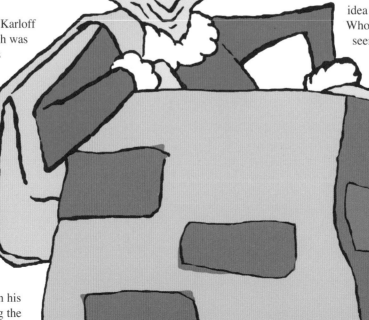

The citizens of Who-ville join hands to sing "Welcome Christmas." © Dr. Seuss Enterprises, L.P.

The Sloo-Slonker

The Jing-Tingler

The Floo-Floober and Tar-Tinker

The Who-Whoover

The game Zoo-Zizzer-Karzay

The Blum-Blooker

177

The Grinch steals Christmas in the Chuck Jones-directed animated special. © Dr. Seuss Enterprises, L.P.

That Mean One, Mr. Grinch, was only the second green-hued menace that Boris Karloff would play in his long career.

The first? Frankenstein's monster.

But it was no great leap when animator Chuck Jones cast the horror movie star as narrator (and the voice of the Grinch) in "How the Grinch Stole Christmas!" With his lilting British accent and mesmerizing lisp, Karloff (1887-1969) possessed one of the most distinctive — and imitated — voices in popular culture. A late-career specialty of Karloff's was as a reader of children's stories on radio and recordings, so this was familiar territory for the star of "Frankenstein," "The Mummy" and "The Black Cat." Karloff, then 78, nailed Geisel's extraordinary rhythms, sailing through the peculiar pronunciations. (Zoo-Zizzer-Karzay, anyone?)

"I didn't want any other voice to come in, because he has a poetic quality, the way he read it, the curious little rhyming patterns that all Dr. Seuss lines have," said Jones (in a 1994 short film about the special). Jones echoed that sentiment in a 1969 letter to Karloff's widow, Eva, shortly after her husband's death.

On MGM letterhead, Jones wrote that the special had become a holiday classic. "In my opinion, the major reason for this is that Mr. Karloff gave such a thoughtful and understanding reading of the script," Jones wrote. "I think it is entirely appropriate that children for many generations will find joy and a deeper understanding of Christmas through the skill of your husband."

Karloff won a Grammy for "The Grinch" in the Best Recording for Children category, but did not attend the ceremony. When Karloff's then-agent, Arthur Kennard, later presented the actor with the award at Kennard's office, Karloff reportedly said, "It looks like a bloody doorstop," and left it on the floor by Kennard's door, never bringing it home.

Karloff's only child, Sara Karloff (born 1938), caught the "Grinch" TV special when it first aired in 1966, a little more than two years before her father's death at age 81. "I loved it the moment I saw it," she told me in 2000, "but I could not foresee the impact it's had on youngsters for generations now."

Sure enough, Sara's grandchildren — Boris Karloff's great-grandchildren — watched the special every Christmas season. "It's a cherished part of our family history and legacy," she said.

As for what Christmas was like growing up with the movies' preeminent monster: "Well, it was probably no different than in any other household. It was certainly not Hollywood-esque. Those Christmases were delightful and marvelous."

"As the Grinch took the tree, as he started to shove / He heard a small sound, like the coo of a dove / He turned around fast, and he saw a small Who / Little Cindy-Lou Who, who was no more than 2."

Wide-eyed Cindy-Lou Who in "How the Grinch Stole Christmas!" embodies the trusting innocence of a child. Despite the Grinch's considerably less-than-jolly appearance as Santa — not to mention the green skin — Cindy-Lou bought his story that "there's a light on the tree that won't light on one side."

As the only character besides the Grinch with dialogue in the classic TV special, Cindy-Lou was entrusted to voice artist June Foray (1917-2017). Foray is best known as the voice of Rocky the Flying Squirrel and Natasha in Jay Ward's political satire "The Rocky and Bullwinkle Show." Foray had hundreds of animation credits from the 1940s until three years before her death at age 99.

"When he (Jones) wanted to do Cindy-Lou Who, whom did he

call but June?" Foray told me in 2000. "He's a very dear friend."

Foray wasn't shown sketches of Cindy-Lou before recording her lines. "Sometimes in animation, if you're voice-testing for something, they show you a 'model sheet,' but they didn't bother," she said. "They know the versatility of an actor and what an actor can do. You say, 'Well, is *this* what you like?' 'That's fine.'"

Foray — who was never in the studio at the same time as Karloff — felt he made a perfect Grinch. "Oh, I thought he was marvelous," Foray said. "Boris Karloff was a consummate actor."

And Foray was grateful that "The Grinch" added another memorable character to her own legacy. "It has become quite a classic," she said. "It's shown every Christmas. The animation is great. The storyline is great. It has a wonderful moral at the end, which is good for children. It's just beautifully done."

"The three words that best describe you are as follows, and I quote: Stink. Stank. Stunk."

As the evil Grinch sews his Santa Claus suit in preparation for burglarizing the citizens of Who-ville, and later as he slithers through their homes, using a magnet to extract stockings hung over the fireplace, we hear a *basso profundo* voice sing those condemning lyrics — a deep, rich voice that is somehow familiar.

It belonged to Thurl Ravenscroft (1914-2005), whose most famous contribution to pop culture was as the voice of Tony the Tiger, mascot for Kellogg's Frosted Flakes cereal. From 1953 until his death, Ravenscroft exclaimed, "They're *gre-e-e-eat!*"

Singing "You're a Mean One, Mr. Grinch" on the TV special "How the Grinch Stole Christmas" — uncredited, yet — was nothing Ravenscroft spent a lot of time preparing for.

"I didn't know anything about it until an hour before I did it," the vocalist told me when we spoke in 2000.

"In fact, when I did it, I was on call with about eight or nine singers. We did all the singing for the people of Who-ville. Then at the end of the session, they said, 'Thurl, here's a solo that we want you to do.' They handed me the music. There was a big orchestra on the big set at MGM. Chuck Jones was there and Dr. Seuss was there, Ted Geisel."

So Ravenscroft had to master a mouthful of typically challenging Seussian lyrics, right on the spot?

"Oh, that was a cinch," he said with a laugh. "I mean, once you get used to Dr. Seuss, you know what he does with lyrics. There was no problem there. I made two or three takes, and that was it."

Ravenscroft also sang in sessions for Bing Crosby, Frank Sinatra and Elvis Presley. "The good lord gave me a very unusual voice," the singer said, "and gave me the opportunity to learn how to use it."

"The Grinch" voice Boris Karloff. Below left: Cindy-Lou Who was voiced by June Foray. Below right: Singer Thurl Ravenscroft.

"How the Grinch Stole Christmas" © Dr. Seuss Enterprises, L.P.

The lyrics were by Geisel, all right, but the melodies for the three songs in "How the Grinch Stole Christmas" — "Trim Up the Tree," "Welcome Christmas" and "You're a Mean One, Mr. Grinch" — were composed by Albert Hague (1920-2001), a Tony winner for "Redhead."

Not that Geisel would have approved Hague for the gig merely because of a fancy award.

Recalled Hague in the 1994 short film about the TV special: "I played him one chorus (of 'You're a Mean One, Mr. Grinch'), and he looked up and said, 'Any man that can slide an octave on the word Grinch gets the job.'"

'The Little Drummer Boy' (1968)

CAN A CHRISTMAS SPECIAL BE religious without being preachy?

Arthur Rankin Jr. and Jules Bass walked that fine line with their first animated special to focus on the religious, rather than the commercial, aspects of Christmas. Without benefit of a single candy cane, sleigh bell or toymaking elf, "The Little Drummer Boy" holds the interest of children of all ages.

The story concerns Aaron (voiced by Ted Eccles), a drummer with a Beatle haircut whose only friends are animals: Joshua the camel, Samson the donkey, and Baba the lamb. These outcasts wander the desert, Aaron tapping his drum while the animals do a joyful kind of dancing march. It's adorable.

Aaron is spotted by Ben Haramed (voiced by José Ferrer), a shifty showman always on the lookout for artists for his traveling revue. Ben kidnaps the talented youngster and his furry friends, and heads toward Jerusalem to mount his next entertainment extravaganza.

But getting Aaron to perform for the public is trickier than Ben imagines. Aaron, you see, hates all people. We find out why in a flashback: Bandits murdered his parents and burned their sheep ranch to the ground.

Little Aaron is the sole survivor of the massacre.

When forced to play for the crowd, Aaron refuses to smile, so — in a sidelong wink to Victor Hugo's "The Man Who Laughs" — Ben paints one on his face. Aaron's act wins the audience over — that is, until he lashes out at them.

But Ben Haramed will make a profit yet. A caravan of three kings is following the Star of Bethlehem. When a camel needs to be replaced, heartless Ben sells them Joshua.

And so Aaron, Samson and Baba also follow the star, in the hopes of retrieving their little friend. En route, a speeding Roman chariot tramples Baba, and the tiny lamb's death seems imminent. Will Baba die?

Ferrer was, of course, an Oscar winner. Eccles was a child star who turned up on "The Beverly Hillbillies" and "The Munsters." The script was by Romeo Muller ("Rudolph the Red-Nosed Reindeer"). And the Vienna Boys Choir (founded in 1498) sang the stirring title song.

The special was narrated in the dulcet tones of Mrs. Miniver herself, Greer Garson, another Oscar winner billed as *"Miss* Greer Garson," just so there's no mistaking this is a classy broad.

Hey, there was no "Mister" billing for Burl Ives. And there was no Greer Garson puppet.

Top: Aaron does his thing in "The Little Drummer Boy." Above: Mary nods as Aaron plays for Baby Jesus. © Rankin/Bass Productions

Frosty leads local children in an impromptu parade. Below: Old-schooler Jimmy Durante growls the title tune. © Rankin/Bass Productions

'Frosty the Snowman' (1969)

"As any child can tell you, there's a certain magic in the very first snow — especially when it falls on the day before Christmas."

These words of wisdom, conveyed in the gravelly Lower-East-Side-ese of Jimmy Durante, set the scene for Rankin/Bass' animated — as in true illustrations, not puppets — special.

Like other veteran entertainers who sat at the microphone of Arthur Rankin Jr. and Jules Bass, Durante won generations of new, pint-sized fans with this one gig.

But "Frosty the Snowman" is kind of a bittersweet affair. For many grown-up children, the special left an indelible impression with its heart-wrenching "Bambi" moment: the scene of a little girl sobbing by a puddle that was once her new friend Frosty, now melted by less-than-frosty temperatures.

Fear not, traumatized kiddies. As promised in the lyrics, Frosty will "be back again some day."

Much of the special's appeal is thanks to Jackie Vernon, a throwback nightclub comedian who, but for the Rankin/Bass special, might have been relegated to the depths of entertainment-world obscurity. Frosty was voiced by Vernon, a recurring presence on "The Ed Sullivan Show," "Tonight" and "The Hollywood Squares" — one of those comics you would see on TV and go, "Oh, *that* guy."

Vernon's casual delivery makes Frosty like an every-oaf — funny and kid-friendly, sure, but somehow forlorn.

Durante — then 76, in his second-to-last film production — was a natural to host the cartoon special, for a full-circle reason.

In 1950, Durante scored a #7 hit with Steve Nelson and Jack Rollins' song "Frosty the Snowman." And like Vernon, Durante sounds a little bit sad, like a grandfather with scant time left on the clock telling a bedtime story.

The young girl was voiced by June Foray, who also voiced Cindy-Lou Who in "The Grinch."

The plot has bumbling magician Professor Hinkel (Billy De Wolfe) hired to entertain a classroom on Christmas Eve. His magic tricks fall flat, but his hat is somehow imbued with real magic, the kind that brings to life a snowman built by the schoolchildren. Frosty — fashioned with his coal eyes, button nose and corncob pipe — utters his first words upon coming to life: "Happy birthday" (presumably to himself).

Hinkel wants to regain his magical hat and cash in, but the kids want Frosty to keep wearing it — and thus, continue to exist. Meanwhile, Hinkel's rabbit, Hocus Pocus, jumps ship and sides with the kids.

The silly story is pure kids' stuff, but when Frosty the Snowman melts, so do you.

181

'Santa Claus is Comin' to Town' (1970)

IMAGINE THE PRESSURE! ANIMATING A dancing doll in the likeness of Hollywood's greatest dancer, Mr. Fred Astaire. The Fred puppet didn't move with the grace and precision Astaire evinced in "Top Hat" or "Shall We Dance," but it got the general idea across.

Astaire narrates and sings in Rankin/Bass' special, which features the voice of another star of golden-age musicals, Mickey Rooney, as Santa.

"Comin' to Town" — which uses the song by J. Fred Coats (music) and Haven Gillespie (lyrics) as its jumping-off point — is an origin story with a cute setup. Astaire voices S.D. Kluger, the North Pole mailman who handles letters from kids asking questions about Santa such as: Why the red suit? Why live at the North Pole? Why go down chimneys?

A long flashback explains all. It seems that Santa was once an infant abandoned at the doorstep of the imperious Burgermeister Meisterburger (voiced by the prolific Paul Frees). BM is a tempestuous tyrant who rules a bleak, monochromatic town square that is fashioned after once-popular American assumptions about Communist Russia — cobblestone streets, tight living quarters, oppressive vibe, jittery citizens. The children even have gray hair.

Said kids are joyless, since the Burgermeister outlawed toys. (Ah, we have our Christmas villain.)

The Burgermeister rejects the baby, but furry little animals —

always hovering on the periphery of a Rankin/Bass special — tote the child to the Kringle family in a remote village. The Kringles are jolly toymakers who wear red suits and, if male, white beards. (File *that* one away for later.)

The Kringles adopt the baby, christen him Kris Kringle, and continue to manufacture toys that, alas, never get delivered. A nearby mountain, alas, is impassible. (File *that* one away, too.)

You guessed it: Kris grows into manhood and crosses the mountain to deliver the toys. En route, he meets a penguin named Topper, and these fast friends encounter the Winter Warlock (voiced by Keenan Wynn). WW is a scary figure, but turns into an old softie when Kris gifts him with something he's always wanted: a "choo-choo."

That's the power of toys for you. Kris has but to present someone with a toy, and their heart goes pit-a-pat. Beautiful, no-nonsense schoolteacher Jessica (voiced by singer Robbie Lester) is touched when Kris gives her a doll. Even old Burgermeister feels a reluctant twinge of joy when Kris hands him a yo-yo.

One by one, the questions in Astaire's letters are answered. Kris keeps tabs on whether kids are "naughty or nice" by monitoring a crystal snowglobe. Reindeer are imbued with the power of flight via a magic coin. The letter-writing begins when kids send thank-you notes to Santa.

And Jessica becomes Mrs. Santa Claus. Yep, Santa, the old dog, locked that down.

Young Kris Kringle (voiced by Mickey Rooney) makes a toy. Top: Fred Astaire as the North Pole's mailman. © Rankin/Bass Productions

Heat Miser, left, and Snow Miser, right, have serious mother issues. Below: Vixen makes an unconvincing dog. © Rankin/Bass Productions

'The Year Without a Santa Claus' (1974)

THERE'S ONLY ONE THING YOU NEED TO KNOW about Rankin/Bass' animated special of 1974, "The Year Without a Santa Claus": The Miser brothers. The flamboyant, competitive, mother-issues-suffering, narcissistic, polar-opposite Miser brothers.

The title of the special is a misnomer. There *is* no year without a Santa Claus, just a year in which he has a bad cold and a bad back, and decides to stay in bed rather than make the brutal Christmas Eve trek. But eventually — spoiler alert — circumstances compel Santa (again voiced by Mickey Rooney) to climb aboard his sleigh and make with the toys.

The title isn't the *only* red herring. The special is "hosted" by Oscar winner Shirley Booth (star of TV's "Hazel"), who voices Mrs. Santa Claus in her final film production. Viewers are led to believe that Mrs. Santa will stand in for her ailing hubby, and deliver the toys herself. Booth even dons Santa "drag" and sings a song about it, "I Could Be Santa Claus."

But the idea is unceremoniously dropped, and the story focuses instead on Mrs. Santa's scheme to draw Santa back into action with help from two goofball elves, Jingle and Jangle, and a baby reindeer, Vixen.

The disruption of weather patterns figures in Mrs. Santa's scheme, so the Miser brothers — Mr. Snow Miser and Mr. Heat Miser — are called upon. And these skirmishing siblings steal the show.

We first meet Mr. Snow Miser who, in the days before "Fame" and "Glee," must have attended some fancy high school for the performing arts. Without provocation, Snow Miser launches into a Broadway-ready production number, heavy on the outstretched arms, cane-twirling, in-unison steps and Rockettes-style strut kicks.

Snow Miser lustily sings and dances wearing a straw hat, icicles dangling from his pointy nose, and — no pun intended — a frozen smile, accompanied by a "mini-me" chorus line fashioned in his image. Sample lyrics: *"He's Mr. Ice Crystals, he's Mr. Ten Below."*

Where Snow Miser is whip-thin and smiley, Heat Miser is pudgy and scowly. Heat Miser's color scheme — red, yellow and orange — evokes a fire motif, as does his Flock of Seagulls hairstyle. Not to be outdone in the ego department, Heat Miser likewise employs a mini-me chorus line. Sample lyrics: *"Whatever I touch, starts to melt in my clutch."*

Back on Earth, in an average American town, stockings are used to hide Vixen's antlers to fool the locals into thinking she is a puppy. The ploy backfires: Vixen is promptly caught and caged by the town dog-catcher. Guess who comes to her rescue? Santa! He's back, baby, and he's better than ever.

This is a rare Rankin/Bass special not based on a popular song, though some are heard on its soundtrack: "Here Comes Santa Claus," "Sleigh Ride" and "Blue Christmas," which was popularized by Elvis Presley. It makes you wonder: What if Presley had "hosted" one of these specials? Can't you just picture The King's swiveling hips in Rankin/Bass animation?

Roger Daltrey as Scrooge in New York City in 1998.

Photo by Kathy Voglesong

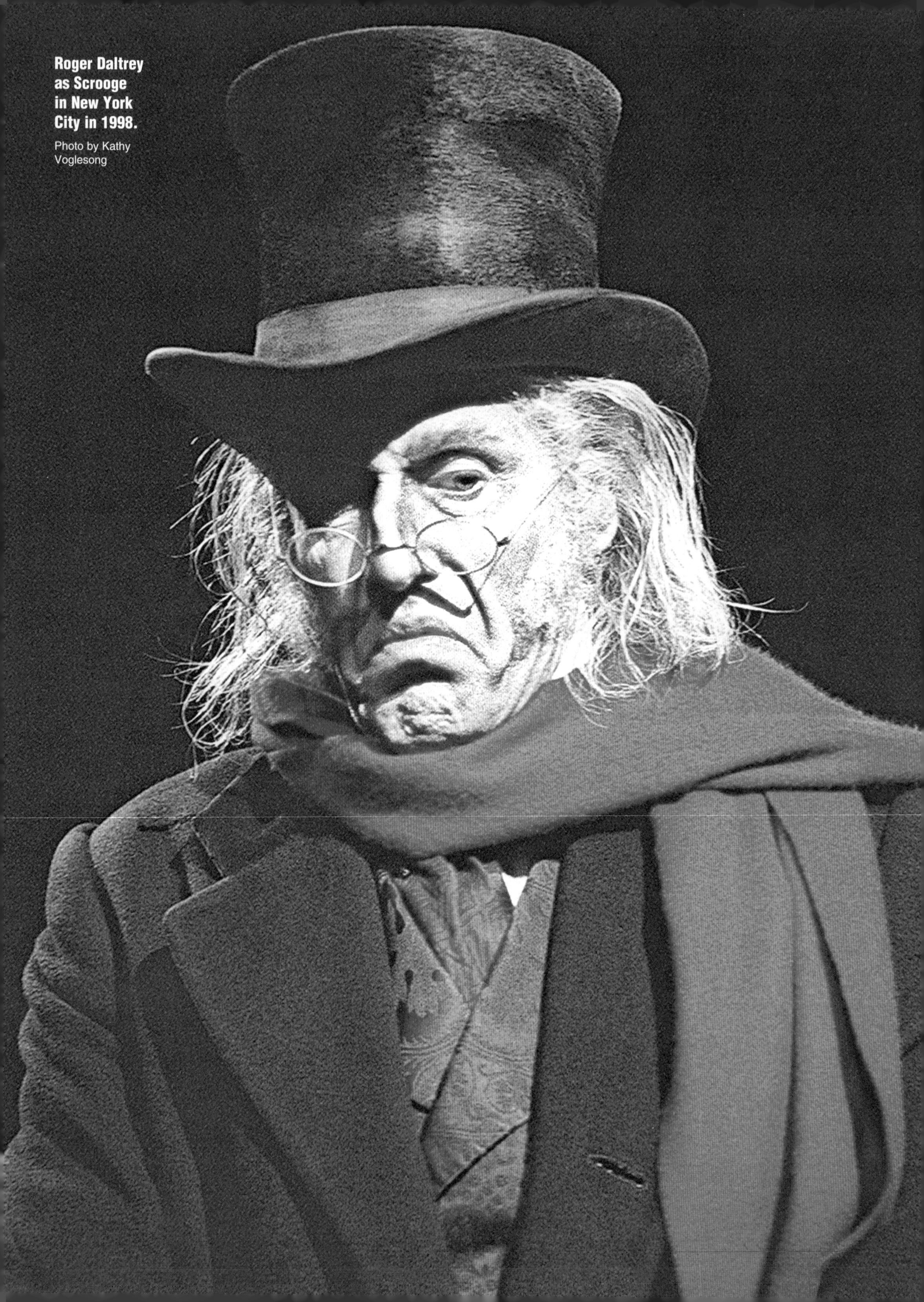

Auld lang syne

Christmas-y memories recalled by celebrities

SOME CELEBRITIES ARE WELL-KNOWN FANS OF Christmas. Elvis Presley famously (and extravagantly) decked out his Memphis homestead Graceland in holiday style, and gave thoughtful (and extravagant) gifts to his family and posse, er, staff. Despite the demands of touring, recording and movie-making, Presley always made it a point to return home for the holiday. From 1962 until his final Christmas in 1976, Presley spent the holiday at Graceland.

Old-guarders such as Frank Sinatra, Liberace and Andy Williams were said to carry their public affection for Christmas into their private lives. Sinatra's daughter Nancy told *Variety* in 2017: "My mom (Nancy Barbato Sinatra) was a tinsel master. My dad and his friends would come over late Christmas Eve after a night of revelry, and they would just throw tinsel at the tree. And my mom and I would undo it afterwards."

Then there's Lou Costello, perhaps the Santa Claus-iest of all celebrity Santa Clauses.

Joe Besser, who played overgrown brat Stinky opposite Costello on the 1950s sitcom "The Abbott and Costello Show," shared a Christmas-centric anecdote involving Costello in his memoir, "Not Just a Stooge" (1984, Excelsior Books).

Besser wrote that, while living in North Hollywood, he was asked by Costello why there were no exterior Christmas lights on his home. Besser replied that he didn't own any lights, and besides, nobody in his neighborhood put lights on their houses.

"These words horrified Lou," Besser wrote, adding that Costello asked him, "What are you, Scrooge or something?"

The next day, Costello showed up at Besser's home carrying 50 boxes of lights — not that Besser could *see* Costello at first.

Wrote Besser: "I removed the top 10 boxes and, sure enough, Lou was behind them. That afternoon, he helped me string the entire house and by nightfall, we witnessed the wonders of our work: the entire house lit up! Lou had me string lights over every window, completely around the house, on the weather drains, across the roof, around the door frames — everywhere. He even brought candy canes to put around the front yard that also lit up. Our home looked like a substation for the electric company!"

Following are celebrity musings on the holiday, derived from interviews I've conducted over the years. Some are about childhood Christmases, some about Christmas-themed productions and professional engagements. A few are memories from the offspring of famous folk — including Presley's daughter, Lisa Marie, and Costello's daughter, Chris.

ROGER DALTREY

The Who singer Roger Daltrey played Scrooge in a New York City production of "A Christmas Carol" in 1998. When Daltrey said the Cratchits' paltry Christmas dinner reminded him of the modest holiday repast of his *own* childhood, he wasn't joking. "It's as big as the chicken we used to have when I was a kid," Daltrey said. "I look at it and think, 'Bloody hell!' The Christmas dinner — that was our year's luxury! It was post-war England. We just about managed to get the windows replaced from the bombing. There are things within the show that bring back memories of my childhood. It really does remind me of how far I've come."

ANNIE HASLAM

"I come from Lancashire," said singer Annie Haslam in 2001. "I remember, when I was a little girl, the Christmas carolers that used to come 'round all the time. It was snowing. You used to take out drinks to the people that came, or take hot mince pies out. It was like something out of Charles Dickens, actually. By the way, I wasn't born in Victorian times. I'm not that old. But that was actually before I even knew that I was going to be a singer. I wanted to be a ballet dancer and all kinds of things that all the little girls wanted to be. But I always remember loving the melodies so much, and them bringing back to that time of year I think is so special. Christmas is one of my favorite times of year anyway."

LOU CHRISTIE

The singer of "Lightnin' Strikes" (#1 in 1966) has Christmas to thank for his earliest gig. "The first time I sang in front of people was 'Away in a Manger' in a first grade Christmas play," Lou Christie said in 2013. "I played Joseph, and this little girl played Mary. Well, she freaked out, so I had to sing it by myself. From there, it was 'O Holy Night,' and then something else. And I got applause! I thought, 'Gosh, this is wonderful.' So I kept on going."

GARY PUCKETT

Long before he sang on such Top 10 hits as "Young Girl" and "Woman, Woman" with his group the Union Gap, Gary Puckett made his first-ever recording as a Christmas message. "As a child, I had this little, little soprano voice," the singer recalled in 1998. "You know, it's God's gift to me. And, of course, it just matured over the years. My mother told me once, she said, 'I just thought that *all* little kids could sing like you could sing.'

"When I was about 8 years old, they used to get a tape recorder about a month before Christmastime. We would record Christmas songs and little messages and things — just talk to my grandparents back in Minnesota. And then they would take the tape recorder back to the place where they rented it, and these people would transfer the tapes onto these little yellow discs. And my folks would send them to my grandparents, so that they could just put them on their record player and listen to them.

"My mom still has a lot of these little records. She has one of me when I was 8 singing 'Rudolph the Red-Nosed Reindeer.' When I listen to it, I just go, 'Man, that's pretty amazing.' Because I had this little soprano voice that was just perfect. So it's not something I really developed. I think the vibrato probably developed over the years. But it was something God placed there."

ANNE MURRAY

As a child, singer Anne Murray ("Snowbird," #8, "Danny's Song," #7) never had to *dream* of a white Christmas.

"Well, I grew up in Nova Scotia, so there was almost always snow at Christmas," Murray said with a chuckle in 2004. "It was just great, you know. I came from a very big family — five brothers — so it was wonderful. I just think of warm and fuzzy when I think of Christmas, because we had a very happy family."

TOMMY JAMES

With his group the Shondells, Tommy James sang on such 1960s Top 10 hits as "Hanky Panky" (#1), "Mony Mony" (#3), and "Crimson and Clover" (#1). The singer spent his youth in Michigan. "Christmases when I was a little kid growing up in the Midwest were tremendous," said James in 2004. "I mean, they really were a major, big deal. When I was 3 years old, my mom took me to the store to see Santa. That just left a real dent in my head."

LISA MARIE PRESLEY

Elvis Presley lived large — and celebrated the holiday the same way.

"He very much loved, loved, loved, loved Christmas," said Presley's daughter, Lisa Marie. "The house was always lit up. I love Christmas as well. I kind of got that, as well, from him. It was always an amazing time. Very happy. Very fun."

JAMES BROWN

In his final interview, conducted four days before his death on Christmas Day 2006, the "Godfather of Soul" was publicizing a Dec. 30 show he never lived to perform. On how he planned to spend the holiday: "Well, my family, they're on the way. They're comin' here now. My wife's gonna look up people." On his happiest memories from childhood: "Christmas. My daddy gave me five dollars on Christmas and a suit of clothes." On whether he had a New Year's resolution: "Yep. We got to learn to love each other." On how that's going to happen: "You keep on practicin' and keep on talkin' about it. I'd appreciate it if *you* keep talkin' about it."

JONATHAN HARRIS

"Lost in Space" star Jonathan Harris, who played conniving Dr. Smith on the 1960s sci-fi series, recalled a Christmas-y anecdote involving his old boss, producer Irwin Allen, and Allen's then-assistant who was named Paul. Said the actor in 1990: "At Christmastime one year, Irwin called Paul into the office and he said, 'I've gotta give some guy a Christmas present. I don't know what the (expletive) I'm gonna give him. Go out and get him a sweater.' Paul said, 'A *particular* sweater?' 'Cashmere.' 'How much do you want to spend?' 'Twenty-five dollars is good enough for him.' 'You can't get cashmere for $25.' 'Well, get *some* kind of sweater.' 'Any particular color?' 'I don't give a damn!' 'Well, I'll go out and do the best I can.' 'Do that. I'm busy.'

"Paul came back with a sweater of sorts. Irwin examined it very carefully and said, 'Good. Now wrap it up. I want to see bows. I want to see streamers.' Paul was very good at packaging.

"He came back with this gorgeous, gorgeous package. Irwin picked it up and examined it. 'Mmm-hmm.' (Here, Harris pretended to be Allen handing the gift back to his assistant.) 'Merry Christmas, Paul.' That's a true story. That's the real Irwin Allen."

LYDIA CORNELL

The Christmas of 1982 was especially memorable for actress Lydia Cornell, who starred in the sitcom "Too Close for Comfort" (1980-87). But not for a reason you might guess. Cornell was part of a troupe of celebrities selected by Bob Hope to entertain troops overseas. "In 1982, I went to Beirut on Christmas Eve to visit the Marines," she recalled during an interview in 2000.

"Bob Hope wasn't going to go that year because he had eye trouble. So I went with Johnny Grant and another actress, Kelly Patterson. We flew into a war zone at midnight. The Marines picked us up at the airport. There was a blackout — no lights were allowed to be on — and a curfew. We drove through minefields. We went down to these burnt-out artillery units and sang 'Silent Night' with all the Marines. We went on all the aircraft carriers the next day. It was a scary, amazing thing. Then we went to this big building where they did a changing-of-the-guard for us.

"Then I came home," Cornell continued. "A month later, a truck bomb blew up that whole building."

CHRIS COSTELLO

Roly-poly comic Lou Costello, of the comedy team Abbott and Costello, was an avowed Christmas fanatic. Recalled Costello's daughter, Chris, in a 2002 conversation: "In 1958 — it was the year before he died — I had wanted a little typewriter. He went out the night before Christmas to find a typewriter for me. He said that there was a mother there at the counter, and a little girl was crying because she wanted this one doll, and the doll was very expensive. My father, being who he was, said to the cashier, 'Just get that doll, wrap it up, and say it's from Santa Claus.' So that's who he was. Always giving. Constantly giving to people."

BELA LUGOSI JR.

"Dracula" star Bela Lugosi once played Santa Claus in a Hollywood parade. What was Christmas like for the *son* of Dracula? "It was a wonderful time," said Lugosi Jr. in 1998. "We always had a huge tree, because my father had a two-story-plus living room. There'd be presents and surprises — a very family-oriented event at our house. We had all the parents and aunts and uncles and cousins and what-not. My mother did a wonderful job decorating the house, like an artist, almost. It was always a very happy time."

GLORIA HENRY

The favorite "Dennis the Menace" moment for Gloria Henry — who played Dennis' mother on the 1959-63 sitcom— happened to be the series' first Christmas episode. Recalled the actress in 2011: "Generally, on every Christmas show, we ended up singing 'Silent Night.' The first time we did, the way it was written, I was to start it. I can't sing! I mean, I love to sing if not a soul is listening," Henry said with a laugh. "But this was my first time, actually, not only on camera, but the first recording of me actually singing a note by myself! So I think *that* was my favorite moment. I'm actually captured, on record, on tape, singing for, I think, two words, and then everybody else joined in. It was my favorite moment, because I always thought I'd never be able to sing publicly, and there I was, singing publicly."

CAROL BURNETT

The doyenne of TV comedy, Carol Burnett often played Christmas skits in her long-running variety series, which aired for 11 seasons beginning in 1967.

"It's always been a special time for me," Burnett said in a 2013 interview.

"Because you remember other Christmases, too. I've got a good memory. I go back to when I was 3. I can remember almost every Christmas. I remember when people were still with us. It's a sentimental time. Everybody seems cheerful," Burnett added with a wry chuckle, "depending on how dysfunctional their family is."

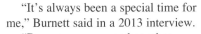

STAN LEE

In discussing stories that inspired him as a youth, Marvel Comics legend Stan Lee cited Charles Dickens' "A Christmas Carol" during a 2004 interview.

"I'm a guy who just loves stories," Lee said. "Everything I've ever seen or read has stuck somewhere in my subconscious, I guess, and inspired me. The song about 'The Little Drummer Boy' — I can't hear that through without getting misty-eyed. I'm not even Christian, and I love the whole Christmas thing," added Lee (who was Jewish).

Well, the writer was told, the world figured out a long time ago that Christmas is for *everybody*. "Absolutely," Lee agreed.

DOROTHY SCHAFFENBERGER

The wife of Fawcett Publications and DC Comics artist Kurt Schaffenberger, Dorothy Schaffenberger sometimes posed as Lois Lane for her husband. In 2008, she fondly recalled weekend get-togethers with other Fawcett creators and their wives, such as C.C. and Hilda Beck; Jack and Olga Binder; and Otto and Ione Binder. "It was the best at Christmastime," Dorothy then said.

"Each woman would make one or two batches of cookie dough. We usually met at Ione Binder's. The boys would be off bowling; it's a wonder they didn't get a ticket on the way home. We all had assignments. One of us would work the oven; one would roll out the dough; one would decorate. By the end of the evening, we had all of our holiday cookies done."

O(yster) holy night

My dad never cooked. Well, rarely. Every Christmas Eve, he made a vile concoction he called, without fanfare, oyster stew. He went to a special place to buy the oysters — if a tiny, run-down shack stinking of fish can be called special.

Early one Christmas Eve, when I was about 9, he took me with him to the oyster shack. There was a line of men my father's age — the World War II generation. Guys who didn't shave every day. Guys who looked like they'd already started celebrating the holiday. My dad, a German-Irish guy who you wouldn't call a demonstrative person, seemed the slightest bit excited when he got his bag of oysters from the indifferent man in the stained apron. We walked out of the shack a tiny bit faster than we'd walked in.

Everyone called my dad "Cholly" — that's South Philly-ese for Charles. My dad was born in South Philadelphia and emigrated to South Jersey, where my sister, little brother and I were born. Five days a week, Charles was a shipping foreman for the Gulf Oil Refinery in Philadelphia. On Friday nights, and practically all day on Saturdays and Sundays, Cholly put on a red vest and tended bar at Dan McShea's Rustic Tavern on Route 70 in Cherry Hill, New Jersey, in the shadow of the Ben Franklin Bridge. In other words, the guy worked seven days a week. The whole time I was growing up, he never had a weekend off, barring some special occasion.

He attended Edgar Allan Poe School in Philadelphia, but never made it past the eighth grade. His parents lost their house during the Great Depression and he went straight into the workforce. He was a Marine during WWII who fought at Iwo Jima and, later on, was part of a complement that patrolled the future Camp David during visits by President Roosevelt.

My dad, and men like him, were what they used to call the "salt of the Earth." They had no time for nonsense. They didn't complain. They didn't like hippies. They never spoke about the war. They bet on ball games. They called refrigerators "ice boxes." They ordered creamed-chipped-beef-on-toast at the diner because it reminded them of the chow Uncle Sam fed them during the war. They drank. My dad liked a cold beer on a hot day, but he wasn't an alcoholic by any stretch. He poured a lot more than he drank.

SO CHOLLY MADE THIS OYSTER STEW ONCE A year. It was for an open house, a giant party, my folks threw every Christmas Eve. They invited the world. This was the 1960s — the golden age of boozy parties that were thick with blueish cigarette smoke and slurred talk. This was normal to us little kids. We didn't know any different. There were a lot of drunk, middle-aged couples at my folks' Christmas Eve parties. The men would pat our heads. Mr. Cumberland always gave the three of us a crisp, new dollar bill each. That was big money for a kid in those days.

It wasn't until we were adults ourselves that we put it together. A lot of those drunk men were customers of my dad's from Dan McShea's Rustic Tavern. They were well-heeled, well-dressed

My folks posed by the rotating Christmas tree in 1967. Family photo

professional men — boozers, nonetheless — with nowhere else to go on Christmas Eve. Or worse, they were avoiding their families.

My mom remembers one of them crying sloppy tears as he watched my dad assemble our Christmas toys, a task usually begun around 2 a.m. (This gentleman obviously didn't know when the party was over.)

Mom: "Why are you crying?" Drunk Man: "I'm thinking of my *own* kids." Mom: "Where are they?" Drunk Man: "Oh, they're at home."

The oyster stew, it turns out, was always a big hit with these men, but no one under the age of 40 would go near the stuff. The stew, you see, would put something in your stomach, but not kill your buzz. My old Irish aunts — all born in the old country — were geniuses at this. That's what soda bread was about — to stave off the burn and weakness of hunger, but not diminish your level of inebriation. You need your strength to drink 'til dawn.

The simple stew my father made every Christmas Eve had a thin, pungent broth. No one under 40 would go near it. Photo by Mark Voger

SOMETHING ELSE ABOUT THOSE CHRISTMAS EVE parties of my parents' — Santa Claus visited them. You see, on Christmas Eve, when Santa rode atop a fire truck through every block in our neighborhood, the truck would stop smack in front of our house. Then Santa Claus, surrounded by a posse of men dressed in fire-fighting garb, would trudge into our house and go downstairs for a sandwich and a drink.

When we kids were so little that we still believed in Santa Claus, we would peek down the stairs and see the Jolly One himself there, eating and drinking and, I recall on one occasion, smoking a cigarette. We thought of Santa's visits as if he was casing the joint, for when he would return overnight with his sack of toys. Other kids in the neighborhood were jealous. We thought our dad must wield great political clout to make this happen.

The food served at those Christmas Eve parties was not approved by the American Heart Association. Besides the icky oyster stew, there was clam dip (cream cheese and canned clams), onion dip (sour cream and Lipton's Onion Soup Mix) and a bizarre *hors d'oeuvre* that involved bologna slices spread with cream cheese, wrapped around sweet gherkins, and cut into coins.

My mom had a three-tiered pewter serving tray she religiously filled with peanuts on top, pretzels in the middle and potato chips on the bottom. There was lots of lunchmeat (including ultra-fake "chicken roll" with mysterious gelatinous specks), breads, condiments, pickles and cheese spreads. (This was before "foodies" and the James Beard Awards.) If my dad wasn't around, we little kids surreptitiously ate the maraschino cherries he used for cocktails. (We left just enough cherries behind that we didn't get busted.) Tom Collins mixer could pass for soda if you pretended real hard.

MY DAD DIED IN 1999, FOLLOWING A SERIES OF strokes over a seven-year period. He didn't walk too well in his last seven years of life, and not at all in his final year. His left arm hung uselessly at his side. But somehow, one Christmas Eve in the middle 1990s, he made one last batch of oyster stew and brought it to the home of my little brother (who'd taken over the Christmas Eve open house tradition). Did we grown children, overcome with nostalgia, get ourselves a steaming bowl of Cholly's Christmas Eve oyster stew? Nope. We *still* didn't go near the stuff.

Not a Christmas Eve goes by that I don't time-trip back to those boozy parties my parents used to throw. I can still hear Mr. Botensten or Mr. Jacobs or Mr. Yarnell, or their Aqua Net-coiffed wives, say, "Hey, Cholly, fix me a highball?" Whiskey sours and highballs were all the rage in the 1960s. If we were lucky, there might be snow outside, and the Christmas lights on our house — the huge, multicolored, glass kind that nowadays are considered "vintage" — would glow warmly from beneath the cold white stuff. We had a tacky, gaudy, wonderful Christmas tree that rotated slowly and played "Silent Night" and "Jingle Bells," music-box style. Incessantly. It drove some people crazy, but we kids loved it. We would have a week off from school. No nuns or teachers for a whole week! All was right with the world. Every Christmas Eve, Channel 12 in Philadelphia would air the 1951 "Scrooge" starring Alastair Sim. Our eyes were glued to the TV as the party raged downstairs. To this day, I watch "Scrooge" every Christmas Eve, and I swear that sometimes I can still hear, ever so faintly beneath the movie's soundtrack, my parents' drunken guests laughing it up as Mr. Scrooge exclaims to Mrs. Dilber, "The spirits must have done everything in one night!"

Index

Bibliography

Bemelmans, Ludwig; "Mad About Madeline" (1993); Viking, New York

Besser, Joe, with Lenburg, Jeff and Greg; "Not Just a Stooge" (1984); Excelsior Books, Orange, California

Brooks, Tim, and Marsh, Earle; "The Complete Directory to Prime Time Network TV Shows 1946-Present" (1988); Ballantine Books, New York

Bruegman, Bill; "Toys of the Sixties" (1996); Toy Scouts, Akron, Ohio

Dickens, Charles; "A Christmas Carol. In Prose. Being a Ghost Story of Christmas" (1843); Chapman & Hall, London

Dickens, Charles; "Stories for Christmas" (facsimile edition published 2001); Platinum Press, New York

Dickens, Charles, writer, and Hearn, Michael Patrick, editor; "The Annotated Christmas Carol: A Christmas Carol in Prose" (2004); W.W. Norton & Company, New York

Eury, Michael; "Captain Action: The Original Super-Hero Action Figure" (2003); TwoMorrows Publishing, Raleigh, North Carolina

Geisel, Theodor (as Dr. Seuss); "How the Grinch Stole Christmas!" (1957); Random House, New York

Goldschmidt, Rick; "The Enchanted World of Rankin/Bass" (1997); Miser Bros. Press, Oak Lawn, Illinois

Grispino, Joseph A., and Terrien, Samuel, and Wice, David H., editors; "The Children's Bible" (1965); Western Publishing Company, Wisconsin

Herbert, Stephen, and McKernan, Luke, editors; "Who's Who of Victorian Cinema: A Worldwide Survey" (1996); The British Film Institute, London

Maltin, Leonard, editor; "TV Movies" (various editions); Signet, New York

Morgan, Judith and Neal; "Dr. Seuss & Mr. Geisel: A Biography" (1996), Da Capo Press, New York

Overstreet, Robert M.; "The Overstreet Comic Book Price Guide" (various editions); Avon Books, New York

Rockwell, Norman; "Norman Rockwell: Artist and Illustrator" (1970); Harry N. Abrams Inc., New York

Schulz, Charles M.; "The Joy of a Peanuts Christmas" (2000); Hallmark Books, Kansas City, Missouri

Smith, Ken; "Ken's Guide to the Bible" (1995); Blast Books, New York

Suit, Kenneth; "James Friedrich and Cathedral Films: The Independent Religious Cinema of the Evangelist of Hollywood, 1939-1966" (2018); Lexington Books, Lanham, Maryland

Sundblom, Haddon; "Dream of Santa: Haddon Sundblom's Advertising Paintings for Christmas, 1932-1964" (1997); Gramercy Publishing, New York

Various authors; "The Thompson Chain-Reference Bible" (1964), B.B. Kirkbride Bible Company, Indianapolis

Whitburn, Joel; "The Billboard Book of Top 40 Hits" (various editions); Billboard Books, New York

Yoe, Craig, editor; "The Great Treasury of Christmas Comic Book Stories" (2010); Yoe Books/IDW, San Diego

Notes

Page 10: "Candy canes are introduced": Spangler Candy Company, Bryan, Ohio

Page 10: "When young reader Virginia O'Hanlon": Newseum.org

Page 11: "Sears, Roebuck and Co. issues its first": the Sears Archive

Page 11: "Blumstein's in Harlem": BBCNews.com, 12/9/2016

Pages 11-13 and 96-103: Charting and release histories of Top 40 records: "The Billboard Book of Top 40 Hits"

Page 20: "Rat-infested warehouse": uncredited introduction, "Stories for Christmas" by Charles Dickens

Page 32: "Presumably depending on the edition": In 2020, the Ruby Lane antique auction website cited Howard Del as the artist of an 1860s edition of "Santa Claus, & His Works"

Page 34: "Cécile concocted the character": Cécile de Brunhoff, 99, Creator of Babar, New York Times obituary, 4/8/2003

Page 38: "I remembered the stories": essay in "Tell Them It Was Wonderful: Selected Writings by Ludwig Bemelmans," Viking Press, 1985

Page 38: "Wasn't the character's first brush": profile of Ludwig Bemelmans by Amy Fine Collins in Vanity Fair, 1998

Page 43: "(Ada) Richter was": International Piano Archives at Maryland, University of Maryland

Page 49: "It was brilliantly lighted": Edison Electric Light Company Bulletin No. 16, dated 2/8/1883

Page 80: "Uncle Scrooge was needed": Carl Barks interview, 1997. Due to Barks' hearing impairment, my questions were faxed to his studio, and his replies were transcribed by his then-managers Bill Grandey and Kathy Morby

Page 102: "His mother, Peggy Jones, insisted": Mary Crosby interview by Stuart Pink in The Sun, 12/20/2019

Page 125: "If they could have dubbed": Rosemary Clooney interview in the short film "White Christmas: A Look Back With Rosemary Clooney," 2000

Pages 150-161: Series broadcast histories: "The Complete Directory to Prime Time Network TV Shows 1946-Present"

Page 172: "Collaborated on an unsold documentary": short film "The Making of 'A Charlie Brown Christmas,'" 2001

Page 173: "Mendelson believed the special might never have aired": Ibid

Page 176: "It was a good story": short film "How the Grinch Stole Christmas! Special Edition," 1994

Page 178: "Any other voice": Ibid

Page 178: "On MGM letterhead": letter from Chuck Jones to Eva Karloff postmarked 2/5/1969, Heritage Auctions

Page 178: "It looks like a bloody doorstop": Sara Karloff interview by Chuck Falzone for Legacy.com, 2016

Page 179: "I played him one chorus": short film "How the Grinch Stole Christmas! Special Edition," 1994

Page 185: "My mom was a tinsel master": Nancy Sinatra interview by Chris Willman in Variety, 2017

Acknowledgments

My heartfelt thanks to some who showed me how to honor Christmas in my heart and keep it all the year (Dickens yet again): my growin'-up family Charles, Mary, Bobbi and Brian Voglesong and Henry Kelly; and the "lay teachers" (that's what they were called) and clergy of Holy Rosary School in the Diocese of Camden, New Jersey (it's not there anymore).

Thanks to John and Pamela Morrow, Eric Nolen-Weathington and everyone at TwoMorrows for, well, everything.

Thanks to the creators of Christmas Culture, and onlookers of same, who graciously submitted to my interrogation, among them Howard Bender, James Brown, Bill Bruegman, Carol Burnett, Lou Christie, Lydia Cornell, Chris Costello, Roger Daltrey, Leonard DeGraaf, June Foray, P.C. Hamerlinck, Jonathan Harris, Annie Haslam, Hollie Heller, Isaac "Ike" Heller, Gloria Henry, Tommy James, Sara Karloff, Jane Kean, The Amazing Kreskin, Stan Lee, Darlene Love, Mike Love, Bela Lugosi Jr., Anne Murray, Antony Peters, Lisa Marie Presley, Gary Puckett, Joyce Randolph, Thurl Ravenscroft, Dorothy Schaffenberger, Charles M. Schulz, Keith Thibodeaux and Andy Williams.

A tip of the visor to journalistic colleagues for editorial favors great and small. Wallace Stroby vetted "Holly Jolly" while revising his ninth novel. Vanessa Johnson lent her ever invaluable editorial advice. Across the pond in Nottinghamshire, Scott Peters proved again to be an ally as well as an eagle-eyed proofreader. Tidings of comfort and joy always to fellow alums of my alma maters The Star-Ledger and The Asbury Park Press, and to my late wife, the photographer Kathy Voglesong.

Toys and games on pages 56-67 came from a variety of sources: conventions, auctions, antique centers, flea markets, garage sales and personal collections.

Thank you to Liberty Hall Museum at Kean University in Union, New Jersey, for giving us a private tour of its "Toys Through Time" exhibit in 2016, and especially to our guide, Rachael Goldberg. The 300 toys and games in the exhibit were the very ones that the children of New Jersey's Kean political dynasty played with — in the very same 18th-century house, to boot — so you felt like you went back in time.

Thanks also to Charles Clayberger, who collected 5,000 board games over a 50-year period, and to auctioneer extraordinaire Col. Bob Randolph, who arranged for us to photograph the Clayberger collection. Hollie Heller brought along armloads of Remco toys to be photographed when I interviewed her father, Remco founder Isaac "Ike" Heller, at his New Jersey home.

The lawn decorations (page 47) are from the extravagantly decorated Gress House of Union Beach, New Jersey. The 1882 photo of Edward Hibberd Johnson's first-ever Christmas tree lights (page 48) is courtesy of Thomas Edison National Historical Park.

I wish I could tell you the name of the artist who painted the exquisite scene of budding Victorian romance on the frontispiece (page 1), or at least the publisher and year. It's a scan of a Christmas card from a private collection I obtained in the 1990s, as are vintage cards seen on pages 24-30. The unnamed collector pasted hundreds of card-fronts into large bound albums, slicing off and discarding the "indicia" halves. Thus, their publishers remain a mystery. But ain't they pretty?

Speaking of mysteries, who painted our cover boy, the smiling Santa from Dell's Four Color #958 (1958)? It's so good, Haddon Sundblom could have sued. Damn you, comic book industry, for not consistently crediting artists until comics became "cool" in the '60s.

Among 19th-century etchings on our left-hand endpapers page are pieces by artist George Cruikshanks (dancers at a ball) and engraver Edmund Evans (outdoor market). Investigate their work! Cartoonist Thomas Nast's central Santa is perhaps the single most influential illustration of the Jolly One.

On our right-hand endpapers page, vintage advertisements from a 1916 Sears catalog (Santa Claus costume, fake snow, tree angels, "kiddie" cards, etc.) are © Sears, Roebuck & Company. More images are © General Electric Co.; © KoKoMo Skates; © F.A.O. Schwarz; © Gamages; © Frederick's of Hollywood; © Philco; © Whitman's; © Prince Albert; and © Paramount Pictures.

Vital information, materials and support were provided by Jeff Colson, Maggie Hoffmann, my brother Brian Voglesong, Brian the Batman Guy (a different Brian), Bender, Hamerlinck, Stroby ... and Edward "Fast Eddie" Zupkus.

Looking for something to play in the background of your Christmas party? Click on https://vimeo.com/34111339, 4.5 hours of Christmas cheer lovingly compiled by my nephew, filmmaker Ian Voglesong (who also created my book trailers). Ian's video compilation inspired the "Not Exactly Christmas Movies" section (pages 144-148).

Disclosure: The memorabilia collages include composite images created from various sources, which I've altered digitally to correct distortion, wear (when clarity was compromised), inconsistent lighting and disruptive cropping.

My hope, Dear Reader, is that you drag out your copy of "Holly Jolly" every Christmas morning and find chocolate smudges on it from the previous year. To me, the saddest song in the world is not "Danny Boy" or "Seasons in the Sun," but "Auld Lang Syne." It means the party's over. But just for this year.

About

Shown in 1961 with his sister Bobbi and Santa Claus, Mark Voger is a 1972 graduate of Holy Rosary School in the diocese of Camden in New Jersey. A seven-time (and counting) balloon handler in the Macy's Thanksgiving Day Parade in New York City, Voger designs pages for At Home New Jersey and lives at the Jersey Shore.

Also by Mark Voger from TwoMorrows Publishing:

■ "Groovy: When Flower Power Bloomed in Pop Culture" (2017)

■ "Monster Mash: The Creepy, Kooky Monster Craze in America 1957-1972" (2015)

■ "The Dark Age: Grim, Great & Gimmicky Post-Modern Comics" (2006)

■ "Hero Gets Girl! The Life and Art of Kurt Schaffenberger" (2003)

When in cyberspace, please visit MarkVoger.com.

Family photo

MORE FROM TWOMORROWS PUBLISHING

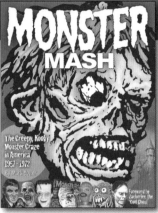

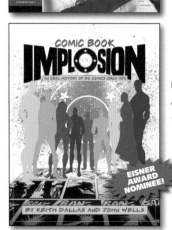

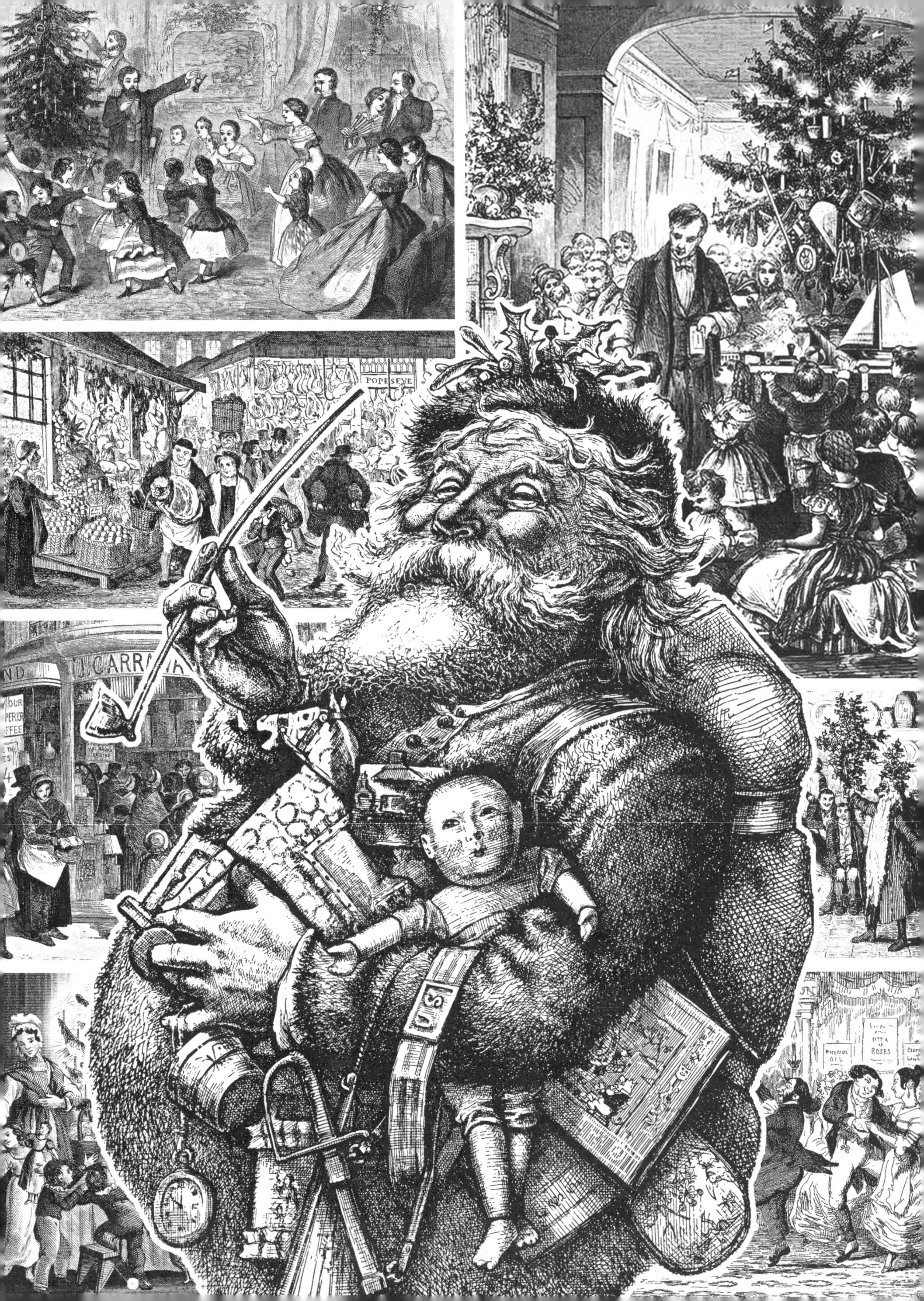
POPESEYE
ROSES